BRIAN LARA

CRICKET'S TROUBLED GENIUS

BRIAN LARA

CRICKET'S TROUBLED GENIUS

BRIAN SCOVELL

First published 2007

STADIA is an imprint of
Tempus Publishing Limited
The Mill, Brimscombe Port,
Stroud, Gloucestershire, GL5 2QG
www.tempus-publishing.com

British Library Cataloguing in Publication Data.
A catalogue record for this book is available from the British Library.

ISBN 978 0 7524 4287 7

Typesetting and origination by Tempus Publishing Limited.
Printed in Great Britain.

Contents

Dedication and Acknowledgements

I have dedicated this book to my very good friend Tony Cozier who has been extremely helpful from the start of this enjoyable venture. We first met in 1963 when he covered his first tour of England by the West Indies and at first I thought he was an Elvis Presley impersonator. He was certainly a lookalike... but without the voice. I soon pressed him into opening with my wandering side the Woodpeckers and he proved to be a talented wicketkeeper and an attacking opening batsman of the Bajan stamp. Unfortunately, he had little time to play because he was also the busiest journalist on the tour.

Over the years he developed into the finest all-round cricket journalist from the Caribbean and latterly there has been no better all-rounder in the world in his three disciplines: writing for newspapers, broadcasting on radio programmes and commentating for various television companies. Truly, he is the Gary Sobers of the cricket media. His finest moment, in my view, was when he was at the mike when the West Indies *v.* England match was abandoned in Sabina Park, Kingston in 1998. When a major story breaks on television, you need a professional who knows his subject and Tony was the man.

He spoke without notes for a long time about the background and the history of catastrophes in previous Test matches and it was a tour de force. These days, former players are monopolising the positions in television coverage but there is always room for a top professional with a good memory and an authoritative style of speaking.

Tony and his wife Jillian come from families who first settled in Barbados in the early eighteenth century, both of Scots origin I believe. The name Cozier meant 'shoemaker'. Their ancestors were cotton plantation overseers who worked for rich owners. Tony's father Edward Lloyd Cozier, known to everyone as Jimmy, was the editor of the *Barbados Advocate* for many years and he too covered an early tour of England by the West Indies. He was much loved throughout the Caribbean along with his wife Maggie, who was an artist. Jillian, a former hockey player and a universally popular business lady who worked in the travel industry, came from the McKinstry family and, like the Coziers, they have had fulfilling and long lives. Their son Craig is now carrying on the tradition: he makes his living from cricket.

One of my best friends, Willie Rodriguez, whom I first met with his wonderfully entertaining wife Beverley on the 1963 tour to England, was a terrific help in organising interviews during my last stay in Trinidad and he acted as my chauffeur among other things. The sports-loving people of Trinidad owe him a huge debt. He has put a tremendous amount back into sport and is the only sportsman who has been capped by Trinidad in both cricket and football. Peter Short, the former president and secretary of the West Indies Cricket Board, has been immensely helpful to me over the years and he is still swimming for eighteen minutes every day from the Barbados Yacht Club in his mid-eighties. I thank him for his kindness. Clive Lloyd provided me with plenty of information about Brian Lara's Test career and Bryan Davis, a friend of mine from his two seasons at Glamorgan, was typically frank about some of Brian's failings and I thank him for his time while I was in Trinidad. I also spent a lot of time with Clive Pantin, one of Lara's principals at Fatima College, and I was very grateful to him for his valued assistance.

Others who gave kind insights into the life and times of Brian Lara and supplied invaluable statistics were Dennis Amiss, Stephen Almandoz, Joey Carew, George Busby, Jonathan Barnett, Philip Bailey, David Manasseh, Alan Smith, John Jameson, Jack Bannister, Martin Crowe, Steve Camacho, Charlie Davis, David Francois, Bill Frindall, Andy Ganteaume, Ed Giddins, Everard Gordon, Wes Hall, Roger Henderson, Ray Julian, Nick Knight, Imran Khan, Ken Medlock, Brian Murgatroyd, Deryck Murray, Royce Moore, Tim Munton, Danny Morrison, Jean Mountler, Keith Piper, Jason Ratcliffe, Anil Roberts, Dermot Reeve, Barry Richards, Scott and Charisse Rodriguez, Raman Subba Row, Ian Stone, Sir Gary Sobers, Michael Slater, Phil Simmons, Valentino Singh, Mike Smith, Gladstone Small, Gloria Valere, Bob Woolmer, Sir Clyde Walcott, Rudi Webster and Everton Weekes.

A number of books have been consulted and I append a list: *Wisden Cricketers' Almanac 1990-2007*; *Who's Who of Cricketers*, edited by Philip Bailey; *Out of My Comfort Zone* by Steve Waugh; *Winning Ways* by Dermot Reeve; *Cricket's Great Expectations* by Henry Blofield; *Sir Viv Richards* by Viv Richards; *Brian Lara – the Story of a Record Breaking Year* by Jack Bannister;

Ashes to Ashes by Keith Fletcher; *Dazzler* by Darren Gough; *A Majestic Innings, Writings on Cricket* by C.L.R. James; *World Cricketers* by Christopher Martin-Jenkins; *Opening Up* by Michael Atherton; *Playing with Fire* by Nasser Hussain; *Phil Tufnell* by Phil Tufnell; *Twenty Years On* by Sir Clyde Walcott; *Woolmer on Cricket* by Bob Woolmer; *White Lightning* by Allan Donald; *The Guinness Book of Test Captains* by David Lemmon; *Everything Under the Sun* by Jeffrey Stollmeyer; *The Cricketers Who's Who 1990-2007*; *A History of West Indies Cricket* by Michael Manley; *Cricket Through the Year* by Christopher Walmsley; *The 300 Men* by Christopher Hilton; and *Beating the Field* by Brian Lara.

I relied heavily on *Wisden* for facts and figures and I compliment their outgoing editor Matthew Engel and staff for producing the finest sports book in the world, which improves every year. The game would be lost without it.

Brian Scovell
Bromley, Kent
March 2007

NOTE: Illustrations have been provided by Ted Blackbrow (plates 10-11, 20-21, 24, 26-27), Gordon Brooks (plates 14, 16-17), PA Photos (plates 7, 9, 12-13, 15, 18-19, 22, 25, 28-32), Ken Medlock (plate 8), the University of Sheffield (plate 23) and John Arnold (scorecard of Lara's 501* innings), with the remainder being from the author's own collection. If any copyright has inadvertently been infringed, the copyright holder should in the first instance contact the publishers.

one

The Greatest?

Records held by Brian Lara:
- Highest individual Test score, West Indies *v.* England, Antigua, 2004: 400*
- Most career Test runs, 1990-2006: 11,953
- Highest first-class score, Warwickshire *v.* Durham, Edgbaston, 1994: 501*
- Most Test runs in an over, off R.J. Peterson, West Indies *v.* South Africa, Johannesburg, 2003/04: 28 (4-6-6-4-4-4)

Is Brian Charles Lara the greatest batsman in the history of cricket? The figures speak for his case. He has scaled cricket's Everest twice – 375 at the St John's Recreation Ground, Antigua in 1994 and 400* on the same ground ten years later – and Sachin Tendulkar, his chief rival of the present day and four years younger, is showing signs of physical frailties. Tendulkar is lagging well behind him, by more than 1,000 runs, on Test aggregate. The Prince of Port of Spain has dominated more matches than any Test batsman in the history of the game, even Sir Donald Bradman when he towered over his teammates in his great Australian side either side of the Second World War. Lara's biggest regret is that he has hasn't won many of these matches.

When Bradman was number one in the world he played for that outstanding team for most of that time, whereas Lara's greatest successes have been achieved when he is the star in a poor side. He is a colossus, often carrying his ailing team. Bradman was on the winning side in six Ashes rubbers against England and was only on the losing side in two. He played just 17 innings against the West Indies, South Africa and India, all at home and out of his 52 Tests, 33 were played in Australia. Lara has played all around the world, from bouncy pitches like Perth and dangerous ones in Sabina Park in Jamaica to low, flat ones in the subcontinent. Matthew Engel, editor of *Wisden*, said of him, 'Though he is a calculator, he is also an instinctive entertainer; in him, the three often irreconcilable aims of a professional cricketer – personal success, collective success and pleasure for the onlooker – come together in glorious conjunction.'

Clive Lloyd, the greatest West Indian captain of all time when measured by results, said:

> In terms of the volume of runs, he's number one: most Test runs, a top score of 501 in first-class cricket and 400 in Tests. People look on Bradman as being a different class from the others and he was but in different eras you can't really judge. They had the same background and they always wanted to play. When Brian started out, the West Indies were the best side in the world and the team was full of stars. It's a pity that we went down so quickly and he was left as the only star. If he had been in a stronger team, he would have been more successful. He kept our cricket alive at a tough time and now we've got some youngsters who might turn them into fine players and he's played a key point in bringing them on. We have to be proud of what he's done.

Sir Garfield Sobers said:

> You can't compare Brian with Sir Don because they played in different eras, playing different type of cricket. The stats proved that Sir Don was best in his time and now Brian's figures show that he is the best man of his time. Brian has excelled in every department and from the time when I first met him in Barbados when he was a young man, I realised he has this hunger to succeed. He loves cricket, he's a great entertainer and a great person and I am very proud of him. Every time he plays, he's under pressure and some of his finest performances have been against the very best bowling.

Bradman and Lara were born in poor, small communities in the country and had a God-given gift, the ability to hit a ball from a very early age. They were natural geniuses, like great composers or musicians. Lara started at three when one of his older brothers, Rudolph, gave him a hand-carved miniature bat. The seventh son in a family of eleven – he is the only one not married – he was the youngest by some distance. Bunty and Pearl, his devoted and strict parents, chose the name Brian and their choice turned out to be very appropriate: 'Brian' is a Celtic name which means 'a strong man of honour'.

They lived in a scrupulously clean bungalow in Mitchell Street, Cantaro in Santa Cruz and it had a large porch with a low wall around it. The boy was often on his own and used to bounce a marble against a wall and hit it with his bat or a ruler. He said, 'There were a lot of pot plants dotted around and I put them in fielding places. When I hit the marble, the idea was to miss them.' That is how he developed into a world-class batsman who hit more boundaries than anyone in his time: because he avoided the fielders. He had also inherited the love of cricket from his father and his grandfather Herbert St Louis, who died from a stroke after listening to a radio report from an Australia *v*. West Indies Test. Lara said:

> My first experience of playing outside was in the street. We had a soft ball or, if it was lost, we used oranges. The other boys would borrow my bat and I let them have a go first because when I went in I usually batted the rest of the day. Like most West Indian boys, I played 'pass out', a street version of cricket where you are out if you miss the ball. An old man, Mr Dorsey, who used to live nearby, would often offer the other boys money for getting me out. It made me all the more determined to bat on as long as possible.

He trained from a young age to play major Test innings.

Bradman started later, when he attended a primary school at Bowral, New South Wales. He said:

> There was little or no organised sport in school. We were left to our own devices and had to play as nature advised, without knowing whether we were adopting orthodox methods or not. During the weekend and after school, I usually found myself without any playmates because no boy lived close to our home. For this reason I had to improvise my own amusement and, during the hours of daylight, almost invariably it centred around the use of a ball. It was either kicking a football, playing tennis against a garage door or an unusual form of cricket which I invented.
>
> Armed with a small cricket stump which I used as a bat, I would throw a golf ball at this brick stand and try to hit the ball on the rebound. The golf ball came back at great speed and to hit it all with the round stump was no easy task. This extraordinary and primitive idea was purely a matter of amusement but looking back I can understand how it must have developed the co-ordination of brain, eye and muscle which was to serve me so well in important matches later on.

These two uncoached, self-made cricketers, through their determination and enthusiasm for the game, reached the top in their early twenties.

Bradman was twenty-two when he became the fifth batsman to take the world's highest individual score, reaching 334 against England at Headingley in 1930. Lara was twenty-five when he became the ninth, scoring 375 against England in Antigua in 1994. For much of his nineteen-year first-class career Lara's strike rate was between 55 and 70 runs per hundred balls and up to the start of the 2007 tour of England it was 60.20. Bradman's rate was 58.61 in a career lasting twenty-one years. Sachin Tendulkar's was 53.75 at the time of writing and Ricky Ponting's 58.95.

Lara has scored quicker than Bradman, and up against far superior fielders. Both Lara and Bradman sought to make fielders redundant and they almost did. Bradman scored a century every three innings while Lara has scored one every 6.8 matches. They shared the ability to pierce any field and Lara was one of the first batsmen who angled his bat while playing shots to avoid fielders. Keith Piper, the former wicketkeeper who shared a stand of 322 when Lara scored his 501* world record, said:

> I first met him when I toured in the West Indies in 1987 and it was clear then that he was an exceptional talent. I have never seen anyone I have batted with or kept wicket to who opens or closes the face of the bat in mid-stroke like he does. That is why he has so many strokes.

When his run charts are examined one fact stands out: he hits the ball to all 360 degrees of the compass. A few of his innovative sweeps have sent the ball flying over the head of the wicketkeeper and hardly anyone has hit the ball all round the circumference of a cricket ground to the same extent. His unique high backlift has enabled him to power the ball to the ropes at tremendous force with a bat weighing, on average, 2lbs 7oz. Most of the game's power hitters, like Graeme Pollock, Clive Lloyd and Ian Botham, used much heavier bats. Another key part of Lara's armoury is that he knows where the stumps are and when he plays defensively he ensures that his leading foot is outside the line when the ball is swinging, obviating the risk of being lbw. C.L.R. James, the eminent West Indian cricket writer who died a year before Lara made his Test debut, wrote in one of his articles, 'I believe Botham to be the hardest hitter of any Test batsman, or for that matter of any Test cricketer of all.' He hadn't seen Lara in action, or he might have changed his mind.

Bob Woolmer, the Kent and England batsman and highly regarded coach of South Africa and Pakistan, now sadly deceased, worked with Lara as Warwickshire's coach in 1994 and 1998, and he said:

He is a gentle, nice man who redefined the art of batting and I think he is the best batsman of his time. Tendulkar is a very fine batsman too but there are plenty of bowlers in Test cricket who couldn't bowl to Brian. I have never seen anyone hit the ball harder than him and his greatest quality is to hit it late and square. It is very difficult to block scoring shots in this area because most field placings are at an angle. His placement comes purely from the top of the hand which controls when he opens and closes the face of the bat. I think he is ready to hit every ball for four until he has to block one. Most batsmen approach things the other way around – that is why he is the most exciting batsman in the world.

Bradman and Lara are among the few batsmen who used their feet regularly when facing slower bowlers. Bradman had the skill of a Fred Astaire as he danced down the pitch; Lara, less artistic, likes to finish his act with a dramatic kill, either a punishing boundary or a toppling six. Doug Insole, the former Essex and England batsman, and president of MCC in 2006/07, is more knowledgeable about the history of cricket and its personalities than almost anyone and he once said:

> Bradman was calculating. He wasn't elegant but he worked out where he could get his runs at one a ball and did it mainly by square cutting and pulling and looking for the ones. He wasn't so much of an off driver. But Lara has more range of shots and has the capacity to challenge Bradman's records by the time he retires.

Insole, now eighty, said that twelve years ago and he has been proved right.

Most experts agree that it is impossible to judge each champion in different eras. Bradman's Test average of 99.94 dwarfed that of the next man in the list, South Africa's Graeme Pollock (60.97). Lara is placed twentieth with an average of 53.86; Tendulkar is fourteenth with an average of 56.71.

In the 2006/07 Ashes series, Ricky Ponting improved his Test batting average to over sixty after averaging 100 in a year. He was compared to Bradman and he dismissed the idea. He is a great player but would he have done so well if he had not played regularly in the best side in the world, playing instead for one of the weaker countries? Ponting is a beautifully balanced player and like most of the current Australian batsmen, he keeps his feet perfectly still until the bowler starts releasing the ball. His right foot is anchored on the crease and his left is aiming towards mid-on. If the ball is short, he is ready to move backwards on to his right foot in one movement to play a shot. If it is well up, he moves on to his left foot, again in one movement. It is the traditional way of great players but for some reason many England bats-men shuffle around and make several movements before they move into line with the ball (perhaps this is why some are taking up roles in BBC1's *Strictly Come Dancing*). The so-called trigger movement on to the front foot before the bowler delivers is against all logic. Lara's problems later in his career were brought about by excessive foot movement, and he still has a tendency to move too soon. Tendulkar, Ponting, Jacques Kallis, Inzamam-ul-Haq and the other current greats all keep still until the ball is released.

Neil Harvey, the great Australian left-hander who believes in old-fashioned batting techniques, scattered the critics during the Adelaide Test in December 2006 like the hundreds of pigeons who paraded around the ground. Asked by an Australian journalist whether he thought Ponting could be compared to Bradman, he said:

> That's garbage, absolute garbage. He wouldn't have got into the Don's 1948 invincibles side. I can name plenty of players better than Ponting. He's a good player, sure, but he is got so many things in his favour now, he should be averaging 60-plus. You've got covered wickets, you've got flat wickets, you've got ridiculously short boundaries and you've got jet-propelled bats – I think it is unfair.

Only two batsmen have ever scored two treble hundreds in Tests: Bradman, with 334 at Headingley in 1930 and 304 four years later on the same ground, and Lara with 375 at St John's in 1994 and 400* on the same ground ten years later. They are in a club of two and though Bradman's average was far superior, Lara's habit of producing exhilarating champagne moments and producing upset wins against the premier side in the world surely backs his claim to being number one when he finally bows out. Bradman, from Anglo-Saxon stock and a Protestant, was the star in a winning side and it was easier for him. Lara, from a more flamboyant background with an easy-going approach to life, played in an average side which veered from occasional highs, mainly inspired by him, to abysmal lows. The Roundhead Bradman accumulated his runs in remorseless fashion whereas the Cavalier Lara is more entertaining.

Both of these great batsmen were small men. In the record books and on websites, Lara is recorded as being 5ft 5ins, while Bradman was 5ft 7ins. Tendulkar is 5ft 4½in, which is why he is known as the 'The Little Master'. Lara insists that he is five feet eight, but it is clearly an advantage to be small. Shorter batsmen can duck under short-pitched bowling, or if they are prepared to move inside the line and hook, they find it easier to hit the ball upwards like the master of that art, Sunil Gavaskar. Lara has virtually stopped trying to use the hook shot. 'When they see me doing it, they have two men out so it's not a good idea to give the fielder a chance,' he said.

Both Bradman and Lara were uncomfortable against genuine pace bowled short of a good length. On the back foot, Lara copies the Sobers style of opening up and playing the ball in front of his body. 'I did that because if the ball catches the edge it doesn't go to the keeper,' Sobers once said. 'It hits me. Good reason for me to middle it!' Batsmen never wore helmets in Bradman's day and the 1932/33 Bodyline tour of Australia, when Douglas Jardine ordered his bowlers to aim at him more than the stumps, caused such animosity that the Commonwealth was in danger of breaking up. Bradman's average dropped to 56 that tour but he still hit four fifties in the four Tests he played, including a century. He was only struck once, by Harold Larwood, the fastest of the England bowlers. The rest of the time he managed to avoid injury by the dexterity of his footwork but a number of his colleagues were less fortunate.

Like Lara, Bradman was a believer in the Corinthian spirit. He thought the game should be played in the right spirit but, as a tough Aussie, he didn't go so far as to 'walk' when he knew he had connected with the ball and the catch was taken. Lara does. He and Adam Gilchrist are the only top-class batsmen who will voluntarily give up their wicket when they know they have got a nick. 'He is the fairest cricketer of his generation,' said one of his former managers, Wes Hall. Sometimes Lara's temper snaps, and between 1992 and 2006 he was penalised twice by the ICC for misdemeanours. Clive Lloyd said, 'He's an honest cricketer and the ICC respect him as one of the few batsmen who walk. He's had a few tantrums but they have been balanced with the occasions when he walks or shows sportsmanship. He hasn't been rude to the ICC.'

The first occasion was when he showed dissent after being stumped against New Zealand in a triangular tournament in India in 1994. He said:

Matthew Hart, the New Zealand left-arm spin bowler was bowling and I went down the pitch to hit him over midwicket but missed. Adam Parore, the New Zealand wicketkeeper, fumbled the ball and I honestly thought I got back into my crease before he removed the bails. Without hesitation the umpire lifted his finger. I thought, this couldn't be happening. The third umpire was available and he could easily have referred the decision to him. I thought there was going to be a referral and I delayed my walk back to the dressing room. The end result was that the umpire made an official complaint about me and the referee, Raman Subba Row, the former England and Surrey batsman, fined me fifty per cent of my fee and suspended me from appearing in the next match and I was severely reprimanded. I could have done without losing the money but at the time I was already completely exhausted and I did not mind missing the match.

Ten years later he also breached section 3, showing dissent in the second Test against England at Port of Spain in March and was fined fifty per cent of his match fee. Graham Thorpe was hit in the hand by Tino Best and umpires Billy Bowden and Daryl Harper offered Thorpe the light. Lara thought that was unfair and said so, using strong language. Earlier in his career he had a row with Gus Logie, one of his heroes, when they were playing together and he was fined TT$500, around £65. Logie was captaining Trinidad against Jamaica when the game was almost over and he brought on a bowler who had been struck for 22 runs. Lara said:

> I said to David Williams, the keeper, that I did not think that was a good idea and he told Gus. The outcome was that I was told not to criticise my captain and a fine was imposed. I was sore about it at the time but it did not affect my good relationship with Gus or David Williams. Those sort of comments are made on the field all round the world.

On another occasion, Lara was having a night out with footballer Dwight Yorke and another friend in Port of Spain when someone else started to be nasty towards his friend and he stepped in to tell him to behave himself. The police were called and they were all taken to a police station and Lara was given a dressing-down. Later he said, 'I would hardly describe it as a dressing-down, especially as I was the innocent party, but what it proved to me was that when you are a well-known figure you have to try to avoid confrontations in public. Since then I have been careful not to do that again.'

Bowlers as fast as Brett Lee, Shoaib Akhtar, Curtly Ambrose and others have tried to ruffle Lara's imperturbability and they have succeeded on a few occasions. He can squirm but he doesn't cave in. His courage has never been doubted. Bradman was just as brave when facing the bouncers. Before the Second World War, Bradman accumulated his runs all round the wicket on pitches which were flattened out, almost rock hard, by rollers weighing several hundredweight. Batsmen dominated and there were few fast bowlers who really won matches. Would Bradman have scored as many runs if he had faced bowlers of the quality and speed of Glenn McGrath, Brett

Lee, Courtney Walsh, Curtly Ambrose, Wasim Akram, Waqar Younis, Allan Donald, Steve Harmison and Shoaib Akhtar, most of whom are well over six feet tall? Reverse swing hadn't been discovered and bowlers spent less time working on the ball than they do today, scuffing up one side and wetting the other, often illegally when they use their fingernails, or applying a form of liquid. There is more cheating today and more bouncers are bowled – the exception was the Bodyline tour. Unlike Lara, Bradman played on uncovered pitches and he acquired a sound defence to counter the effect of the ball rising sharply off the ground. He still made big scores on them and there is no reason why Lara should not have done the same.

Would Bradman have countered the skills of Muttiah Muralitharan, bowling with a straightening arm which in a previous generation would have incurred a shout of 'no ball!' from the umpire? Lara's way of unravelling the bowling of Murali is, 'I watch only his fingers; not his run up, not his arm, just the fingers.' Bradman led the campaign in the late 1950s to stamp out chucking and the throwers were barred. With a fifteen per cent tolerance on bowling actions now legalised by the ICC, many of today's spin bowlers are using methods which in a previous generations would have been prohibited.

Most years Lara has averaged twice as many Test matches as Bradman did in his heyday and he also plays around thirty or so one-day internationals each year. The cumulative hours spent in aircraft has taken a toll on modern cricketers and Lara is no exception. Clive Lloyd recalled:

> I persuaded the West Indies Board to fly the players in club class in the early nineties. These fellows like Courtney Walsh, Curtly Ambrose and Ian Bishop are so big that it was impossible for them to sit comfortably in economy. We always had single [hotel] rooms if players wanted them. Youngsters sometimes prefer to share. It's a much tougher life now than in Bradman's day. Today's players have to play back-to-back Tests and the mental side of it is very taxing. I wonder how Fred Trueman would have coped with today's pressures? Would he put in the same amount of effort day in and day out and keep flying all round the world? Would these old-time stars play thirty or so one day internationals in a year?

Few top cricketers go into a match without any strains or bruises and Lara takes every precaution to avoid more serious injuries. He is not a fanatical trainer and often he misses the more rigorous routines. For much of his career, Bradman travelled in luxury liners to his tours, which gave him plenty of time to rest. Medical experts now admit that excessive air travel is bad for the health, particularly for top-class sportsmen. One of Lara's prizes for setting the then 375 world record in 1994 was to be presented with a letter from British West Indies Airways, the Caribbean international airline, giving him TT\$375,000 for free air miles. His agent Jonathan Barnett contacted BWIA and asked if it could be first-class. 'They told him it would be first-class only to discover that there was no first-class on BWIA,' said Barnett. 'He had to put up with business class.'

Lara is not keen on playing one-day cricket and dismisses it as 'not proper cricket'. Unless he is competing for the World Cup or the Champions Trophy he is reluctant to play mundane one-day games. He said:

> I am not an admirer of one-day cricket because it is not a true test of ability. But I do see the need for it because it brings in much-needed revenue and attracts large crowds. Night cricket, the wearing of coloured clothing and the use of the white ball have contributed to the popularisation of the sport. I think these ideas add to the excitement and they are good for the heartbeat. But when one-day cricket starts to take over and Test cricket is cut back to accommodate it, then the time has come for the authorities to act. In limited overs the batsman has to take risks to score quickly from the start and they easily pick up bad habits. Like most West Indians I play the same way. I do not adjust because it is a limited-overs game.

For much of his career, he has scored faster in Test cricket than in one-day internationals because of the defensive fields in ODIs. Bradman never played competitive one-day matches and he was a strong opponent of the Kerry Packer World Series Cricket innovation in 1978.

Today's cricketers are much fitter than those of the past. Bradman's players never dived for the ball in the outfield. They did for catches but not to stop runs. Catching and throwing have improved immeasurably and Bradman would find it tougher to score at his customary rate. And no one sat at a computer studying the evidence needed to block the runs of a batsman. Today there is a science evolving to counteract the best batsmen. In Bradman's day he used his intuition and skill to avoid fielders.

Bradman showed no mercy to bowlers and he never eased off irrespective of the circumstances. One of Lara's weaknesses is that if the opposition is unchallenging he can lose interest. He will forfeit his wicket with a reckless shot and won't worry so much about his average whereas Bradman was the opposite. But up against the very best sides he will rise up and dictate the tempo of the match. Everton Weekes, the last of the 'Three Ws', now eighty-two, said:

Don Bradman was unbelievable. He would say, 'You are not going to get me out,' and they didn't, not too often. Brian has the same philosophy. He is a genius. He sees the ball so early and he knows where he is going to put it. But he does get caught more than he should. I only hit one six in my career and I used to say, 'If you don't hit the ball into the air, you're not going to be caught.'

Brian Lara ended any speculation that he was retiring from Test cricket during his triumphant tour of Pakistan in the November and December of 2006. On 21 November at the central Pakistan city of Multan, he became the sixth Test player to score a Test hundred (his 34th) before lunch, off 77 balls. He went on to score 216. It was his ninth double-century to Bradman's twelve. He struck seven sixes, one more than Bradman had in his 52 Tests. 'This match could be used as a template for us,' said Lara, 'because we played fifteen hard sessions of cricket and that is needed for any team to draw or win a match.' The high-scoring game duly ended in a draw and, considering the away record of the West Indies since the end of the Lloyd and Richards dynasties, that was seen as a triumph. Fazeer Mohammed of the *Trinidad Express* said, 'Lara's batsmanship at Multan was an experience that transcends the petty boundaries of nationalism and it would have left the Pakistan crowd with an empty feeling had he completed his final tour of Paikistan without leaving a lasting impression.'

Lara has never been afraid to use his feet and loft the ball out of the ground and his tally of sixes up to the start of the 2007 series in England was 88, a figure only surpassed by Adam Gilchrist's 97. His third six against Pakistan took him past the 84 of Viv Richards; his seventh and last of that match took him to second place, beating Chris Cairns' 87. Lara has edged ahead of Gilchrist in one-day internationals, scoring 128 sixes in 290 appearances to Gilchrist's 126 in 257 matches. The risk factor attached to six-hitting is almost unique to him. Bradman wouldn't take the same gamble. Once, in a Test in Antigua, facing Brett Lee, the second fastest bowler of all time if the timing devices are to be believed, Lara opened his score with a searing six over point. Bradman would never have thought of doing that; he tried to keep the ball on the ground to avoid the risk of being caught.

Lara is a complex man with natural charm who sometimes upsets his colleagues and bosses. Bradman was very similar. They believed they were right to do what they did. Bradman, a private person who had an idyllic marriage which he protected from press intrusion, had several disputes with the Australian Board as a player over the years, whereas Lara has experienced many more in his turbulent career. People who didn't know Bradman called him a loner and it was true that he shunned the trappings of celebrity. W.G. Grace was the first major cricketing celebrity; Bradman was the second and he couldn't really handle it. He angered some of his teammates by retiring to his bedroom after a day's play, preferring to order a pot of tea and write his diary rather than joining them for a drink. At the time he was teetotal and at home he was happiest with his devoted wife Jessie and family. For many years, his son John changed his surname to avoid recognition. Now John has reverted to his original name and is proud of it.

Two of Bradman's colleagues, Bill O'Reilly and Jack Fingleton, made a living out of journalism after they retired from cricket and they showed their sour feelings about Bradman in a number of critical books and articles. According to Jim Swanton, a lifelong friend (both Swanton and Bradman died in their nineties):

> While he did not put his hand in his pocket or in any way court popularity with his colleagues, he was alive from the first to the financial opportunities that fame was bringing. Depression was deep in Australia. His ambition was to achieve a degree of security that enabled him to marry his childhood friend.

Lara, who is generous with his friends and younger colleagues, commands respect but has yet to capture the hearts of all cricket lovers around the world. That may well come. Chris Gayle, the Jamaican left-handed opener, says, 'Brian is my player, my batsman. He was the only one I used to watch before I started playing cricket.' Lloyd recalled, 'He's a kind host and on tours he often used to take the younger players to dinner. And in India on one occasion when the temperature was in the forties he gave them one-over spells to protect them.'

Bradman was revered in his later years when he became an administrator, selector, author and journalist and the nation came to a standstill at his funeral in early 2001. The admired Australian writer Gideon Haigh said of him, 'He probably signed more autographs than anyone in history.' Before a Lord's Taverners dinner in London in 1974 he signed every one of the 900 menus and up to the end of his life he was still typing letters in response to admirers all around the world. The author received a letter from Bradman two months before his death, apologising that 'my typing isn't quite up to writing an article for the Forty Club Handbook – I've just been recovering from a stroke – but I wish them well.' Lara is a devoted signer of autographs but he doesn't always go in for answering his sometimes voluminous mail.

Lara, who has never been married and lacks a stable private life, has been disciplined seven times by the West Indies Board of Control and they still keep coming back and reinstating him as captain; he is now in his third spell. When you are self-made, you aren't keen to listen to the orders of someone else, especially if they are lesser people or cricketers of modest accomplishments. He has a set of close friends, like the footballers Dwight Yorke and Russell Latapy, and he rings them constantly. He has been called a loner, wrongly, but like Bradman he avoids mixing with people outside of his close circle. The pressure of fame hit him in 1994, and in 2000 he withdrew from the game and finished up at a treatment centre in Florida. He complained of mental exhaustion and needed several months of rest before he resumed his career.

Two factors have helped to mould Lara's personality: the loss of his father, who died from a heart attack in 1988 when Lara was first in the West Indies' Test squad; and the absence, as yet, of a wife or long-term partner. Peter Roebuck, the former Somerset captain and journalist, now living in Pietermaritzburg, summed up the situation perfectly:

> Happiness remains elusive for him. He once said cricket was ruining his life and he meant it. Such a sentiment might have escaped Donald Bradman when he was sick in 1930 after being flung from simplicity to stardom and on towards a young grave. But Bradman recovered, found a wife, and worked as a stockbroker and found relief in the wide-streeted Adelaide. And his batting flowed again. Lara has found no such respite and continues in turbulence, torn between indulgence and application, a mixture of laughter and petulance so that he can seem less a formed character but a sculpture whose clay is still soft.
>
> He has been unable to check himself or improve himself. The story of his life was an immature ego and an unshaped genius. Until manhood has been properly achieved, most boys need a father's influence. Sachin Tendulkar's father is a professor, Viv Richards's dad was a prison warder and Chanderpaul had his practical fisherman father at home. But Lara's father, a stern-looking gentleman, was taken away too soon and he never seemed as stable again.

It is fair to say that Lara has now changed as his career nears its end. He has mellowed and is much more supportive of his colleagues. He has always been a team man but off the field his life is still chaotic on occasions and he still apparently finds it difficult to live with fame.

Bradman's career was dogged by different concerns, mainly health. Near the end of the 1934 tour of England he felt excruciating pain in the abdomen and his life was in danger before an emergency operation saved him from the ravages of peritonitis. He played no more cricket for a year. During the Second World War he had a health breakdown and was transferred from the RAAF to a non-combatant role with the Army, incurring complaints that he had been excused from fighting in the front line.

Bradman is still rated as the greatest batsman of all time but as Lara's career reaches its final chapter it is time to re-examine this. The Prince of Trinidad has performed many great deeds which no one else can match. He has thrilled and inspired millions of cricket lovers around the world and the vast majority can forgive his past sins, like calling a strike before a tour of South Africa, threatening to retire on a number of occasions, including twice in Tests and failing to turn up on time on countless occasions. Geniuses can sometimes be excused; mortals can't.

In 1999 Matthew Engel, the occasionally abrasive and highly amusing editor of *Wisden*, had the idea of a poll to identify the best five cricketers of the twentieth century. He recruited 100 people to take part in cricket's worldwide general election, ranging from Sir Alec Bedser, Steve Waugh, Ali Bacher, Clive Lloyd, Sunil Gavaskar, Polly Umrigar, Walter Hadlee, Hanif Mohammad and Sri Lankan ICC Referee Ranjan Madugalle to Dickie Bird, Netta Rheinberg, Richard Cashman, Cec Starr, Norman Gordon, Reddy Krish, Sir Carlisle Burton, Donna Simmonds, Kris Srikkanth and Lindsey Weir. There were two certainties, Sir Donald Bradman (100 votes) and Sir Garfield Sobers (90). One wondered about the sanity of the other ten who failed to vote for Gary! In third place came Sir Jack Hobbs (30) and that was a reasonable decision because this nice, gentlemanly chap scored more centuries and more runs than any of his contemporaries.

The fourth selection was much more controversial – 27 people voted for Shane Warne, the greatest leg-spinner of all time, now on his way to immortality. In the words of Australian Prime Minister John Howard, 'He is a larrikin.' But Warne probably deserves the honour. A man who is generous in his views about players, Warne once said, 'The hardest batsmen I've played against would be Brian Lara and Sachin Tendulkar, the two best of my era.'

Number five was Sir Vivian Richards (25). Again, a fair shout. In the top ten Dennis Lillee and Sir Frank Worrell shared sixth spot (both received 19 votes). Eighth was the little-loved Walter Hammond, the finest all-rounder of his day, ninth was Denis Compton, the matinee idol who everyone loved, and tenth position was shared by Sir Richard Hadlee, with his late father Wally voting for him, and Imran Khan, the Pakistan all-rounder who may well have been underrated by some judges. Readers of *Wisden* must have been searching for the name of B.C. Lara when their copies arrived. No such luck. The only Trinidadian who attracted a vote, and a single one, was Learie Constantine who rose to become Lord Constantine and earned a worldwide reputation as a lawyer, governor of the BBC and a fierce fighter against racial discrimination.

No disrespect to Learie because he was a dynamic all-rounder who always delighted his audiences, but was his contribution in his eighteen Tests greater than Brian Lara's? There were some interesting cricketers who were given a single vote, including B.J.T. Bosanquet, the inventor of the googly, Bruce Mitchell, K.S. Ranjitsinhji, Maurice Tate and Sir Pelham Warner, none of whom set world records. Matthew Engel wrote:

> A total of forty-nine players received one vote. And the difficulty of the choice can be gauged by the quality of some of those who failed to get on the score sheet at all: Keith Miller (who received many mentions in despatches), Barry Richards, Greg Chappell, Gooch, Laker, Lara, Hanif, C.B. Fry…

These gentlemen were very worthy candidates but, except for Jim Laker, none of them rewrote the record book as Lara has done.

The chief reason why Lara was totally and shamefully ignored was probably because of his reputation. Many of the judges must have thought him an awkward customer – which he is. He is not a conformist. But he is a record-breaker and a unique cricketer. He might not be loved by everyone (although many ladies would like to love him) but when he retires, which may well be soon, his position in the lists should be amended, even putting his name right to the top. He ought at least to be considered for a spot in the leading five, possibly in place of Sir Jack Hobbs, if there were to be a recount.

In the high summer of 2005 Birmingham's Symphony Hall staged a celebration of the seventy-fifth anniversary of the election of the West Indies as a Test-playing team and a panel of experts, mainly from the Caribbean and from *Wisden*, voted for the top five West Indians in that period. Bowlers were virtually ignored, which was odd. The five were Sir Viv Richards, Sir Frank Worrell, George Headley (known as 'The Black Bradman' before political correctness took over), Sir Garfield Sobers and Brian Lara. Lara had finally gained some recognition and he spoke with feeling about his late father, his love of cricket and the need to play as a team. Even on such a special night for him, he turned up half an hour late and was the only person not to wear the official maroon blazer. Punctuality has been his chief failing and one of his many agents said, 'If he arranges an appointment for himself, he'll be on time. If someone else fixes it, he always turns up late.' One of his awards was for the best innings by a West Indian – his 153 in Barbados in 1999, which enabled the West Indies to beat the Australians by one wicket in one of Test cricket's greatest encounters.

Viv Richards used the occasion to berate Lara's teammates. 'You guys have something serious to represent and don't ever forget that,' he said. 'Because of the inspiration factor of the past, let us hope you guys understand what it is to represent the West Indies. Cricket began a long time ago, let us not forget why you guys are here, okay?' In a different time Lara might have used a similar speech but he is too diplomatic.

Late in the summer of 1994, when he was caught up in the commercial frenzy after being the top scorer in Tests against England, Lara was credited as saying:

> I do love cricket and I pray that I can stay fit enough to play for a number of years to come. Unfortunately, I don't see myself still playing cricket when I am forty. I admire those players who have done it but hopefully I will have enjoyed myself enough to be able to bow out before then and enjoy the rest of my life.

Bradman played until he was forty. Lara, who was thirty-eight on 2 May 2007, might just last out. Don Bennett, the respected and long serving Middlesex coach, gave an interesting insight into Lara's fitness and how he has kept playing at the highest level:

> He's never had a serious injury. He rarely misses a game and he looks after himself, pacing himself. He doesn't go in for hard training. His fitness comes from playing long innings. He's very similar to Gary Sobers, who used to enjoy a late night. I'd pick Gary ahead of Don Bradman in my World XI because he was such a great bowler and still won matches with the bat. Gary was virtually finished at twenty-eight because of his knee. Surgery wasn't too clever in his day. I remember seeing Denis Compton's knee after one of his operations when Bill Tucker took his kneecap away. There wasn't much left. Denis couldn't get much flexion in the knee and they used a bit of rope to attach to his ankle and pull on it to get his knee working better. After ten minutes Denis' shirt was soaked with sweat. Every time he played afterwards he played in pain. He was never fit again.

Compton's crippling injuries were caused by playing football in Arsenal's first team. Bennett also played for Arsenal and he too had knee surgery. 'Bowlers who bowled hundreds of overs every year expected the arrival of the surgeon's knife!' he said. 'Lara hasn't those kind of problems. He's a fit person.' Bennett went on to say:

> I think Lara is another Tiger Woods. He's so far ahead of the rest and when he wants to do it, he'll just do it. Other times his concentration goes a bit against the lesser sides otherwise his average would be in the seventies, not the fifties.

Nick Knight, the former England, Essex and Warwickshire batsman, now working for Sky, shares Bennett's view:

> He is phenomenal. When I played with him I realised that he was playing a different game to mine. I was trying to score but if he thought he wanted to score a boundary, or hit a six, he would. No bowler can stop him. He likes a chat in the middle and I was always asking for advice. He didn't really know most of the players in England but he could spot instantly what their weaknesses were and he would tell our bowlers how to get them out. I was desperate to learn from him but I was just an ordinary player whereas he is a genius. It's unfair to talk about comparing him with Bradman but I think he's right up with the best batsmen of all time.

Yorkshire and former England bowler Darren Gough believes Lara is undervalued by the experts.

> For some reason, when it comes to the legends of cricket, we go for people from the 1940s and 1950s. Yes, there were some great batsmen then but we overlook players from this era, such as Lara, who has to be in the top three batsmen of all time. You can't break two world Test records and score 501 in the county game without being included. Luckily I wasn't involved on the two occasions he broke the Test record against England. I told him that had I played, he wouldn't have got them. I have taken his Test wicket six times.

Martin Crowe, possibly New Zealand's greatest batsman, said:

> Lara's strength was his freaky backlift and timing of strokes. Unique and unstoppable when on song, which was often, he sometimes used excessive foot movement when early in his innings and he could be vulnerable. A comparison

with Braddles [Bradman] is a tough one, especially with an era such as the twenties to the late forties. I don't think anyone would have stopped Bradman on a Bunsen [a pitch which takes plenty of spin]. More range of shots? No way. If Bradman had batted on that pitch at Antigua against that England attack he would have scored 600. These days bowlers are pretty average, with the exception of Murali and also the now-retired Warne. Pitches are flat, too. They play more cricket now and Bradman never had a bad patch like Lara has had at times, like three or four failures in a row. It's too hard to compare eras for a start, I'm afraid, but he is up there with the greatest as he is the best of his time, as Hobbs, Bradman, Viv and Barry Richards, Greg Chappell and Tendulkar have been in their time.

Keith Fletcher, the England coach in charge when Lara scored his 375 at Antigua, agrees with Crowe that Lara isn't in the same class as Bradman. But in his book *Ashes to Ashes* he surprisingly voted for another candidate as the greatest ever batsman, as opposed to an all-rounder: Gary Sobers. He said:

I never saw Bradman but I cannot image there could have been a better batsman than Sobers. He possessed the rare ability to drive through the line of the ball without moving his feet more than absolutely necessary. At St John's, Sobers strode to the middle to embrace Lara for posed pictures and the match came to a complete standstill. Still, you could forgive Gary anything. He is the most generous of individuals and regarded Lara as a worthy batsman to beat his record.

Lara is an overrated batsman. He is not in the same class as Ponting, Kallis, Tendulkar, Richards or Greenidge. It was an extremely flat pitch and Ambrose and Walsh bowled 80 overs between them in one innings and took just one wicket. Lara can destroy an attack in these conditions but he is less adept on pitches with bounce and pace. He is unorthodox and has not eradicated a weakness against the ball above waist height.'

A few miles away from Fletcher's house, another cricket lover living in Vange, Essex, came up with a contrary view. Writing in *The Wisden Cricketer*, Mr N. Dhesney wrote:

It is now beyond reasonable doubt that Brian Lara is the greatest batsman that ever played the game. His tour of Pakistan has proved this. The 216 he scored at Multan was almost as good as his 277 at Sydney in 1993. His foot movement, timing, placement and power have never been bettered. Are there any records left he will not break? Mr Bradman, in my eyes, doesn't even come close.

two

Crime and Not Punishment

Early in his career, Brian Lara had his cricket bag stolen by a thief. The robbery was extensively reported in the Caribbean media and the thief soon realised that he had made a huge mistake. He rang up the police to pass on the information about the whereabouts of the prized bag. It was returned to Lara the next day.

Hardly a day passes in Trinidad and Tobago without the sun shining. The temperature rarely drops below 20°C and never reaches the late thirties. The effects of global warming have only just begun to arrive and, though the humidity can be a distraction, the climate is almost idyllic. The multinational culture of the islands took root centuries ago, long before West Indians started migrating to England in the aftermath of the Second World War. Trinidad and Tobago were plundered by a succession of invaders, Spanish, French, Dutch, Portuguese and English and the capital is still named Port of Spain.

The name Lara comes from the Spanish and there are forty-three Laras listed in the telephone book including Brian Charles Lara, who is rarely at home. Way back, members of the Spanish branch of his family took up with the heirs of slaves who were snatched from Africa, packed into wooden ships and transported to the West Indies in the most inhumane fashion, but the official records do not go back far enough to trace the Prince's ancestry. Once DNA testing is introduced in Trinidad – which may take some time – we will know the full facts about the country's greatest celebrity.

DNA testing is sorely needed to convict criminals because crime is rife and it is ruining the country. The 1.3 million inhabitants dread being robbed, mugged, kidnapped or murdered; in 2006 there was a murder every day on average, yet only forty people were arrested. The previous year there were a record 386 murders, thirty-six per cent up on 2004. There were a record 235 kidnappings in 2005, up nearly a third on 2004. Amnesty International reported that only twenty per cent of 12,919 complaints made against the police from 1999 to 2004 were investigated. Stephen Cadiz, a Trinidadian businessman and chief of the Keith Noel 136 Committee, an anti-crime pressure group, said, 'An island paradise? It's the killing fields!' In terms of murders per 100,000 population, Trinidad is now approaching the figures of Jamaica, which has three times the population and where 1,200 murders were recorded in 2006. One of the victims was shot dead on the Brian Lara Promenade in the posher part of the city. The figures for the UK recorded 766 murders in a population of 60 million people in 2005.

The mixture of nationalities within Trinidad has produced a race of people with a strong sense of humour who live life to the full. They love dancing in the streets in carnival each February, a lot like the Brazilians, except the carnival in Rio de Janeiro is bigger and brasher than Trinidad's. Many of the women are beautiful and personable, the men are laddish and amusing and they cherish sport, particularly cricket. The middle-class and the wealthy barricade their houses and often have to hire security guards to patrol their roads. Few parties take place without them. In a country with an inflation rate of nine per cent, the growing number of security staff are earning little more than the minimum hourly wage of less than a pound, and not many are qualified to be armed. They are sitting targets. The sugar industry is coming to an end in 2007 with 7,500 farmers and their workers losing their jobs but there is a demand for labour because a proportion don't like working and others live on the drug trade. Drugs come from crooks in Venezuela, just six miles from Trinidad at the nearest point, and Colombia, the main source. The unemployment rate is five per cent, reasonable for a Third World country.

Brian Lara is a generous host, staging plenty of parties at his castle-style house overlooking the Savannah at Knaggs Hill. He stages a fête, a party with loud music, food and laughter, before carnival and charges up to TT$1,000 (about £80) per ticket with a substantial amount of the proceeds going towards his Bunty/Pearl Cancer Foundation. One of the people who 'jumps' at these fêtes – he is always being seen at them – is the seventy-year-old President, Professor Max Richards, who is a good friend of Lara's.

Deryck Murray, the former West Indies wicketkeeper who is president of the Trinidad and Tobago Cricket Board and one of the directors of the West Indies Board, lives in one of the protected areas at Westmoorings and he said of the problems in his country:

> We need a catalyst. One horrific thing is being followed by another but I am
> an eternal optimist and I believe the politicians and the collective will of the

people can do what New York did in the nineties and turn it round. The prisons are full up and there is a backlog of 23,000 cases. It's a terrible problem. Everyone you know has been a victim or knows who the attackers are.

Lara is untouchable and doesn't need personal guards except for his fêtes. But someone told of an incident which might well have turned nasty. He went to a 'pan' night (a steel band show) and found himself being confronted by one of the gang leaders – most of them are well known to the public – and the man said, 'Have a drink, Lara!' Lara accepted – he probably had no choice in the matter – and two more men, known as 'robots' who work for the leader, approached and stood either side of him and gave him a hard stare. These men could shoot on sight when told but nothing happened. After a short while, the men left.

Everard Gordon, the seventy-four-year-old cricket writer on *The Guardian* who is one of the best authorities on West Indies cricket and its history, said:

> Brian is a national hero many times over but not everyone worships him. I'd say seventy-five per cent love him and the rest are anti. Many of us were very bitter about the way he refused to play for his country, Trinidad & Tobago, after his 375. We thought that was an insult. He used to come up with medical certificates to say he was unfit and at one game he arrived late at Queen's Park saying 'I'm full of flu' and went off. People were furious and they had to put up with it. There was a rule that Test players had to play a certain number of games in the regional tournament and if they didn't, they would be dropped by the West Indies selectors. That could have applied to Brian. Imagine the selectors doing that! They'd be lynched. One of them was Joey Carew, his mentor! No, it was a cop out. He was playing for Lara, not for the country who made him.

Bryan Davis, the former Trinidadian opening batsman who played four Tests and was one of Lara's coaches at school, said:

> He picked and chose his games but after his 375 he came up with a variety of excuses and the selectors had to kowtow to him. He would say 'I don't care, I am Brian Lara.' This very pleasant boy had turned into something else, he'd become arrogant and I was sad to see it.

The British Government is spending £13 million between 2006 and 2009 to recruit thirty-nine British police officers to teach the Trinidad police better policing methods. It has been a painfully slow exercise but legislation is now being passed through Parliament legalising the use of DNA testing and drink-driving prevention measures; there are currently no speed cameras nor breath tests in Trinidad and Tobago, and the road accident figures are horrendous.

An associate of Lara said, 'He used to take the motorcycle he won in Australia round town. People didn't recognise him behind his helmet. Just before the 2004 series against England he fell off and hurt his knee and he doesn't use it now.' Lara has had knee trouble since he played for Warwickshire in 1994 and Valentino Singh, the sports editor of the *Trinidad Guardian* said:

> He wasn't fit for that England series and that explained why Steve Harmison gave him such bother. He was cussing but being able to bat on a very flat pitch at Antigua helped him get back in the runs to make his 400 record. He trains hard to keep in condition, often jogging the four miles up Chancellor Hill.

Trinidad and Tobago still has capital punishment. Eleven years ago nine members of the Dole Chadee gang were hanged after four members of the Baboolal family were gunned down at the Williamsburg massacre and they were the last to be executed. Early in 2007 there was a newspaper headline that read 'TWO WOUNDED IN HILTON HOTEL CAR PARK – DINER SHOT FOR NOT PAYING'. It was a slight error. A twenty-one-year-old man had run up £13,000 debts at the city's best known hotel on a stolen credit card and when approached by a security guard, he reached towards a pocket and the guard shot him. Another ricocheted shot struck a Surinamese Minister. In the past, Lara has stayed at the Hilton Hotel, built on a hill with the reception at the top and the rooms below. Most of the Test squads stay there and it has a strong force of security men, mostly armed.

The day after the shooting a forty-eight-year-old WPC, Elizabeth Sutherland, along with her husband Ivan, aged fifty-nine, her twenty-one-year-old daughter and another man were slaughtered in another massacre, at Morvant. At their funeral, conducted with full military rites and attended by thousands, Pastor Ethelbert Charles condemned the activities of Amnesty International saying:

> It is time the murderers must be hanged. Corporal punishment must be brought back and because this country is an independent republic state and

no human rights association can come forward and say no and have all the members of the Cabinet arrested. Death row must be emptied. [There are dozens of killers sentenced to death still in jail.]

The Minister of Education should also repeal the law that states that children cannot be beaten because there is too much immorality and disrespect that is going on within school walls. We have reached a stage of spiritual bankruptcy. We have to start with the petty things because it leads to the bigger ones.

Fitzgerald Hinds, Junior Minister of National Security, said the police are being threatened daily and witnesses are terrified to give evidence.

One of the most famous victims of the gangsters was Jeffrey Stollmeyer, the former Test opener and captain who was a leading administrator, businessman and a much-loved man. He was born at Mon Valmount, a great house built in 1880 in a valley not far from the Lara family in Santa Cruz in 1921, and was one of the first to spot Brian's talent. He was driving to a race meeting when he saw a tiny boy playing some amazing shots in a junior game near his home and it was Bunty's son Brian. 'I've never seen such talent,' he said. 'He will be a Test player without doubt.' Stollmeyer stayed so long that he was late for the first meeting. And unlike the Prince, he had never been late before that day.

In 1989 Stollmeyer was at his home when two men knocked at the door. 'Where's the money, I want money,' said one, brandishing a gun. Stollmeyer tried to shut the door but he was gunned down. He was flown to America for treatment but died a few days later. It shocked the nation. The Stollmeyers were one of the leading families in Trinidad and Jeffrey's grandfather had built a magnificent castle next to Queen's Park which is now owned by the Government. Jeffrey was a Senator in Parliament, managed tours, was president of the West Indies Board and worked for the ICC. Above all, he was a sportsman who promoted the Corinthian spirit. He invited Muhammed Ali to pay his first visit to Lord's for the 1966 Test and Ali was impressed with the conduct of the players. Whether this was because there was little sledging that day, or a great deal of it, is unknown. Ali was an inveterate sledger in the ring and he kept up a battery of insults aimed at his opponents. Everard Gordon said: 'He used to call them rubbish but if they were rubbish and he beat them that wouldn't enhance his own reputation. If you respect your opponent and praise him, and you defeat them, your stock rises. So why do you need to belittle someone?' That was a creed preached by Stollmeyer, Gerry Gomez, Denis Atkinson, John Goddard, George Headley, Sir Frank Worrell, Sir Clyde Walcott and other great Caribbean cricketers. The flag bearer was Sir Gary Sobers who always 'walked' when he knew he was out. 'Brian Lara always walks,' said Sir Gary. 'And I believe that is a hallmark of a great player. I am proud that he is one of the few of today's players who walks.' Lara is not a sledger by choice. Sometimes he has been angered by comments from Australians and has replied in kind but it is not his style. Real champions honour their opponents, not denigrate them.

One of Stollmeyer's duties as president was to calm tempers during the West Indies' tour of New Zealand in 1980 when Clive Lloyd's players wanted to quit after being victims of some disgraceful umpiring decisions. Michael Holding kicked the stumps down in a Test in protest and Colin Croft deliberately charged into umpire Fred Goodall as he ran in to bowl. Four senior players booked tickets to go home on the last day and manager Willie Rodriguez told Stollmeyer, 'They have decided to go home.' Stollmeyer talked them out of departing and afterwards he restored peace when he ordered them to write an apology to the New Zealand Board. No one was fined or suspended and it was a great coup by Stollmeyer. However, a day before the West Indies team were going to assemble for the start of England's tour several weeks later, he received a call saying the players weren't going unless their payments were improved. Another round of calls produced a minimal increase in pay and the strike was called off. As a man who knows the history of West Indian cricket, Lara has been a rebel leader in these situations, playing a key role in the 1999 Heathrow strike. Cricket in the Caribbean is the most exciting, and sometimes the most explosive, in the world, both on and off the field, which is why it holds the esteem of the bulk of the population. It is never boring. But there have been far too many disputes which should have settled by diplomacy rather than threats and walkouts.

Stollmeyer dedicated his book *Everything in the Sun*, published in 1983, to 'Sara and all cricketers' wives'. He was lucky to be in a happy marriage and it was appropriate that he never forgot the wives. In the final chapter he wrote about the essential difference between English and West Indian cricket:

> With crowds needed, Test cricket must put much more of an emphasis on winning. Those teams which play the more positive cricket have been the successful ones. Isn't that a moral in this for England? Their selection has tended towards safety first and the stroke player has not been sufficiently encouraged. So many of the imported players in county cricket, including West Indians, show the way to success by playing their shots. Our bowlers attack as well and here lies to the secret of our success.

Latterly, the secret has been lost, and this is primarily due to indiscipline because there is plenty of talent around. And some cricket lovers in the Caribbean believe that Lara has helped foster the indiscipline among the present generation of cricketers by setting a poor example.

Friday 27 July 1990 was a day of infamy in Trinidad when 114 Muslim terrorists seized the Parliament building after a suicide bomber drove a truck full of explosives into the main police station a few yards across the road, destroying it. Radio and television stations were stormed at the same time and the Parliament building was forcibly occupied. Prime Minister Arthur Robinson was shot in the leg and an MP died later of his wounds. A group called Jamaat-al-Muslimeen brought the nation to a standstill for a week, threatening to blow up Parliament unless their demands were met. The leader of the group, a former policeman named Lennox Philip, latterly known as Abu Bakr, told startled television viewers, 'We are now in control of the country.'

Clive Pantin, who was Minister of Education from 1981 to 1990 and the principal of Lara's school Fatima College until 1981, was sitting at home watching television. He said:

> I thought it was a play. I couldn't believe what I was seeing. I was the only member of the Cabinet not being held and I went to the Army camp to talk to the commander about what we could do. The terrorists were threatening to kill everyone and blow up this beautiful old building. Abu Bakr sought an amnesty and we refused. We weren't getting very far but one of our lawyers drew up the amnesty agreement and there wasn't much that he could do. Maybe the amnesty wasn't the right answer. The President and several other top officials were all out of the country. It was so fraught. We had to think of the safety of so many people.

The siege was lifted and, astonishingly, the men were released. The Government appealed to the court to nullify the amnesty and a sole judge heard it and upheld it. And he ruled there was to be no appeal to a higher court. It was like a Dario Foy play except that it wasn't funny. Abu Bakr is still living in Trinidad and is playing a prominent part in its affairs. He owns a quarry and it provides a good living for him and his men with the Government paying him for his wares. The Government sued him for TT$21 million for the destruction he caused and in return he is suing them for the damage he claimed was brought about by police seeking to find weapons in his compound which included a mosque along one of the main highways out of Port of Spain. There were no weapons. The court battles are still being played out.

These extraordinary happenings have been blamed for Trinidad's slide towards anarchy. If terrorists who have committed treason, and who according to the law should have been hanged, are still at large, what message does this send out to the young? There are those in Trinidad who believe that discipline has eroded enormously, not just in schools but in every sector: the Government, the police, the poor... and in cricket. There is little respect for elders, no respect for decent behaviour. Malcolm Marshall, possibly the greatest of the Barbadian fast bowlers, who died of cancer at the age of forty-two, said, 'Everything seems to be going down the drain. There is no respect, no manners.' Brian Lara was just about setting out on his journey as a Test player in 1990 and one wonders whether this affected him. Was he caught up in the tide too?

Basdeo Panday, Prime Minister between 1995 and 2001, was recently sentenced to two years in prison and fined TT$20,000 dollars for not declaring details of his bank account in the affair of the redevelopment of Piarco International Airport. He claimed that the money was given to him by a political supporter to provide scholarships for the education of his two daughters. As a Parliamentarian and public figure he would have had to declare his assets to the Integrity Commission. He is appealing but as he was ordered to pay his costs his chances of success are dim. Chief Justice Satnarine Sharma is another facing the prospect of jail. He was accused of interfering in a murder case when a surgeon and his third wife were charged with arranging a contract murder of his second wife. Sharma advised that there was no case to answer and he was overruled. An official said, 'We've got a Prime Minister and a Chief Justice Minister facing jail – what kind of country is this?'

Pantin, aged seventy-four but looking fifteen years younger, is related to the Archbishop of Port of Spain and trained as a priest in Dublin when he was young. He said: 'I fear for my country. The politicians are failing the people. So many of them are close to starvation.' Now retired, he runs a charitable kind of miniature Trinidadian Salvation Army named FEEL, catering for 3,000 destitute people. He is a fine man and his country needs men of his calibre.

Oil is providing riches and much of the wealth is being devoted to the wrong parts. Some is spent on erecting huge, ghastly buildings; some goes into the back pockets of profiteers, gangsters and their protectors. Some £4 million is being spent on a house for Prime Minister Patrick Manning. With the US deporting criminals at will, there is a constant stream of them arriving in Trinidad, often not having come from the island in the first place. They augment the other gangs and it is like a tumour strangling the life out of the country. The gangs are controlled by so-called 'elders' who are given financial backing from official sources to 'reform' deprived areas. Law-abiding citizens feel powerless. Only their innate sense of fun, rising to the annual climax at carnival in February, keeps their spirits high. Low-level criminals are sometimes arrested but those at the top are rarely touched.

In the same week of the Morvant massacre, Inshan Ishmael. owner of the Islamic Broadcast Network, was arrested for distributing leaflets appealing to the public to join in a shut-down throughout the country to protest against rising crime. At first he was charged under anti-terrorist legislation, but later he was instead charged for failing to put his name and address on his leaflets. He is not an extremist. Morvant is in one of the worst areas for crime and in June 2005 a sixteen-year-old boy was killed there when someone threw a petrol bomb into his small home. Another man was fatally shot and a father was slaughtered in front of his four-year-old son while swimming. Frankie Francis, a football coach at the Russell Latapy Secondary School in Morvant said: 'There are some positives here. We have our youth and our football.' The name of the school was changed to honour one of the finest Soca Warriors stars – ostensibly as a role model for the coming generation. Latapy agrees with his friend Lara that heroes need to be used in the fight against crime.

As in England, schools in Trinidad are cutting down on sporting activities and Lara's proposed scheme to fund coaching for children and encourage them to take up sport could fill a void. One leading academic said:

> It is becoming so dangerous that kids can't go out to play and if they are not playing organised sport at school it is going to lead to a serious situation. Trinidadians love sport but where are the next Laras coming from? Cricket bats cost up to TT$2,000 and only rich parents can equip boys properly. The rest rely on donations or cast-offs or make their own.

Valentino Singh said:

> Brian is very serious about this. He is going to give most of his time to it when he retires from cricket. He has talked to me about ideas about paying youngsters to take up sport and give them hope in their lives. It will need corporate support and he hopes it will happen.

Imran Khan, who captained Pakistan to victory in the 1992 World Cup, beating Graham Gooch's England at Melbourne by 22 runs, led his Justice

Party in the 1997 election in Pakistan and was heavily beaten by Nawaz Sharif. He fought on an anti-corruption ticket but his party was virtually wiped out. Charles Fry, not the 2006 MCC president but Charles Burgess Fry, the England Test cricketer born in West Croydon and renowned international sportsman, was once offered the position of King of Albania but declined. Not many famous cricketers become leading politicians but Singh believes Brian Lara could do it and be a success. 'I think he could be Prime Minister of Trinidad eventually,' he said. 'He speaks well and he cares for young people and he sees it as his mission. If he put up he would definitely win. He's the most admired person in the country.'

One lady who would win his vote is the English wife of a leading businessman in Port of Spain who was once was attacked by a hooded man in her holiday home in Tobago. The man held a knife to her throat and threatened to kill her, then took her wedding ring and engagement ring and bound her and left her on the floor before departing. Before she managed to free herself, he returned with more demands. It was a terrifying experience but it ended when the man ran off. She said:

> I'm certain Lara could be Prime Minister. He has made plenty of mistakes in his life but he is now mature and confident. He is loved by most of the people and with the right people helping him he could turn the country around. If Arnold Schwarzenegger can become Governor of California and Ronald Reagan be President of the USA, I am sure he can do it.

Someone close to the current Prime Minister Patrick Manning had a different opinion to the English lady's view. 'Brian says all the right things but often he does the opposite,' he said. Deryck Murray said: 'I know that Brian can inspire young people but I haven't heard that he is interested in going into politics. I would be surprised.' Ato Boldon, the Trinidadian sprinter who won five Olympic medals, is a successful politician in Trinidad. He is a friend of Lara's and is a highly valued member of the Senate. He could show him the way, although he may go into sports production before the imminent election. The organisation of the existing parties would probably preclude a Prime Minister from outside the two main parties and a new party would have to get grassroots support to succeed. But with the right backing, Lara would have a good chance if he felt he was up to it.

three

Not Quite Born With a Bat in his Hand – But Almost

Following England's Ashes triumph of 2005 there were cases of babies in South London's 'Nappy Valley' – the stretch of land between Wandsworth Common and Clapham Common – being given miniature cricket bats at an early age. One father, living in Clapham, gave one to his son on his first birthday and within a short time the toddler had started whacking a plastic ball around, even before learning to walk or use the potty. He might be another Brian Lara... or maybe not.

Starting at three with the miniature bat made for him by his brother, the Prince of Trinidad was a late starter by Nappy Valley standards. However, Brian Lara was bestowed with a number of God-given gifts which turned him into a cricketing genius, like being left-handed (making it awkward for opposing bowlers); his love of the sport, inherited from his loving father Bunty and his grandfather Herbert St Louis; his fanatical determination to practise all day, often on his own (following the example of Don Bradman); a dynamic hand-eye co-ordination which enabled him to pick the line and length of the ball so early; and finally, his genes, which gave him a hardy physique.

He always knew what he wanted: to be the best. Before she died, Lara's mother, Pearl, told Colin Wills of the *Sunday Mirror*:

There was never any problem keeping him amused. He did it all himself. Cricket found him when he was three and never left him. All I heard was the tap-tap-tap of the marbles hitting against the wood. He did that in the yard as well, using dustbins as fielders. It was cricket all the time. There were times when I wished he'd never heard of cricket. He would break windows regularly. Once we were sitting down having dinner when there was a huge crash and a ball landed in the stew!

Mrs Lara told another journalist, the *Daily Mail*'s George Gordon:

> When there wasn't anyone to play he played on his own. As he grew older, he used a tennis ball and knocked it against the walls. No one ever had to tell Brian where to put his feet or how to hold a bat. For him, the right way was just instinctive.
>
> He would often stay out late, well after dark fell. I would be crazy with worry. Then he would arrive and I would give him such a slap and tell him never to do that again. He'd say 'Yes Mum' but it was no use. I was just worried for him, that something dreadful might have happened. It is the same now in a way. He is famous, I know, but I still have this fear. I know cricket can be a dangerous game, that injuries happen. I just want him to come home like he always did, healthy and smiling. I'd like him to marry one day and perhaps have children. But not yet. It wouldn't be fair on a wife. All the travelling, all the parties.

When he was young, Pearl dressed him up in his best clothes and took him to church every Sunday. Pearl was a Seventh Day Adventist but now Brian rarely attends a church.

In his six years at Fatima College, Brian Lara was voted Player of the Year several times, scored sixteen centuries – including four by the age of fourteen – and won countless trophies. He also won regular trophies at Harvard Cricket School and the front room was full of them. Since first hitting a marble with his miniature bat, he has graduated through rubber balls and tennis balls to cricket balls, but Keith Gomez, a neighbour, recalled: 'When he was four he came down into the orange grove because no one would bowl to him. He asked the orange pickers to throw a few oranges so that he could hit them.'

Born on 2 May 1969, he was the eleventh and last-born of the family and was the seventh son. He weighed seven pounds exactly. At thirty-eight he is still the favourite; the eldest is now fifty-seven. With a wide gap in age, some of the others took a personal interest in his sporting future, particularly his sister Agnes Cyrus. Some close to the Laras say he was somewhat spoiled, a claim which he doesn't contest. Agnes told *The Guardian*:

> When he was playing in the porch, he used to execute every stroke perfectly. When he was six, I saw an advertisement in the local newspaper asking for youngsters who were interested in cricket coaching at the Harvard School. I filled the coupon in and took him along. I bought him a little green cap, some white clothes and his first proper bat. I took him down for the first two

Sundays and then my father took over, wholly and solely. He never missed a practice or a match of Brian's until the day he died.

Bunty would collect him from school at three o'clock to drive him to the Harvard School in time to start practising at four. Hugo Day was in his seventies and he took the boys, with the help of a few volunteers. There were no competitive matches. Most of the time was spent practising and that suited the small boy. Edward Gordon, one of the coaches, said:

> When I first saw him I thought, 'What a scrawny shrimp – he's too small to play.' When he was eleven he looked about eight, but when you put a bat in his hand he was a child transformed. He was better than fifteen-year-olds. He practised and practised until the last ball was bowled and the last rays of sunshine disappeared.

At his first school, St Joseph's Roman Catholic Primary School, Lara was in the first team at the age of eight but the deputy headmistress, Mrs Merle Joel, wanted him to study more instead of playing so much cricket. 'He will never make a career out of cricket,' she said. Vernon Lyons, the sports master, disagreed and he won the battle. Steve Vissesser, the principal, said: 'Brian was a bright boy and was a good cricketer when he was there but he was never brilliant. That was to come later.' Lara wanted to move to Fatima College at eleven but, with his marks too low to qualify for a place, he was earmarked for another school. Bunty took him see the principal, Clive Pantin, and pleaded with him to admit his son. Pantin said:

> I explained to him that the school has very high standards both academically and in behaviour. He said to me, 'That is the reason I want Brian to be at your school.' Bunty was a very impressive and a humble man. Brian went to the Second Form and he studied diligently but it was obvious to us that he wanted to be a cricketer. I remember seeing him trying to put his pads on. He was so small and the top of his pad was up to his stomach. He was always practising and if a boy bowled a little short the ball would go over his head. They didn't have helmets.

Mervyn Moore, who succeeded Pantin, said:

> We all thought he might be a little small to make it as a cricketer. It frustrated him. I was once told he had burst into tears because of it. But his potential

greatness soon became clear in the Under-14 Giants League. He was marvellous in 'pass out', where there is no wicket and you are out if you miss the ball. He would be in all day.

Lara recalled:

> My height was definitely a handicap. I was only five feet tall until my mid-teens and I remember in one match I went to the wicket with pads almost up to my thighs, and baggy pants, and when I took guard there was a chuckle behind me as one of the fielders said, 'It will be just a matter of time before this guy is out.' It was a matter of time – quite some time! When bowlers tried to exploit my lack of height by bouncing me it made me all the more determined to do well. The school matches started on Fridays at 3.30 and continued on Saturdays and there wasn't much time to get a result, which put pressure on batsmen to score quickly. I did my best to oblige.

His sixteen centuries at Fatima were almost invariably scored at a rate of around one run a minute. Moore told *The Guardian*'s Richard Williams:

> I remember going to Barbados for a tournament in 1987 involving schools from the West Indies, Canada and England. Sir Garfield Sobers was there. He said then that Lara was the finest talent he had seen for a long time. Our team wasn't that good. But Brian could really motivate the boys and get the best out of each of them. He was fiercely competitive, but I never heard him shout. He just had this calm authority which everybody responded to. He never lorded it over anybody. I always remember him with a little smile on his face. He was very well mannered. I never had to discipline him.

Harry Ramdass, the Dean of the Lower Form, was in charge of the Under-14 team and he pointed out a skill in Lara's approach to the game which helped him to be captain of the school, then Trinidad and finally the West Indies:

> He knew exactly where the field was when he was batting. He even seemed to know who was weak on what side, which players who weren't quick. No one told him. He knew. The opposing side's coach said he thought it was a fluke at first. But then he realised it was deliberate. He had never seen anything like it before. Brian was his toughest critic. If he was having a problem with a particular shot he would tie a ball on a string to the nets so that it was

coming in at the difficult angle, and he would hit them until he had beaten the problem.

Another of the school's cricket coaches, Francisco Santos, the Under-16 coach, said:

> I didn't need to coach Brian. It was just a joy to umpire and to watch him at close range. He never seemed to hit the ball to the boundary. He just stroked it. It was sheer delight. I remember reading that Bradman would practise with a stump and a golf ball or that Sobers would use a stump and a tennis ball. Lara used a small bat, or a ruler sometimes, and hit a marble against a wall. Can you imagine? He never forgets to come here to say hello. He is very amiable, with a joke. We have a saying in Trinidad: go and lime. It means to relax, have a few drinks and enjoy yourself. Maybe he feels he can do that better here than in England.

Lara is sensitive about the suggestion that he came from a poor family. 'But with eleven children my father had no money to spend on luxuries,' he said. 'He was a manager employed by the Ministry of Agriculture and it was one of the top jobs in the village. He had to make sacrifices to buy shoes and clothes and school books.' Bunty wanted to be a cricketer himself but Lara recalled:

> He might have gone on to do it but after being asked to play in a regional match he was stranded because according to him the donkey cart couldn't get there to pick him up. He told me once he played in a game in which his side was all out for six, and he made four!

Denied the opportunity to play himself, Bunty devoted himself to helping his youngest son. He drove the boy all over the island in his dilapidated Morris Cambridge to ensure he was on time. He also started a junior cricket league for boys on a nearby ground and the pitch was red clay with matting. Matting pitches were common in Trinidad and many still survive because of the low cost of maintenance. Grass pitches need regular attention, whereas matting lasts for a long time.

When he was young there was no television in the bungalow and he and his father used to listen to the cricket commentaries on the radio, especially from Australia. He said:

My father would be listening to his radio in the lounge and I knew he would
be upset if he felt I was missing out on sleep because of school next day. But
I used to listen to a transistor which I hid under my pillow. I imagined myself
as Roy Fredericks. Roy was the Guyana and West Indies left-handed opener
who was at the height of his career. He appealed to me because he played so
many flamboyant shots. I was so obsessed about him and his exploits that the
other boys called me Roy Fredericks. I wore my shirt buttoned at the wrist,
just like him.

I also idolised Viv Richards for the exciting way he played. I realised that it
was probably better for my own game if I shaped up like Gordon Greenidge
who played straighter, but Viv had wonderful eyesight and was able to get
away with playing across the line when he played the ball to the leg side.
Listening to these players enthralled me. I wanted to learn everything about
them. When I eventually met Roy, who had become a selector, I found it
frightening. But he gave me plenty of good advice.

His grandfather actually died from a stroke while listening to a Australia
v. West Indies series at the age of seventy. When television arrived in that
part of Trinidad, he would study the techniques of the West Indian batting
stars, players like Seymour Nurse, Conrad Hunte and Gordon Greenidge,
all stylists. Lara was a useful footballer, although his size counted against him.
Once he cut his knee playing football in the street and his father was angry
with him. He didn't want him to play a rough game which might stop him
playing the game he loved. Lara said:

> I played football regularly and represented the Trinidad and Tobago Under-14
> side in the same year as my great friends Dwight Yorke and Russell Latapy. I was
> a forward who relied on speed. Another of my friends and former colleagues
> was Shaka Hislop, the Trinidadian goalkeeper who played for Reading and
> West Ham. My footballing career finished around that time because it became
> clear that cricket was what I was destined for. My father was delighted.

Shaka, named from the Zulu kings, said: 'Brian was a very good footballer
but he knew that cricket was his destiny. He was a good, all-round sportsman. He played tennis, squash and table tennis and later he took up golf,
which he loves.' Bryan Davis, the former West Indies and Glamorgan opening batsman, played a major part in Lara's development, urging him to play
straight and keep the ball along the ground:

I was a coach at Fatima and when he arrived at the nets I took one look at him and said to myself, 'Jeez, this little lad is going places.' He was very pleasant, very eager. One day he said to me, 'Are you going to be coach for next year Sir?' and when I said yes he replied, 'Hurrah!' That made feel good because not many coaches are told anything praiseworthy by their pupils. I didn't have to tell him much. He knew it himself. Early on I had to put him down to five in the order because he slowed down the run rate with his short legs. On another occasion he said to me, 'Why has Gary Sobers' record of 365 not been broken after all these years?' I explained that captains were declaring to win games and it's becoming harder to set records. He replied, 'It's one of my goals. I want to beat his record.'

In most successful sporting careers there is often a moment, a turning point, which changes their lives. Lara's came when his father introduced him to Michael Conrad Carew, known as Joey, when his son was being coached at Harvard Clinic. Joey, a left-hander, played 19 Tests for the West Indies between 1963 and 1972, averaging 34.15, and his nineteen-year career with Trinidad had just ended when he became Brian Lara's mentor, filling the boy's mind with his own knowledge and love for the game. Later Lara said:

When it was late and difficult to make the journey back home, sometimes lasting an hour, Joey invited us to stay the night at his home. Joey would talk cricket to us for hours, we watched videos of matches and he would talk about what made the great players so good. I learned a lot from him and he still gives me very good advice.

Carew became chief executive at the Queen's Park Cricket Club – the equivalent of the MCC – in Port of Spain and was a Test selector for many years. 'Brian's talent was God-given,' said Carew. 'He was born this way.' Lara, who became a firm friend of his cricketing son Michael, said: 'He was a father figure to me and I appreciate everything he has done for me.' In subsequent years when Lara has been in trouble he turns to Carew for advice. They are still good friends.

Bryan Davis offers the opinion that the Carew influence wasn't as beneficial as most people think:

Brian was away from home at a young age and Joey is a bit of a cynic. Joey would talk about the abilities of captains, criticising them and Brian probably picked up the same habit when he led the West Indies and later lost the captaincy. And Joey was a gambler and still is and his son Michael, who could have been a Test player, also gambled.

David Francois, a coach and mentor, was another key person in the Lara story. He said:

> By seventeen he was the outstanding young batsman in Trinidad and he set Under-19 cricket afire with his performances. He wasn't going to go to university and he wanted to play cricket for a living. I was working with Angostura Bitters and we arranged a job and some sponsorship with him to enable him to play cricket. I found him an extremely nice boy, soft spoken. He used to give money to his mother.

Lara made his debut for Trinidad at the age of eighteen against the Leeward Islands, and he made an undistinguished start, being dismissed for 14 and 22, firstly caught and then stumped by wicketkeeper L.L. Harris off the slow left-arm bowling of the first cricketer from the small island of Nevis (population 15,000) to play for the West Indies – thirty-five-year-old Elquemedo Tonito Willett, who made five international appearances. A week later he faced Malcolm Marshall and Joel Garner and scored 92, showing immense fortitude against two of the greatest bowlers who has ever played the game. He was on his way.

four

A Turbulent Start to a Test Career

Brian Lara was captain of Trinidad at the age of twenty and most people forecast that he would skipper the West Indies within a couple of years. In fact he had to wait nine years before that happened. There were various reasons why he failed to meet the objective, including his inconsistent pattern of scoring early on and scepticism among some selectors, who felt he was temperamental and had a chip on his shoulder which was weighing him down. So they kept him waiting and resentment built up.

Clive Lloyd, who has managed four West Indian tours, offered this explanation:

> We had some good batsmen at that time. Viv was still there, Desmond Haynes, Carl Hooper, Richie Richardson, Gus Logie, and it was a good side. I rated him but I only saw the limited television coverage of that time. Perhaps some other people didn't think he had set the world alight yet. They saw him as a one-day player and he played in the 1992 World Cup and they used him as an opener. And he wasn't keen on opening.

When Lara left school he worked for a while as a clerk with Angostura Bitters, his first sponsor when he finally made the grade as a professional cricketer. At the age of eighteen – his hero Gary Sobers was capped at the age of seventeen years 245 days – he was appointed captain of the Trinidad side for the World Youth Cup in Australia, a one-off tournament that helped the cricketing education of no fewer than five Test captains: Mike Atherton, who was fourteen months older than Lara, Nasser Hussain, Inzamam-ul-Haq, Jimmy Adams and Brian Lara himself. Atherton and he are still good friends despite the Lancastrian changing his opinion of Lara from 'a genius' to 'a flawed genius'. In his award-winning book *Playing with Fire* Nasser Hussain wrote:

He was a good friend at the time. I had been out for a drink with him in Adelaide. There was no doubt that Brian changed after his 501. He became more wary and didn't know who he could trust and who his real friends were anymore and I sort of drifted away from him. I suppose in his 375 he went from mere mortal to the greatest batsman in the world and it was bound to have an effect on him.

The following spring, Lara scored 182 against India in a friendly and it started a pattern which still survives in his career: a few low scores, then a massive one, and back to ordinary totals before going back up the mountain again. To date, he has failed to exceed 20 on 89 occasions out of 232 innings. That innings of 182 persuaded the Test selectors to add his name to the squad for the third Test against India at Queen's Park and he was named as twelfth man. At the end of the second day, 15 April 1989, his father Bunty died of a heart attack at the age of sixty-two. He had had two previous heart attacks and was forced to stop work at the age of fifty-five. Lara said:

> It was the saddest time of my life. He had done so much for me and in his latter years he devoted his life to helping my goals. It was a tragedy that he died when I was so close to attaining them. He always said to me that if you wanted to achieve anything in life you must have dedication, discipline and determination. I have tried to be faithful to that creed, and when I scored my 375 I dedicated my innings to him.

It was one of sport's most loving father-son relationships, and losing his father at a comparatively young age left his heart permanently scarred. In crucial times of his career, like when he walked out of the team in 1995, he has burst into tears when faced by officials of the West Indian Board of Control. A friend said, 'It's called post-traumatic stress and if you've lost someone very close to you and that you love very deeply, it can last all your life. Your emotions are closer to the surface and when confronted by a stressful situation, you are likely to break down.' Bunty's funeral was a sombre affair and it was attended by the whole of the West Indies squad.

At the end of 1989, at the age of nineteen, Lara was appointed captain of the West Indies 'B' side in Zimbabwe and in his three innings he scored 145, 35 and 7. Carl Hooper, whom he called 'the most elegant player I played with', described his 145 as 'the worst century you've scored'. Lara said, 'For once I couldn't disagree. I played and missed countless times and kept finding the edge but I maintain that being captain carried me through. Leading from the front brings the best out of me.'

In Trinidad's first year under Lara's captaincy, they lost all four matches in the Red Stripe competition of 1990, and he was promptly sacked. He blamed 'a bad run of scores', contending also that 'many of the older players resented that I was a little boy made captain ahead of them and they never gave me 100% support.' Gus Logie, nine years older, who once presented him with a bat, took over as captain. Lara was seething and said years later, 'The experience affected me deeply and it took four years to get the job back.' Two months after his sacking, he impressed the England selectors, if not the Trinidadian ones, by scoring a sumptuous 134 against England for the West Indies Board President's XI at the oil town of Pointe-a-Pierre, forty miles south of Trinidad.

Logie returned after injury to keep him out of the Test squad and it was a frustrating time, almost a year, before he eventually made his Test debut. Luck went his way for once. Pakistan were supposed to be touring India at the end of 1990 but the countries failed to agree terms and the West Indies were invited to fill the slot in the calendar. Their squad took a tortuous route to Pakistan, playing in a tournament in Toronto first. The day after they arrived, they played a one-day international in Karachi. Lara came in at five with the score at 137 for three and with Waqar Younis on a hat-trick. Lara hadn't faced a bowler of his pace and hostility up to then. The noise was deafening with 25,000 Pakistanis chanting 'Waqar, Waqar, Waqar'. 'I did well to get 11,' Lara reflected.

He knew he needed runs with Logie and Carlisle Best ahead of him as middle-order candidates and against a Combined XI at Sargodha he chipped out 139 off 270 balls on a slow pitch. He was excluded from the first two Tests which left him low in spirits but when Best cut the webbing of a hand he took over at number four. Best had scored only 22 in four innings and Lara should really have been picked earlier. He went to the wicket at 24 for two and with Wasim Akram moving the ball both ways, had him caught off a no ball and almost caught at short leg. He took twenty minutes to get off the mark. Around this time the Waqar–Wasim duo had perfected ordinary and reverse swing with a old ball roughed up on one side and treated with spit on the other. In his autobiography, Lara said, 'As a newcomer, I didn't feel it was my place to get involved and the umpires rarely examined the ball.' But Lance Gibbs, the West Indian manager, protested to the Pakistan Board about the interference with the ball. Also, there were twenty-five lbws awarded by the umpires in that series and only four of them were against Pakistan. It proved to be a good baptism for the coming star.

After two hours of toil, Lara was caught off the bowling of that great leg-spin bowler Abdul Qadir. 'I was quite pleased with myself,' he said, going on to reflect: 'Pakistan is a dangerous place to play cricket. Courtney Walsh was struck a painful blow on the back from a missile and had to go off for treatment. Some players were hit by apples.' The man who threw the missile was arrested and given a thorough beating. Walsh was so angry that he charged to the middle, pulled out a stump and held it high in his hand, giving the impression that he was ready to hit any more possible assailants. This writer reported the incident in the *Daily Mail*, which drew the threat of a lawsuit from Walsh's lawyer. The graphic accompanying picture told the story though, and there was no further action.

Lara finished top of the batting averages in the Pakistan tour with an average of 70.66 from four innings and must have thought he had an outstanding chance of being picked for the visit of Allan Border's Australians three months later, especially when he set a record of 627 runs, averaging 69.66, for the 1991 Red Stripe competition. Desmond Haynes raised it to 654 a week later but even so, being number two in the list was a fine achievement. He was picked in the squad for the first Test against Australia at Kingston only to learn on the day before it started that he was twelfth man. 'That killed my spirits,' he said. 'I didn't know what I had to do to impress the selectors.' More than anything, this brought on the 'attitude' which affected him around this time. Observers in Trinidad felt he had changed for the worse. There were more sulks than smiles.

As captain of the Under-23 side – the West Indies have a good record of staging matches to advance the careers of younger players – he played in three warm-up games against the Australians, scoring 33, 22 and four for the Under-23s and 56 and 36 for the President's XI. He thought he should have been the next batsman to be promoted. Unfortunately for him, there were some serious contenders: Gordon Greenidge, who was reprieved after averaging 9.66 in Pakistan, Haynes, Richie Richardson, Carl Hooper, Logie, who scored an unbeaten 77 in the first Test and the kingly Viv Richards.

His next match was a friendly for Trinidad against the tourists at Pointe-a-Pierre and he scored 33 without convincing the selectors that someone else had to be sacrificed to bring him in. Heavy rain ruined the match and the Australians asked the West Indies Board to lay on a one-day game, ostensibly to provide some exercise for their lanky opening bowler Bruce Reid. The Board generously agreed and Lara seized his chance, scoring 91. The local Press called for his instant promotion but he failed to get the call. His supporters claimed he had been discriminated against and Lara admitted this was one of his lowest times.

Viv Richards was the captain and he assured him that he would be chosen for the tour of England in the summer. 'You'll be in the sixteen,' he told him. Lara was doubtful. 'I didn't see myself as a certainty,' he said. 'I hadn't played at all in the series but I was in the best form of my life and some of the players who played in all five matches hadn't established themselves.' Viv was right and Lara was selected. He was given every opportunity early in the tour to stake a claim. He scored just 15 in a one-day opening game at Arundel against the Duchess of Norfolk's XI, with the West Indies losing; he scored 30 against Gloucestershire at Bristol and struggled against swing bowler Phil Newport at Worcester, reaching 26. He wasn't chosen for the first two Texaco Cup ODIs but his mood improved when he was picked as replacement for the injured Greenidge at Lord's. On an excellent pitch, he played too early and was caught and bowled for 23 by Richard Illingworth, the Worcestershire slow left-arm bowler. Yet again he failed to make a meaningful score. A classy 93 at Taunton raised his hopes again until he began to worry about the introduction of the twenty-nine-year-old Guyanan left-handed opener Clayton Lambert for the injured Greenidge. Lambert, a slap-banger with a good one-day record, wasn't in the same class as Lara but the selectors brought him in at five in the final Test at the Oval. Called up from Blackhall, the North Yorkshire and Durham League club, it proved to be Lambert's only Test that summer, although he played two more against England in 1998 and two against South Africa.

By now Lara was out injured. Phil Simmons, his friend from Port of Spain, was used as opener with Haynes and he averaged just 18.10 from his five Tests. Lara was bowling to Viv Richards in the indoor nets at Edgbaston when the ball was driven back to him with such power that he fell awkwardly and badly sprained an ankle trying to avoid it. His foot was so painful that he couldn't put any weight on his leg and had to be helped to the dressing-room. As he sat down he burst into tears and said to Lance Gibbs, the tour manager who bore a slight resemblance to Bunty, his father, 'I want my air ticket to go home. I've had enough!'

It wasn't just the accident, he explained, but all the frustration he had experienced in the past year or so. 'I was twenty-two and eager to advance my career and I hadn't been given a chance,' he said later. 'Calm down,' said Lance. 'Tell me what happened.' Lara mentioned that he was always batting last in the nets, facing the net bowlers not the mainline ones. And he claimed that some of the senior players hadn't shown respect to him. Lara's recollection of this was: 'One of them made a remark to the effect "that I only got into the side because Joey Carew was a selector". This was a senior player whom I idolised and it disturbed me greatly. I was thoroughly dismayed at the atmosphere around this time.' What he said was perfectly true but was he developing a persecution complex? And did he need to grow up a bit more? Some people thought so.

Nowadays the major cricketing countries employ a sports psychologist and though Dr Rudi Webster did some stints with the West Indies, the former world champions did not employ a full-time one. In 1991 Lara needed someone to sit down and talk with him. And Gibbs wasn't the man to do it. Lara brought up an incident in an Indian restaurant in Leeds after England won the first Test, a game in which Graham Gooch scored a magnificent 154. He told the others that he didn't think the West Indies had batted well. According to him, Gibbs dismissed his view, saying, 'A player like you wouldn't have scored many anyway at Leeds. You would have been a failure.' Lara wrote later: 'He might have been a great bowler for the West Indies but I don't think he was a good manager. His handling of certain players, me included, could have been much better. Once he told me, "You think you can bat like Gary Sobers."' After that, Lara kept away from Gibbs: they were two proud and stubborn men who didn't, and wouldn't, get together to talk things through.

Lara's foot was put into plaster and the management allowed him to return home. His miserable tour yielded 344 runs at an average of 24.57. Not enough, as Gibbs would have told him. The injury took time to heal and he played only three Red Stripe matches that season – one century in five innings – before he was chosen for the West Indies squad for the World Cup in Australia and New Zealand in 1992. The West Indies failed to qualify for the final stage but Lara's figures were impressive as an opener. In the first qualifier against Pakistan in Melbourne he was on 88 when he was painfully struck on a foot by a yorker bowled by Wasim Akram, the bowler he rated the best bowler he has ever faced. Batsmen protect their private parts, their legs, their chests, their forearms and their heads but they don't wear adequate boots that can withstand a ball delivered at 90mph. With his face contorted with pain, he went off and Richie Richardson came in to shepherd the West Indies to a ten-wicket win.

Despite his injury, Lara went in against England's Chris Lewis and Phil DeFreitas with the ball swinging prodigiously a few days later and was struck in the box by Lewis's first ball and caught by keeper Alec Stewart from the second. At the end of the World Cup, which Pakistan's tigers won, driven on by their captain Imran Khan, Viv Richards retired, Gus Logie was about to do the same, and Lara was ready for a Test recall.

five

The Floodgates Open

Between 5 December 1990 when Brian Lara made his Test debut in Karachi and 18 April 1992 when he played his second Test, against South Africa at the Kensington Oval, Barbados, he experienced 524 days without playing any Test cricket. Out of the other greats of world cricket – Bradman, Tendulkar, Hutton, Compton, Hanif Mohammad, the Three Ws – none of them were capped at a young age and then put into hibernation. The only great batsman in that class to be treated like that was Lara.

One senior player had a theory about Lara's exclusion order – he put the blame on skipper Viv Richards. He said:

Brian's main motivation to establish himself as a Test player was Viv. He was ready to play for his country but Viv kept him out for two years. Viv is a good man, not vindictive, but he saw Brian as a threat. Brian's aim was to prove him wrong. Viv claimed he wanted to protect him and stick him in at the right time. Bullshit! He stopped him playing for reasons of his own ego. Brian has a big ego too and for a while Viv put his own ego in front of West Indies cricket. Most people knew that he should have been brought in a long time before.

In his autobiography *Sir Vivian*, Richards said:

Brian probably felt I had been a bit harsh with him when he was first making his way into the team. There were many who thought he should have been in the team a lot earlier but I didn't select him as often as he would have liked because I was one of those captains who were very faithful to the players, the players who had helped to take us places and with whom we were still winning. It was in my thoughts to bring him into the team every now and again, include him in the squad and gradually work him in but there were many others who wanted to rush him. It wasn't that he was not ready but he needed to see how we operated, to see what was going on within the squad and witness the discipline and other aspects of the team. A lot of things happened to Brian very fast and he learned some hard lessons. I tried to be a father figure to him because I could see a wonderful talent in him and I felt that after I retired he could be the one to take over and help keep West Indies cricket at the top. I believed that as captain I had to play my part in laying out discipline and certain guidelines, and to this end I used to invite him to join me and talk about the responsibilities.

When I spoke with him, I found him a mature lad who could hold his own in any company but we all make little mistakes and there are times when he was a bit casual. My advice was to become a little more aloof and more professional, though it is hard to do when you have been one of the boys. He needed to be more forceful and be first on the bus, first to arrive at practice and take a genuine interest in being leader of the team. He will never have the respect of his peers if he misses aeroplanes, is late for meetings and doesn't turn up for practice, no matter how good he is out in the middle.

Lara's second Test was a truly memorable and controversial match, the inaugural game between West Indies and South Africa after the abolition of apartheid when the South Africa electors voted for it three weeks earlier. In the lead-up to the game a kind of reverse apartheid was brought in with the home supporters deciding to boycott the Test because Anderson Cummins, a fast medium bowler from Barbados, was left out of the West Indies side. It would only happen in the West Indies. The late Sir Clyde Walcott, who was about to be made president of the ICC, said in his autobiography:

> The various regions of the Caribbean have always had an insular approach to the selection of the West Indies and now we were to see one of the worst manifestations of it. It was a depressing saga that brought only embarrassment and no credit to Barbados. I thought the selectors were perfectly entitled to leave Cummins out and with Curtly Ambrose and Courtney Walsh sharing all ten wickets in the second innings that was conclusively proved. As chairman of the Board, the public wanted me to overrule the selectors and include Cummins. I wasn't empowered to do that and would not have done so anyway because I didn't think Cummins was worth a pick.

Several other issues had also contributed to the boycott: the dropping of Carlisle Best, a Bajan, from the previous Bridgetown Test, the exclusion of

Malcolm Marshall from the last World Cup squad and Desmond Haynes being overlooked as captain of the West Indies.

On the final day there were fewer than 500 people at the ground, bringing the overall total up to around 6,000 and the South Africans were close to victory. They were 122 for two, needing to reach 201, but Ambrose and Walsh took the last eight wickets for only 26 runs on a flat pitch, maintaining the unbeaten record in Tests at Bridgetown stretching back fifty-seven years. There were astonishing scenes, with the unprepared South Africans slinking back to the dressing-room to be berated by their dour captain Kepler Wessels while Richie Richardson's players did an emotional lap of honour holding hands, as Richardson said, 'to show the people of the Caribbean how united we are'.

Lara's contributions, 17 and 64, plus five slip catches, were very useful ones but after the presentations, Sir Clyde went up to him and said, 'I hear you are the person who should be the man of the match.' The award was shared by Curtly Ambrose and Andrew Hudson. Lara looked surprised. Sir Clyde went on 'I hear you had the South Africans out until four in the morning,' he laughed. 'Actually it was two o'clock, not four,' said Lara.

At this stage of his career Lara liked to have late nights during big games and that was one of the reasons why the selectors were reluctant to pick him. In the World Cup in Australia Deryck Murray, the manager, brought in a curfew but Lara said, 'Personally I don't think curfews work because there is always the temptation to break them. Each individual will know what is best for him.' Since then he has been more restrained, especially after he took over as captain.

A Bajan nightspot, 'Harbour Lights' was the venue for his night out on the eve of the final day of the inaugural South Africa Test. It is right on a beach and the noise of the band was ear-splitting. He was having a drink when some of the South African players came in. He shouted to them, 'Don't drink too much, you'll be batting early in the morning.' One of them, a bowler, shouted back, 'I don't think so.' Another said, 'You won't be wide awake to take a catch.' Lara soon proved him wrong. He dived to make one of the best catches of his career, ending the innings of Wessels, who top-scored with 74. That started the collapse.

As the South Africans arrived, Lara told them, 'You remember what I told you – you've got it coming!' The game ended twenty minutes from lunch with the West Indies winning by 52 runs. The South Africans were short of preparation and their lack of professionalism let them down. Lara had an up-and-down relationship with Allan Donald, South Africa's fiery, unsmiling fast bowler, and there were angry words from him and some of his colleagues when Lara appeared to knock a bail off as he set off for a run. He had just reached his first half-century in Tests as he turned a ball from Tertius Bosch down to fine leg for a single. Hansie Cronje shouted from gully, 'Hey, the bail is off.' Lara said he 'felt something' but he thought he had completed his shot. He claimed he was 'confused' but he was right to stay at the crease and await the verdict. In those days there was no third umpire watching a monitor, otherwise he might have been given out. Umpires Steve Bucknor and Dan Archer conferred and, not having seen the incident, they allowed Lara to resume his innings. Donald was not amused. Lara's back foot goes a long way when he plays off the back foot and this was the first occasion he had knocked off a bail.

When he was on 64, and fairly confident of reaching his maiden century, he was given out, caught by wicketkeeper Dave Richardson off Donald's bowling. Lara was sure that the ball had struck a pad rather than his bat and hesitated before he departed. Donald was overjoyed. Later when the two protagonists met up, Donald admitted that he didn't think the ball nicked the bat. Someday a bowler may say to the umpire, 'Hey, it wasn't out! Cancel the appeal!' Well, perhaps not.

six

His Greatest Innings: 277 Run Out

Brian Lara still insists that his greatest innings was played at Sydney in early January, 1993, and it meant so much to him that his daughter was named Sydney after Australia's most popular tourist city. His 375 and his 501* were fantastic efforts of stamina and mental strength but his 277 against Australia in the third Test had panache, style and beauty and admiring rival skipper Allan Border said, 'and he never hit the ball over the top!' Rohan Kanhai, the former West Indies Test batsman, said, 'It is one of the best innings I've ever seen.' Border told Tony Cozier:

> It was just a phenomenal knock for a bloke who is so young to show that maturity. He was just relentless in that he kept it on the ground all the way through. You felt that when he got into the hundreds he would start looking to go over the top. But he never did. Just for sheer crisp hitting of the ball into the gaps, it was as good as you would ever want to see.

Mike Coward, the most expressive cricket writer in Australia, said:

> It was more than an innings of power and astonishing beauty, a regal innings befitting a prince, albeit a pint-sized one who stands at just 5ft 5ins tall. This was Lara's theme. This was the cricketing equivalent of a grand opera, a performance which took the art of batting to a higher plane. Such was the skill and refinement of Lara's innings that everyone at the ground was compelled to ask whether they had ever seen the like.

Lara's tour de force reinvigorated the West Indies team to such an extent that they went on to win the series, claiming their sixth World Series limited-overs title, their fifth in as many attempts against Australia. Did Bradman turn a Test around single-handedly to win a series? The answer has to be no. Border was so shocked at what he had seen that he finished the series, which the West Indies won 2-1, by being dismissed for a pair in the final Test, the first time in his 138 Test appearances. He was also twice in trouble with the ICC referees Raman Subba Row and Donald Carr for dissent. In the first Test he had half his fee docked and in the last one he was reprimanded by a lenient Carr. It was the eighth time in a row that Australia failed to win the Worrell Trophy. 'Lara's unforgettable performance changed the whole course of the series,' said Cozier. Lara said:

> The context of the innings – we were 1-0 down, the Australians scored 503-9 in their first innings after winning the toss and I came in at 31-2 – my stroke-play and the eventual role played in the outcome of the series make it the innings I would most like to replay. Personally I don't like describing my batting but I have to say it was a gem.

Pitches at Sydney traditionally help spin and Carl Hooper, the West Indies off-spinner, bowled 45.4 overs for his 3-137 and Shane Warne's figures were 1-116. Greg Matthews, the home side's off-spinner, bowled more overs than anyone, 59, for figures of 2-169. Lara described the pitch as 'non-responsive'. The new year started with rain and there were a number of interruptions in play. Conditions didn't really help bowlers on either side, particularly the slow bowlers. On the end of the first day Border's side struggled to 272 for five after Steve Waugh grafted through four and a half hours, scoring only five boundaries. Waugh was dismissed for 100, David Boon became the eighth Australian to pass 5,000 Test runs with his 76 and Waugh's twin Mark was run out for 57 – he at least played a few entertaining shots. The cricket matched the weather.

Border and Greg Matthews resumed on day two both on nought and they added 155 in four hours before the captain, 74, and his partner, 79, both fell to Hooper's spin. When he reached 21, Border passed 10,000 runs, the second man to do it behind Sunil Gavaskar. The three giant West Indian bowlers, Ambrose, Walsh and Ian Bishop, had similar figures: Ambrose 2-87, Walsh 0-86 and Bishop 2-87. At this time Bishop was emerging into a classy and very fast bowler with steep bounce who could have joined the list of all-time great Caribbean fast bowlers, but two years earlier he had withdrawn after cracking a lower vertebra. An intelligent man who gained an MA after retiring from cricket, and a staunch Christian, he underwent a year-long rehabilitation helped with plenty of swimming and prayer. A year later he played for Derbyshire and captured 64 wickets at 17.46 apiece. Back problems continued to hold him back and he retired after playing in only 43 Tests. His 161 wickets at 24.27 earned him tenth position in the list of West Indian Test bowlers and only four players bettered his average: Ambrose, Malcolm Marshall, Joel Garner and Michael Holding. His chief income now comes from cricket commentating and he is rated one of the best in the world in his field.

At the end of the second day, the West Indies were 24-1 and when Desmond Haynes was bowled for 22 by Matthews, in came Lara for his fifth Test appearance. From the first ball he was in charge, which was rare for him because most experts believe that he isn't a great starter, especially facing fast bowlers of 85mph or more. In his biography he said, 'Why this innings was so special was because I am sitting here trying to recall something that stood out more than the rest and I found it very difficult because there was hardly a false shot. I was amazed by my timing and strokeplay from the very start.' He is not a bumptious man. He was telling the truth.

When he was on 35 the teams came in after a rain break and, sitting in the dressing-room, he heard the telephone ring. Sir Garfield Sobers was on the line. Along with several other former Test stars, Sir Gary was promoting Barbados as a tourist attraction Down Under and he told Lara, 'This is your day, son. Just keep going.' Earlier, in another break, Lara had watched a film on television of some of the great innings of Sobers from the tour of 1960/61, the most famous Test series between the countries. It may well have inspired Lara to go on to great deeds. Back out in the middle, the new captain Richie Richardson told him to keep thinking about the team score, rather than his own, once he passed fifty. In each of his previous three Tests he had passed fifty without going much further. Lara's fifty came in only 43 balls and he was outscoring his captain.

In Trinidad thousands of cricket lovers were sitting up watching the television programme through the night and some of them were probably boys who played with him in the street and when he monopolised the batting in Mitchell Street, Cantaro. *Wisden* recorded:

> In between breaks for rain he unleashed a dazzling array of strokes. He needed only 125 balls to reach his maiden Test century, turning a ball from Matthews to short fine leg, and by the end of the day he was 121 and with his partner Richardson 94, they put on 217 for the third wicket, a record for the West Indies.

Richardson reached his fifteenth Test hundred the next morning, and nine runs later he was caught by Warne at deep square leg off a hook from the bowling of Merv Hughes. Afterwards Richardson told the waiting journalists,

'I can hardly remember my innings. It was difficult playing and being a specta-
tor at the same time.' Keith Arthurton, another left-hander, came in to support
the rampant Lara, who dominated the fourth-wicket stand of 124 before he
was caught by Ian Healy off Matthews for 47. The stocky Arthurton was only
the third Test player from the tiny island of Nevis and he had a difficult time
before becoming a professional cricketer because his father opposed his decision to take up cricket. Fortunately for him, his mother favoured the other
approach and with Sir Gary Sobers backing him, he finally made it.

Matthews and Mike Whitney, the well-built Australian left-arm fast
bowler, thought up Lara's nickname on the 1991 tour to the West Indies:
'the Prince'. These two charismatic men occasionally took him to clubs
and that may well been a reason that the Test selectors were cautious about
picking him at an early age. Coward said, 'As a young man with a smile that
lights the way home from any discotheque – and it regularly does – Lara is
supremely sure of himself and of his ability to influence events.'

Lara passed 150 with a square drive off Greg Matthews which he said later
'was one of my best that day'. On 172 he tried to square cut when Hughes
came on with the second new ball and it went straight to the normally reliable Steve Waugh at gully, where the fielder has more time to see the ball
than at slip. Lara said, 'To my amazement he dropped it and I counted myself
lucky to be still there.'

He had never scored a double hundred in any class of cricket. He had
made 193 against the Jamaican Under-19 side in 1988 and 182 against the
Indian touring side for the West Indies Under-23 side and now he was on
199. He showed no sign of stress. Warne was bowling and he stopped for a
while looking at him before he walked deliberately in and delivered a stock
ball, a leg-break. Lara flicked it down to fine leg for three and as he raced in
for the third he threw his arms high in the air. The ground was well under
half full but they gave him a rousing reception with many of the members
on their feet. Lara recalled:

> I had never felt so much in control of an innings and when I passed 250 I began
> counting down on Sir Gary's 365. At 277 I played the ball towards cover and
> called for a run. I was halfway down the pitch when Carl Hooper called no and I
> knew I had no chance of beating Damien Martyn's throw. It was one of the few
> occasions when I have been run out. Normally I consider myself a good judge
> of a run and I believe I could have got in. I was not angry or resentful about it.

Shane Warne said, 'The only way he could get out was to be run out.'

The electronic scoreboard flashed up his records. His 277 came off 372 balls with 38 boundaries, and the fourth highest score in Test cricket for a West Indian and the third highest against Australia behind Sir Len Hutton's 364 and Reg 'Tip' Foster's 287 in 1903. His runs came from 450 balls in the West Indies' total of 606 for five. One record he fell short of was Bob Cowper's 307 against England in Melbourne in 1966 which is the highest Test score in Australia. He beat Gordon Greenidge's score of 226 for the West Indies against Australia, recorded two years earlier. He was modest in his interviews. 'The pitch was a total batsman's paradise,' he said. 'And their spinners had difficulty in gripping the ball because of the drizzle.' Lara batted six minutes short of eight hours and sitting in the audience were David Gower, Doug Walters, Arthur Morris and Neil Harvey.

The confidence of Lara and his colleagues soared to new heights after that match. They were ready to win the war. However, the Sydney Test petered out into a draw, with Australia finishing on 117-0 in their second innings. The majority of the 83,115 spectators, however, will never forget Lara's magnificent innings. Lara called the series 'the best I have ever played in at that period and fortunately for me that contained two memorable Test matches'.

Before the start of the tour, Viv Richards, Gordon Greenidge, Jeff Dujon and Malcolm Marshall were all omitted, deemed past their best, and Lara wondered whether he would be chosen in the opening match. He was asked to open against New South Wales, a position which he doesn't like, even in one-day cricket. He failed in both innings. 'I wasn't happy about opening,' he said. 'When you open, you have to play in front of the wicket more and I find that restricting. If you open the face of the bat you stand more chance of being caught.' He was relieved when Richardson discarded that plan and he came in at four in the first Test at Brisbane. Phil Simmons opened with Desmond Haynes.

It proved to be a controversial match and in the first innings he was given out stumped for 58. Greg Matthews, whose career was soon to end, bowled a flat off-spinner down the leg side and, with Lara out of his ground, wicketkeeper Ian Healy fumbled the ball before knocking it back into the stumps. Umpire T.A. Prue raised the finger and Lara had to leave. But television replays showed that the bails were removed by the Healy's gloves and the keeper claimed later that he told the umpire, 'That wasn't a fair cop.' That was no consolation to Lara, who followed up with a duck in the second innings.

Lara was involved in another controversy in the first innings in Melbourne when umpire Randell gave him lbw for 52 and he objected. He said, 'I raised

my bat, signalling that I thought I had hit it.' Under the latest ICC disciplinary code, Lara would have been penalised for dissent but he thought the
ICC had got it wrong. 'In the NatWest final a similar thing happened and I
showed my bat to Tom Moody to indicate that I hadn't hit the ball,' he said.
'That time I was given not out and I didn't see anything wrong with that.
It is not blatant dissent. It would be different if a batsmen knew he hadn't
hit the ball and was trying to con the umpire.' He was against the idea of
the 'snickometer' to record a nick and so far the ICC have yet to adopt it
because it is imperfect. 'In my view decisions should be left to the umpires
wherever possible,' he said. His contested decision at Melbourne was one of
many instances of Lara thinking he is right and the game's rulers are wrong,
but he has a good point. As a self-appointed custodian of the spirit of the
game he believes he should speak up on these ticklish issues – and more
often than not he is right.

Australia took a 1-0 series lead when Warne bowled the West Indies
out in the second Test. Warne and Lara have a lot in common. They both
cherish cricket and though they do many silly things off the field, their
cricketing instincts are sound. Vic Marks, the former Somerset and England
off-spin bowler and cricket correspondent of *The Observer*, wrote of Warne,
'Nobody in sport that I can think of so embodies the oddity of being simul-
taneously an idiot and a genius.' Lara isn't an idiot but he has been guilty of
some irresponsible actions.

Lara was one of the first players to call for neutral umpires in the 1992/93
series and both teams felt it was odd that there were only eleven lbws given
out in the five Tests. They thought there should have been more. Prue and
Steve Randell were both Australians and it was ironic that the Australians
complained more than Richardson's players. There was less controversy in
the Adelaide Test which followed Lara's imperious innings of 277 at Sydney
but the West Indies bowlers, particularly the moody Curtly Ambrose,
became agitated by the way Mark Waugh kept stepping away to the leg side
and cutting the ball over the slips. Ambrose was more upset when Waugh
was twice dropped off his bowling. Steve Waugh said in his book: 'The West
Indies quicks were incensed, claiming cowardice and perceiving it as an
insult to play this way, but it was an effective and sustainable solution to
their brutal assaults on the body.' Chipping the ball over the slips is not one
of Lara's regular shots. Like the hook shot, it gives a chance to the fielders
and his philosophy is not to hand out presents.

It was a wet summer in Australia that year and most of the pitches were
poor. Adelaide is normally flat and easy paced but this time it was uneven

with irregular bounce. Justin Langer made his debut, and his new helmet was soon cracked by a bouncer from Ian Bishop. Ambrose was at the very peak of his powers in that series – almost unplayable by ordinary batsmen. With two days remaining, Australia only had to score 186 but at 72 for five they were about to lose the chance of regaining the Sir Frank Worrell Trophy. Langer, 54, and Tim May, 42 not out, turned the innings round to 184 for nine with three runs required. Craig McDermott, 18, clipped a delivery from Courtney Walsh powerfully to leg and it bounced back off the shin pads of Desmond Haynes. An inch or two either way and it would have been a win for Border's men. Millions were watching the live broadcast throughout Australia and thousands of Adelaide cricket lovers turned up to see what they thought would be a piece of history. Lara said:

> The tension out there was the tautest I can remember. The fielders were urging Courtney on and the last ball of the 79th over, bowled in murky light, was short and rising. McDermott pulled back from it. We all went up in the slips, confident that his glove had made contact.

Everyone looked at the portly frame of Darrell Hair. He put up the finger. The West Indies had won by one run, the narrowest victory since Tests were first played. Lara later admitted he felt like crying for joy. Umpire Hair, now 'resting' after being harshly dealt with by the ICC over the Pakistan ball-tampering affair at The Oval in 2006, is Lara's most cuddlesome official. He stood at the Sydney Test when he scored his 277 and he was also the neutral umpire at the St John's Recreation Ground when Lara made his 375. The West Indians were so boisterous in the dressing-room afterwards that they were later presented an invoice for AUS$1,000 to pay for the damage.

Lara made only a token contribution to his side's crushing innings-and-25-run victory at Perth – just 16 – and Ambrose was the match-winner with an explosive spell of seven for one off 32 balls as Australia collapsed from 85 for two to 119 all out. When Ambrose's first delivery to Steve Waugh sailed higher and higher into the upraised gloves of Junior Murray some twenty-five yards back, his colleagues must have felt a tremor shaking the home dressing-room. Waugh admitted, 'I was cooked mentally, like a pulverised boxer waiting the death knell.' But it was Bishop, just as fast, just as dangerous, who dismissed him twice, for 13 and 0. After the celebrations, Lara praised Richardson, who is a devout Christian, and who encouraged prayer sessions before daily team meetings, saying: 'His handling of the bowlers was first class and he showed great tactical skill throughout a fiercely competitive series. As a motivator, he ranked very high, always getting the best out of his players with his positive thinking.' Two years later, Lara's opinion of Richardson changed abruptly.

As he joined in the parade at the WACA, with Man of the Series Ambrose sitting at the wheel of the station wagon which he won, Lara was full of smiles. Tony Cozier said, 'Unlike the previous series which was marred with antagonism, the spirit in this one was very amicable, due to Richardson's attitude and the presence of the ICC referees.' It was a frictionless series, almost.

After his 277 Lara changed from a young man who still had to prove his capabilities to the selectors and the critics into a truly great batsman challenging the giants in the history of the game. And he was ready to leave a mark or two in the record books.

seven

The Record

St John's Recreation Ground, Antigua, 18 April 1994
The Prince c. Jack Russell b. Andrew Caddick 375
766 minutes, 538 balls, 45 fours, 0 sixes and one tired body

At the start of 1994 when he was voted Trinidad's Sportsman of the Year, Brian Lara made a short speech and said that after recording his best innings of 277, a turning point in his hitherto inconsistent career, he would like to score a few double hundreds or even a triple. Two months later he scored 206 for Trinidad against Barbados at Queen's Park, taking his aggregate of runs to 715, a record for the domestic competition, the Red Stripe Cup. Three months later he scored a triple and set a new world Test record score of 375, beating Sir Garfield Sobers' 365 which had stood for thirty-six years.

On 18 April Lara resumed batting on the third day of the fifth Test against England on 320* and when he levelled on the Sobers record, driving a four off Andrew Caddick to extra cover, he suspected that the moody England fast bowler Christopher Clairmonte Lewis, son of a church minister born in Georgetown, Guyana and a friend of Lara, was going to bowl a short delivery from the Factory End. At the start of the tour Lewis had suffered sunstroke after shaving his head. He had recovered in time to play and now, predictably, he bowled short. The time was 11.46 a.m.

But few people in the screaming, shouting mass of people at the old ground realised that as Lara swivelled to his right to pull a four through mid-wicket in the direction of the cathedral, his right pad brushed against the off stump. The off bail quivered before it settled back into its groove. There is a picture of him looking guiltily to the stumps, with his bat held high like a periscope. If it hadn't been for that piece of luck – the only significant one of that monumental innings – he would only have shared Sir Gary's record. There was an edged shot that landed a foot or so from wicketkeeper Jack Russell and near the end a delivery from the perspiring, frustrated Angus Fraser beat his bat. Fraser, who bowled 43 overs, said with a grin, 'Arsey bastard – but I don't suppose I can call you a lucky bugger when you're 340!'

Michael Atherton, the England captain, who was continuing to play while recovering from tonsillitis, said in his book *Opening Up*:

> I knew him from the 1988 World Cup in Australia and we were quite friendly. As the series was meandering to a close it was tempting to sit back and admire his play. But I didn't want to make things easy for him and we tried to prevent him taking singles. For the first time, he began to look nervous. 'Come on Athers, you're making it hard for me,' he said. On this flattest of pitches, it was almost as though he realised from the start that a giant score was in the offing. He played faultlessly. On 291, I took the first slip out for the first time and he nicked Caddick's next ball through the gaping hole. He could quite conceivably have been taking the mickey. I wouldn't know because the scale of his talent was away outside my understanding. He was certainly the most thrilling player of my generation.

Ken Medlock, OBE, JP, DL, who was chairman of the Co-operative Wholesale Society which owned *Wisden* for some years, was sitting in one of the rickety stands and he had been invited by the MCC to attend and to present the Wisden Trophy to Lara. Ken, a former cricketer and golfer, said:

> I knew Learie Constantine very well and he thought there should be a trophy to the winners of Test series between England and the West Indies. I wrote to Billy Griffith, the MCC secretary about it but he replied that he didn't think it was necessary. Learie got back to Billy and that soon changed. The trophy was commissioned from a silvermaker's company in Birmingham and was presented to Frank Worrell after the West Indies won the series in 1963, the hundredth anniversary of the launching of *Wisden*. There are three cricketers on it: John Wisden, known as 'The Wonder', in the middle, one similar to Jack Hobbs on one side and Harold Larwood on the right.

And no sign of a West Indian! Nasser Hussain, who fielded for a day and a half as a substitute for the sick Mark Ramprakash while Lara was batting, said: 'Brian was awesome. I thought it was perhaps the best innings of all time. But little did I know that ten years later, I would be back, still playing and in the field at the same ground, when he topped it and took the record to 400.' In his book *Playing with Fire*, Hussain said: 'He was just in a different world from the likes of me. Ath would move a fielder and Brian would place the next ball where the fielder had just been He was an absolute genius.'

As dozens of exuberant West Indies supporters and local police rushed up to him to try and embrace him – his batting partner Shivnarine Chanderpaul managed it first before a limping Sir Garfield Sobers arrived under police escort – there was a whiff in the air. He wore the same trousers, shirt, socks and jockstrap that he had started in two and a bit days earlier. 'It must have been very smelly,' he said. 'I did that because of superstition and I didn't want to change a thing. I had my kit washed later and got it signed by my teammates and I've kept it.'

As the ball crossed the boundary, he punched the air in celebration, with his bat in one hand and his cap in another. For much of the innings he discarded his helmet because the pitch was obligingly benign. 'It was like marble,' he said. His shirt sleeves were down to his wrists, to protect against the glare of the sun. Sir Gary clasped him and the radio men and photographers heard him say, 'I am very proud of you. I knew you could do it, son. You were always the one.' Lara, not normally overtly expressive in his use of words, said: 'The moment for me, the way I felt, was indescribable, a moment in my lifetime maybe never to be repeated – elation, wonderment, pure joy – the ultimate of my career. Everything that happened was like a dream.'

Umpire Darrell Hair started to grab spectators and tell them to get off the square – it turned out one of them was the groundsman. As the police moved the invaders back Lara bent down to kiss the pitch which had been trampled on but fortunately not damaged in any way. 'Kissing the pitch came instinctively to me,' he said. 'I also wanted to wrap the pitch up and take it around with me but that wasn't possible.' He thought of his father Bunty, who inspired him to become a great cricketer. Speaking after the match, tears welled in his eyes as he said:

> Just to have him here today would have made me the happiest person in the world. My mind went back to all the many sacrifices he made for me, not for me to go on to break world records, but see me happy and also to see his favourite son make full use of his life.

Lara used the same bat he had played with in the Red Stripe competition a few weeks previously – despite it having been stolen in the meantime. As a cutter and puller and a batsman with the highest backlift of any contemporary player, he prefers a medium to light bat (2lbs 7oz) as opposed to a heavy one which suits the strong drivers like Clive Lloyd, Graeme Pollock and Graham Gooch. Constantly picking up a 3lbs bat would use too much energy.

Courtney Walsh was captaining the West Indies for the first time in place of the injured Richie Richardson and the absent vice-captain Desmond Haynes, and he won the toss, to the annoyance of Atherton, who wanted to take advantage of the conditions and regain some esteem after going 3-0 down in the series. The loquacious Bajan opener Stuart Williams stood in for Haynes and was soon out hooking for three. Lara came in to a carnival-style welcome with the All Saints Band in full volume; Chickie's Disco instruments rent the air with deafening noise on the other side, repeating the refrain of the tour theme – 'Feeling hot, hot, hot'. St John's was not an attractive venue but it led in another field, as one of the most animated and intimidating cricket grounds in the world, and it was one of Lara's favourites. On a steaming hot day with decibels reaching record highs, it can leave fielders with bad headaches.

Phil Simmons was soon lbw to Caddick and on a near-perfect pitch the West Indies were 12 for two. Lara decided to take his time to confirm his booking out in the middle, taking 51 deliveries before he reached double figures. Caddick and Fraser were both 6ft 5ins tall and their medium fast bowling had to be carefully watched before the hardness wore off the ball. Lewis, almost as tall, couldn't bounce the ball as high as the other two and held little threat. Phil Tufnell admitted he was going through a bad time because of his love life, or lack of one, and in his book *What Now?* he said:

> Chris Lewis got him jumping about with a couple of short ones and Lara sent for some eye drops. 'Oh yeah, right,' we thought, 'something in your eye there Brian, like a little bit of fear, perhaps?' Next thing we knew he was making the ball scream for mercy and several hours later, so were we.
>
> After he played and missed, Gus decided to rattle him with some sledging. First he stood there staring at the great man from only a few yards away, then, as we waited to hear what he could possibly come up with that would make the slightest impression, Gus burst out laughing. Someone said, 'What's the matter, big man?' 'Well, I was going to call him a lucky bastard but I've just seen the score. And that's the first time the ball hasn't hit the middle of the bat.'

Lara could have reached the record quicker but for the state of the grass. 'Most of the outfield was covered with long, coarse grass,' he said. Mike

Smith, the England manager and former England and Warwickshire captain, said:

> There was an interesting story about that grass. When we flew into Antigua for the first match of the tour, against Leeward Islands, I was looking out as the plane passed over the ground and noticed that wasn't a blade of grass on the outfield. I thought to myself, 'Lara and company could run up a huge total on that.' But a short time later, they decided to returf the whole ground, using turf from the USA. It makes one wonder how many runs Lara would have scored on the grassless outfield!

The imported turf accounted for the comparatively low first day total of 274 for three with Lara on 164. Jimmy Adams had to work hard for his 59 runs before he was caught by Hussain. Lara's dominance was shown by the fours count: Lara 24, the rest six — but Adams did hit two sixes. Lara normally stays up reasonably late but, realising he needed to rest for the next day's exertions, he had a rare early night. Junior Murray, the popular and quiet wicketkeeper, was sharing his room at the Royal Ramada Hotel and he was the ideal man for the occasion.

Unable to sleep through the night, Lara was up at 5.30 a.m. and went off to the golf course and hit a few drives to relax him. 'For me there is no better way of clearing my mind and focusing on the day ahead,' he said. 'I felt that something was special going to happen.' Scores of people mobbed him as he arrived at the ground, wishing him good luck. The fourth-wicket stand of 185 ended with the injured Keith Arthurton out for 47 and a fourth left-hander, Chanderpaul, came in. Lara didn't say much and the nineteen-year-old Chanderpaul kept saying to him, 'Keep going, don't throw it away.' The composed Chanderpaul was batting as well as Lara as the score raced ahead.

When Lara passed 200 he qualifed for a sponsor's prize of £50,000 and put the money into the team pool. The West Indies had been heavily fined for their over rate in the previous Test in Barbados and some of the prize money was used to pay for the fines. Also, Ambrose was fined £1,000 for knocking over the stumps when he was bowled by Chris Lewis. Like almost every Test side, the West Indies players always share the proceeds among the squad. There were two rain interruptions and Lara spent the time with his feet up in a stiff-backed chair with a fan going next to him. Twenty-three overs were lost — Lara might have beaten the Sobers record before nightfall. As it was, he was 320 not out at the close.

Back at the hotel, scores of well-wishers were encamped, urging him on to make history. He went to his room and Junior Murray, acting as his valet, brought in a plate of West Indian food for him The phone kept ringing and Murray told the callers, 'He's asleep.' Lara had a disturbed night. He was thinking about the record and who had played the big innings in Test cricket and how they did it. At four o'clock he was wide awake and his hands were sweaty. Nerves had finally caught up with him. Typically, he almost missed the team bus. The crowd were let in at eight and the 10,000 crowd were in their positions in a short space of time. The brightly coloured sunshades were up and the music was playing.

Out in the middle, his nerves interfered with his timing of the ball and when Atherton took the third new ball he mistimed a cover drive which sailed over a fielder for his fortieth boundary. Caddick cursed him. Then he edged the ball to third man before he middled a square cut off Lewis to pass Graham Gooch's 333 and Bradman's 334 at Leeds sixty-four years earlier. He drove Fraser to his favourite extra cover to overtake Hammond's 336 and Hanif Mohammad's 337. Another sign of nerves came when he tried to run two off a ball fielded by Ramprakash on the square leg boundary. Jack Russell appealed for a run out off the Surrey fielder's throw but Lara knew he was in. A flashy attempted drive failed to connect with the ball, almost hitting the off stump. Chanderpaul came down the pitch, urging caution. Another extra cover shot off Caddick raced to the boundary to take him past Len Hutton's 364 and level with Sobers' 365.

Medlock, now ninety-three and the oldest member of England's veteran club, the Forty Club, said, 'I don't think Brian would have got the runs but for Chanderpaul. Brian was an nervous as a kitten and Chanderpaul kept coming down the pitch to tell him, "Wait for it, don't take any chances."'

After history was made, from his trademark pull swivel shot, his concentration finally broke and on 375 he was caught by Russell off the persevering Caddick who let out a roar of delight. There were scenes of bedlam all round the ground. Medlock was vainly trying to find his way out of the pavilion to join the presentation party on the field until a 6ft 6ins Army officer came to his rescue (he was eighty at the time). He said:

This huge man picked me up and lifted me over a fence, and that's how I got out there. I am thirteen stone so he was an extremely strong man. It was chaos, with the amplification breaking down as David Gower was making his speech for the presentations. I spoke to Lara's mother and she was so proud of her boy. Brian has a wonderful eye and I've seen the greats since the early twenties and I haven't seen a better batsman. I was at The Oval in 1934 and watched Don Bradman and that was a marvellous experience. There used to be massive queues outside The Oval and unemployed people would be paid to queue up for hours. That's how I got my tickets, walking up to one of them at the front and taking his place.

Viv Richards, the local hero, was one of the first to congratulate Lara in the dressing-room, followed by Desmond Haynes and Mrs Jean Pierre, Trinidad and Tobago's Minister for Sport. Another player took off Lara's pads and the hero's tiredness was evident. He gulped down several pints of sports drinks. Faxes started pouring in and he listened to some of them as they were read out. Then he went off for a soothing bath. With two sessions and two days remaining, he faced a long stay in the field but he was excused most of it. It was 2 a.m. before he returned to his hotel room with Junior Murray, who had failed to reach the crease after the declaration on 593 for five. As usual, Lara hardly slept, replaying every shot in his mind. Everything else was an anti-climax, with England equalling the West Indies total before they were bowled with 34 overs remaining. Twenty-four were used as Phil Simmons and Stuart Williams reached 43-0. Lara was supposed to be number three but he wasn't padded up. He had done his bit. 'It was a tame draw,' said Medlock.

That night Lara flew to Port of Spain and was welcomed by the Prime Minister Patrick Manning and half of his Goverment, accompanied by thousands of ecstatic Trinidadians. He was handed a microphone and he said a few words of thanks. A motorcade was laid on, starting in Arima in the east of the island and stopping at City Hall two hours later, where he was presented with the keys to the city. The final destination was the Queen's Park Oval; most of the audience there were children who had been given the day off school. Later, Mr Manning held a reception for him at his home and the President, Noor Hassanali, presented him with Trinidad's highest honour.

eight

Waiting for Brian

We were sitting in a large and luxurious room in an exclusive block of flats off Birmingham's Hagley Road when Brian Lara interrupted me and said, 'Can you come back at eleven?' I was compiling some notes about him for his 1995 autobiography *Beating the Field*, or trying to, and we had just completed a couple of hours, mainly taken up by a stream of calls on his mobile phone. 'You mean tomorrow?' I asked. 'No,' he said, 'tonight.' 'Well, I don't know about you, I usually think about going to bed at eleven,' I said.

I had only met him for the first time a week previously and I soon realised that he wasn't your usual superstar sportsman. Or was he still on Trinidad time, four hours behind? He had just lifted cricket's individual batting record to 375 in Antigua and he felt his world was spinning in orbit. Warwickshire had signed him as their overseas player a month earlier and everyone wanted to interview him. He bore a hunted look, as though he needed a good holiday in Tobago, the hideaway isle which forms the alliance with his native Trinidad, instead of starting a gruelling season in English county cricket. The stylishly decorated room appeared as if a gang of robbers had ransacked it. Hundreds of letters, packages and bits of paper were strewn around, most of them unopened.

While he went to the kitchen to find the coffee, I looked round the debris. Behind a large settee, I could see what appeared to be the back of a body lying half buried under it. 'There's a body there!' I said. 'That's Russell, Russell Latapy, my friend,' he said. Latapy was a professional footballer who played for Trinidad, with Hibernian and Porto among his club sides. Later I learned that Latapy shared Lara's relaxed attitude and enjoyed a kip even if he was lying prostrate on the floor. A month later Lara turned up at a sponsorship function at the Honourable Artillery Company in the heart of the City of London along with Latapy, half an hour late, and someone said he was due to report back to Porto for training. I asked Lara about this. 'Yes, he's catching the plane at 12.30 at Heathrow.' It was then 11.30. 'It will take him at least and hour and a half,' I said. Another half-hour elapsed before the pair set off. Latapy duly missed the plane and Sir Bobby Robson, who was the coach at the time, promptly suspended him. If Warwickshire had followed his example, Lara's mad summer of 1994, when he missed the start of count-less engagements, even cricket matches, might have been very different. The indulgent Warwickshire staff treated him in the same way Sir Matt Busby treated George Best in his heyday at Manchester United, generally excusing his excesses because he was a genius. In the next four years, between the summers of 1994 and 1998 when Lara played for Warwickshire, one close observer announced that the Prince had missed twenty-three flights.

I declined Lara's offer to work on his autobiography through the early part of the night and arranged an appointment at 9 a.m. Next morning we were ready to start when he apologised and said, 'I've just got to find a letter from Germany about my car.' Wading through his earlier mail, now joined with another batch, took some time. Finally we started work. The phone went. When he had first arrived in Birmingham, the club put him into a pokey flat which had a broken window. An exhausted Lara fell asleep on a settee watching television and when he rose the next morning he asked his agent if he could have a proper flat. Now David Manasseh, one of his agents, was calling to ask whether he liked the new one which he had found so quickly. Yes, he did like it but it needed a housekeeper, he said. Now we were ready to resume. His mobile rang. 'Your car is ready,' someone said. 'I'll have to get it,' he said. 'Sorry about this; I should be back at twelve.'

Off he went to buy his first flashy car, at the age of twenty-four, a BMW convertible. The new flat, owned by a diplomat who was working abroad, was in one of the areas in the city where cars are broken into on a regular basis. Fortunately, it survived and he kept that BMW for a while before buying a Mercedes SL 280. He said, 'I remember at that time there were only two people in Trinidad who owned one – the High Commissioner and me!' He eventually replaced it with another Mercedes, an SL 55 AMG with red leather interior. 'Unfortunately the satellite navigation didn't work in Trinidad,' he said, adding:

> We don't have any speed cameras, although the police use laser guns on the highways. The roads aren't suitable for speeding, although you wouldn't believe it the way some people drive. They either jump the lights or come out at you from junctions and you just have to keep cool. And there are no laws for drink-driving.

He thought he was a careful driver, but some might disagree.

He was an hour late when he arrived back at the Edgbaston flat with his new BMW. He was always polite. 'Sorry about that,' he said. 'I've got to get used to these roads.' He had no navigational aids at that time. He made some sandwiches and coffee and we were ready for the interrogation. His mobile rang: Dwight Yorke was on the line. Now it was coming up to three in the afternoon and he said, 'I've got one or two things to do, can you pop out for a couple of hours and we can get down to it at five?' He came over as such a nice little man. You just had to accept his peculiar habits.

When I returned I asked him a few questions before he said he had to go out for dinner, so another day passed without much interviewing. 'He likes a night out,' said one of the Warwickshire players when I called in at the Edgbaston ground the next morning. Dennis Amiss, who had taken over as chief executive at Warwickshire said: 'The good thing about Brian was that he wasn't a big drinker. Otherwise we would have been in trouble. There was a club nearby that Dwight Yorke took him to and he was often there in the early hours.'

When Lara gave his first press conference after his arrival on 23 April, he turned up an hour late because his agent Jonathan Barnett arranged an interview at Pebble Mill en route. Public relations people were charging around, shepherding the sixty-five media men and women and assuring them that everything was under control. Suddenly one of the PR ladies shouted out, 'He's on his way.' Lara duly appeared outside the small hall, which had been decked out with the club's colours and two life-size cardboard cut-out images of the new signing. Alongside him were earnest-looking men in dark suits, looking like bodyguards. Lara was doing his best to smile as a dozen or more cameras were trained on him. He was dressed in a light blue jacket, black shirt without a tie and dark trousers. He sat on the raised table inside, flanked by Amiss and Warwickshire chairman Mike Smith. 'One of the reasons why I chose Warwickshire was because I will be living near to Dwight,' he said, pointing to the gap-toothed Yorke. Yorke was currently in Aston Villa's reserves. Lara was courteous throughout and smiled frequently, albeit nervously.

Stuart Robertson, the club's commercial manager, arranged a picture shoot of Lara standing next to his silver sponsored car bearing the registration L375 ARA. Then he posed under the scoreboard, which showed 375 against his name. As Lara was being escorted out of the hall, another official took off the registration plate and replaced the original one, L289 URW. Michael Calvin of the *Daily Telegraph* wrote, 'It was a subtly revealing moment which underlined that unvarnished truth tends to be the first casualty of sudden fame. Corners are cut. Style supercedes substance.'The quietly spoken Mike Smith presented Lara with a salver to commemorate his world record. 'I have so many things presented to me with 375 on it,' Lara said.They missed engraving 375 on his heart. Dermot Reeve, the captain, gave him his Warwickshire cap. 'He's the first to be capped before he actually plays,' he said.

David Manasseh, son of Maurice who played for Oxford University and Middlesex, was coy when it came to the cash Lara was likely to pick up from his sponsorships. He said:

> There's a clothing company, Joe Bloggs, a golf club contract, a soft drinks deal, a finance house and then obviously his cricket bat and kit contract with Gray-Nicolls which is due to expire in September. That's got to be renegotiated and I think a world record deserves a world figure. We don't want him playing second fiddle to anyone. He also has a sunglasses deal with Oakley and he will be one of the first cricketers to be paid using sunglasses.

When pressed, he admitted that the whole package would bring in around £250,000. The *Daily Mail* paid him £40,000 for his weekly column and when he started scoring centuries and setting more records, the columns were quickly doubled and then trebled each week. 'He insisted that he wanted to do something for children, like doing a coaching column,' said Manasseh. 'He wants to put something back.'Transworld paid an advance of around £60,000 for the book, which was entitled *Beating the Field* because he finds the gaps better than any other player.

'Warwickshire got him on the cheap,' said Jonathan Barnett. 'My company Stellar signed him up before he made his 375. David [Manasseh] met him at a charity game in England three years earlier and got to know him well and they liked each other and they've been close friends ever since.' The figure for his first summer's work on the cricket grounds of England was around £45,000, a reasonable sum for that time.While playing in South Africa in 1992, Lara met Keith Piper, the Warwickshire wicketkeeper, and told him he was keen on joining Warwickshire. Later it transpired that Allan Donald, their overseas player, would be playing for South Africa in 1994 and there was a vacancy. Piper passed the news on but Warwickshire first had talks with Phil Simmons. Simmons wanted a longer contract, the talks collapsed and the all-rounder joined Leicestershire instead.

The unlucky Simmons was nearly killed on the 1988 West Indian tour of England when he was struck in the head by a delivery from David Lawrence when he wasn't wearing a helmet. 'That was the first time I met Brian, playing for Trinidad against Guyana,' he said. 'You knew he was going to be a great player. All great players are hard driven. They've got to be and Brian had the same mental approach as Viv Richards, He knew what he wanted: records.'

Warwickshire officials contacted David Boon and Shane Warne in Australia, offering the overseas place in their 1994 squad; neither was available. Lara had previously played against Dermot Reeve but instead of backing Lara's candidature, Reeve said he wanted an all-rounder and named the Indian Manoj Prabhakar, who occasionally opened both batting and bowling for his country. Warwickshire's committee took Reeve's recommendation and they signed Prabhakar on a one-year contract, but in February, Prabhakar strained an ankle in New Zealand and Dennis Amiss invited him to Birmingham for a physical check-up. The doctor who saw him felt he wouldn't last a rigorous season and the committee decided to cancel his contract and pay him a sum in compensation. It was only then that the committee decided to go for Lara. Rohan Kanhai, who played for Warwickshire for ten years with great distinction, saw Mike Smith, who was manager of the England side, at the Barbados Test in early April and told him, 'Brian would be ideal for you.' Smith said: 'We've had a history of signing West Indians, Lance Gibbs, Alvin Kallicharran, Deryck Murray, Bill Bourne and others and they've all been easy to get on with. They don't live like monks and they like to socialise. Brian should fit in well.' Tony Cross, the prominent committeeman who was later discredited and left, was sent to the Caribbean to conduct the negotiations. They did not take too long. A few days later Lara's 375 gave him a Bradmanesque average of 99.75 in the series against England and he was on his way.

Now Warwickshire's new signing was cricket's hottest property. Jonathan Barnett said:

> His biggest earner was Mercury Asset Management, one Britain's biggest investment companies. They signed him up for £130,000 in a deal worth up to £400,000. All he had to do was to wear his baseball cap with MAM on it and make personal appearances around the world when he was not playing cricket. He insisted that any bonuses paid out if he breaks more records should go to charity.

The day of the launch he duly arrived, late, and instead of wearing his cap, he was dressed in a City grey suit and a bowler hat carrying a brolly, although it wasn't raining. Most of the big sporting sponsorship deals tend to be exaggerated and when some shareholders of MAM read headlines like 'LARA DEAL IS WORTH £500,000' they were straight on to the telephone complaining. An executive penned a letter to the newspapers saying, 'While you gave magnificent exposure to the story, the figure of £500,000 is completely wrong. We are actually paying £100,000 from July to September 1996.' The Lara phenomenon was mushrooming fast, but not that fast. However, the *Financial Times* printed the figure of £500,000 and some shareholders believed it. Manasseh regretted that his client was working in the cricketing world rather than the USA. 'If he had been, he would be another Michael Johnson,' he said.

'He's a great guy, a well-mannered young, confident man made of steel,' said Barnett, the agent who has around 500 clients, including footballer Ashley Cole. Barnett was banned from working as an agent for eighteen months (later reduced to twelve on appeal) and fined £100,000 by the FA in 2006 over a 'tapping-up' scandal involving Cole. Barnett and particularly Manasseh found it difficult to keep up with Lara's activities and his failure to arrive on time brought an end of to their business arrangement after a few years. Since then a succession of agents have come and gone, yet Barnett and Manasseh remain good friends with the cricketer.

Lara is still earning from sponsorships, including around £100,000 a year from a PlayStation game and $500,000 a year from MRF, the Indian company sponsoring his bats. MRF also sponsor Sachin Tendulkar, who is paid a similar amount. They are well ahead of any other cricketers who receive bat payments. Jason Ratcliffe, the former Warwickshire and Surrey player who is now an executive with the Professional Cricketers' Association, said, 'Most batsmen have a favourite bat and take care of it but Brian had seven or eight ordinary Gray-Nicolls Scoop bats lying around in the dressing-room and picked up one of them went he went out to bat.'

Lara found the Press intimidating. He's not shy but he isn't a showman and he said, 'I was there to play cricket but I was being treated like some kind of world famous celebrity and found it rather frightening.' Amiss said:

> He was looking like a little boy lost. I think Jonathan got him on the cheap so he wanted to pile up as many deals as possible on him. He wasn't used to the traffic in England and he thought it would take ten minutes to drive a couple of miles but in the rush hour he'd take forty and was always late.

The day after his arrival, the jet-lagged Lara was out in the field at the start of Warwickshire's opening Britannic Assurance County Championship match and spent a boring day watching Glamorgan scoring 291 for six. Thirty-two male journalists and one female writer sitting in the Press box were unhappy at the lack of anything significant to report. 'This will need some ingenuity,' said one. Ian Wooldridge, the outstanding sport writer of his generation, noticed that Lara was practising his golf swing at first slip. 'He's right-handed,' someone announced. At his peak, Lara reduced his handicap to low single figures but lack of opportunities has taken it back up to ten. 'He's got a beautiful swing,' said Manasseh. 'If he had taken golf up seriously he could have been a star.'

Lara began exercising his right arm as though he wanted to bowl. At 16.06 Dermot Reeve, an adventurous captain who always tried to gamble, asked him to bowl. Lara claimed to be a leg-spinner but he showed no sign of being another Shane Warne. His sole over cost seven runs. The next day he earned a slice of his £45,000 fee, hitting 147 off 160 balls, including an extraordinary 23 fours and two sixes. Glamorgan's Colin Metson said, 'Not one of us has had to dive to stop any of his shots. They all found the gap.' Roger Twose, the Cornishman now living in New Zealand, outscored him, reaching an unbeaten 277. The humorous Twose addressed a note to the new recruit saying, 'Welcome to Edgbaston, from the best left-handed batsman in the club!' and stuck it in the dressing-room.

Lara is one of the rare people who can lie down and go off to sleep at any time, wherever he is. Some of his colleagues were surprised to see him sleeping on the treatment table, sometimes even under the table, between breaks. Hugh Morris, the Glamorgan captain and ECB deputy chief executive, said, 'I never thought I would see anyone better than Viv but now I am not too sure.' That night, Lara joined some friends for a Chinese meal. He loves Chinese food, and Italian. Bob Woolmer thought that Lara did his best work of that summer in a county match against Leicestershire, 106 out of 254 and 120* out of 206 for seven to earn the win in a rain-affected match. Reeve said in his autobiography *Winning Ways*:

> In the second innings we faced defeat on a fast pitch with cracks appearing all over the place. Every other batsman was either rapped on the knuckles or tried to jab down on shooters but at the other end Brian made it look a doddle. The next score was 20. He seemed from another planet and we couldn't believe our luck.

Tim Munton said:

> That was his finest innings of the season and he showed that he was a true
> committed team man because he turned down four singles to long on and
> long off while 99. 99% of batsmen would have taken the first one but he
> didn't. He was thinking of his team.

Lara agreed with Reeve and Munton that it was a special day for him.
However, a rift was soon appearing between the star and his captain. Lara
thought his side should press on to score quickly, rather than acquiring runs
patiently, and then rely on declarations to win matches. He felt Reeve's
tactics produced a lot of boring cricket – and anyone who believes in the
right values of the game would agree. However, in the early days he kept
quiet.

Having scored four centuries in a row, he could have added one or two in
the next game at Oxford University but he decided to take a short holiday
in Port of Spain, courtesy of BWIA. 'There was a lot of publicity about
my chances to equal the world record of six successive hundreds but I
wasn't bothered,' he said. 'I have never consciously thought about going for
records.'

The next day he declared himself fit for the Benson & Hedges quarter-
final against Kent at Edgbaston. The umpires ruled that the ground was
too wet after the famous 'Brumbrella', the huge tarpaulin which normally
covered most of the ground was left off over the weekend and the authorities wanted the tie switched to Derby. Warwickshire declined and under the
rules a bowl-out was organised in the indoor school in secret. The sponsors
objected and the Press were allowed in to see it and Warwickshire won 5-4
when Nigel Llong, now a successful umpire, missed the stumps by no more
than an inch. Lara stood in the back after saying he wasn't willing to take
part.

Twenty-four hours later he was at Lord's for another championship
game, this time against Middlesex. No play took place because of rain and
that day he accepted an invitation from Robert Sangster to join him and
his guests at Tramp's. Most clubs are patrolled by paparazzi who act on tips
from the door staff. This time Lara found himself photographed and several
newspapers published the story, opining that he shouldn't have been in a
nightclub the night before a match. His response was, 'I do drink, but not
excessively, and this time I restricted myself to mineral water. It was in the
early hours of the morning before I returned to the team hotel and with

more rain forecast I didn't think the match would start on time. I didn't feel I was acting unprofessionally.'

The Lord's covers, probably the best in the country, enabled a prompt start and Lara was soon at the crease, intent on scoring a sixth successive century. The ball was moving both ways in the air and off the pitch but he was going well when he edged a loose ball down the leg side from Richard Johnson, who later played for England, and was caught by Keith Brown – once a promising boxer with the nickname 'Scarface' – on 26. He didn't wait for the decision. He was very angry at being dismissed by a bad ball. 'I shouldn't have played it,' he said. He experienced a double dose of bad luck because Johnson wasn't originally in the Middlesex side. Kevin Shine, later to become the ECB bowling coach, was due to play instead but once Mike Gatting saw the conditions he demoted Shine and promoted Johnson. The previous day Lara had been bowled first ball by Mark Feltham in a Sunday League game. *The Sun* offered £1,000 to the first bowler to do it and Lara paid his membership to the Primary Club – which collects money from cricketers who are out first ball and gives it to blind cricketers. On the Monday the sun came out and Lara was back in charge, racing to 140 off 147 balls before he was caught and bowled by John Emburey. 'It was almost impossible to bowl to him,' said Emburey. 'Only one cricketer has hit the ball over the Lord's Pavilion, Albert Trott, off the Australians in 1899 and Lara almost did it. One of his sixes struck the guttering of the South Turret. Another yard or two and it would have cleared it.'

There was now clamour for Lara to try and hit the ball out of The Oval, a feat which has never been achieved. Foster's, the sponsors, put up £50,000 for the first Surrey player to do it and, asked why Lara wasn't eligible, a spokesman said, 'We'll have to arrange something but it could be fifty thousand cans of Foster's.'

His six centuries in seven games equalled a record jointly held by seven other batsman, including Don Bradman. 'When I came back to the pavilion I felt goose pimples on my arms,' he said. The crowd rose to him and they were still clapping as he went up the sepia-coloured steps up to the visiting dressing-room. Several members shouted encouragement to him and others tried to pat him on the back. Lara had just enough time for a shower and a rub-down before Reeve declared, leaving a target of 269 in 50 overs, a generous declaration – too generous perhaps, with Middlesex's Mike Roseberry soon on the way to a second century. But Tim Munton removed Roseberry and Mike Gatting slowed the pace down. Reeve responded by asking Lara to bowl to open the game up again.

When Reeve started setting an attacking field, Lara became agitated. 'I had to put my foot down and insist,' said Reeve, continuing:

> His two overs went for 31 and I didn't mind. It perked Middlesex up and they finished 24 short with the last man Angus Fraser blocking the last three balls. Fair enough, it was an effort on both sides but Brian wasn't happy. As soon he had finished his second over, he pointed to his knee, signalled to the umpire David Constant and walked off the field. When he got back to the dressing-room, he sounded off and told [coach Bob] Woolmer, 'This isn't the way the game should be played.'

The West Indian batsman and the peppy, enthusiastic captain weren't the same after that. Lara was resentful of the way Reeve was pushing him. Reeve thought Lara was a bit of a lead-swinger. 'He was pretty quick running for his own runs out there,' he said. Born in Hong Kong, Reeve had made his debut for Sussex at the age of twenty before joining Warwickshire in 1988. He was made captain of the Bears in 1993 and voted their Player of the Year. His private life was in a bad state after a divorce and he was living life at a very fast pace. 'He was an outstanding leader, very innovative, but I think he was insecure,' said Woolmer. Lara's greatest year, in 1994, was now being soured and it changed his approach. He wasn't enjoying it. Dennis Amiss said:

> I had regular chats with him, trying to get him on time but it was difficult to get through to him. We never fell out over it but Bobby Woolmer and Derek Reeve were being driven to distraction. I remember once he was supposed to be playing at Scarborough and I eventually got through and he said, 'I've just arrived.' I said, 'But the match is about to start. You should have arrived an hour or two before.' Reeve wanted to do something about it, like disciplining him. I took a soft approach. I said, 'He's scoring quick hundreds winning us matches and we'll have to put up with the pain. He's a superstar.' If we had won the toss in the NatWest final to Worcestershire we would have won all four competitions. Even so, winning three was an amazing performance.

Some of the players were complaining, saying that team spirit was suffering. Amiss said:

> I don't think it really got nasty. Reeve or Bobby would have a go and one or other would move on. I had Brian in my office on many occasions telling him

things would have to change. He was such a nice guy that you couldn't get too upset. He'd smile and say, 'Okay, I'll be there.' Next time he was still late. After the affair in Northampton – when he had a go at Reeve on the field – I tried another tack. I rang him and asked to fix up a game of golf at The Belfry and we could talk privately, the two us in my golf buggy. It was just before the Benson & Hedges final and the players were upset about things. He said sorry and that he would do something – and he did because on the morning of the B&H he apologised to the players and said he would make amends. The players were impressed. He didn't want to disrupt the team.

If an ordinary cricketer had missed so many deadlines he would have been fired. Cricket bosses don't like people who fail to arrive on time and as cricketers are poorly paid compared to Premiership footballers they know that the decision wouldn't be contested in the High Court. Not many run-of-the-mill players have agents to help them in any disputes. But the Warwickshire committee decided to go along with the conciliatory approach of their chief executive. Knowing what happened in 1994, it was astonishing that they hired him again four years later but Smith said:

He's a genius and you have to accommodate geniuses. No cricketer has ever had a greater impact on a season than Brian in 1994 with six centuries out of seven and a world record of 501. It gave us a tremendous fillip and for some time Warwickshire was the leading county. He puts bat to ball, like most West Indians. Being a left-hander was an advantage, like Gary Sobers. They have more time to hit the ball as it goes across them and they tend to be more flamboyant. Most top bowlers now go round the wicket to bowl the ball into him and that has been a problem to him. But it hasn't stopped him.

The signing of Allan Donald was a catalyst for the club. Ali Bacher, the former South African captain and secretary of the SA Board recommended him as an overseas player and we hadn't heard of him. But what a great signing he was! In 1994 Donald was playing for South Africa touring England and that led to Brian's arrival.

Smith summed up Lara's record-breaking season at Edgbaston saying, 'No one has ever done what he did.'

nine

The Record II

Edgbaston, Birmingham, 6 June 1994
B.C. Lara 501★
484 minutes, 427 balls, 62 fours, 10 sixes

Sunday 5 June 1994 proved to be a mundane cricketing day. The fourth Test at Trent Bridge between England and New Zealand was heading towards an innings victory in Ray Illingworth's first match as chairman of selectors and unchallenged dictator of the English cricket team, while over at Edgbaston Brian Lara scored just six in Warwickshire's unremarkable 84-run win in the AXA Equity and Law League. Illingworth was insisting on strict new rules banning the use of mobile phones and sunglasses, and he also gave the order to keep the Revd Andrew Wingfield Digby out of the dressing-room, saying, 'If any of the players need a shoulder to cry on, they're not the men to go out and stuff the Aussies next winter.' The popular Wingfield Digby had been the team's spiritual adviser for the past three years.

New Zealand ended another miserable day on 184 for seven, needing 132 runs to make England bat again. Gus Fraser and Phil DeFreitas mopped up the last three wickets on the Monday and the match ended well before lunch on the fiftieth anniversary of D-Day. At Trent Bridge the sixty or so cricketing media men were about to finish their work and get away early. With the possible exception of Jack Bannister, the cricket correspondent of the *Birmingham Post* and radio commentator who had had a distinguished career as a bowler with Warwickshire, no one was thinking about driving over to Edgbaston to watch the final day of the Britannic Assurance Championship match.

The game was dying with no prospect of a result. Durham had scored 556 for eight on a pitch which umpires Trevor Jesty and Peter Wight described as 'too good for batting' in their report to the ECB and after play was washed out on the Saturday, Warwickshire resumed on 210 for two with Lara 111★.

Lara is not an overly superstitious cricketer, otherwise he might have worried – 111 is, like 87, an unlucky score in the eyes of many cricketers, even the better ones. Few spectators were present at the start on a hot, balmy day and only eight journalists were present. Dermot Reeve spoke to Phil Bainbridge, the conservative captain of Durham, and suggested a deal to enable him to chase a total. Bainbridge said, 'No chance, I've got two bowlers injured.' One was forty-one-year-old David Graveney, who had been his side's best bowler the day before until he tweaked a muscle. Reeve was distinctly unhappy.

Lara was almost out to the first ball he faced on Friday, delivered by the Barbadian bowler Anderson Cummins who had a short Test career of three matches. Cummins was better known as the man who was left out of the inaugural West Indies *v.* South Africa Test in Barbados in 1992 after the apartheid ban was lifted. Cummins said in *Wisden*:

> Knowing the type of player Brian is, I knew he would go for it if I angled one in. It lobbed off the end of his bat just out of my reach. Then I bowled him on ten but Peter Wight called no ball. I tried a leg-stump yorker and he stepped inside it. But he started to play really well after about ninety minutes at the crease. I had batted on the pitch and scored 62 and I knew it was as flat as hell and the way the game went it was set up for him to do something like a big score. Things usually go better for people who really believe in themselves. He was helped by a short boundary which meant he could clip the ball off his stumps and it would go for a six.

Lara admitted:

> Luck went my way. When I was on 18 Simon Brown, Durham's medium fast left-arm over-the-wicket bowler, had me playing down the wrong line and I edged an easy chance straight to Chris Scott, their keeper. Thinking I was out, I walked a couple of steps towards the pavilion only to realise he had dropped it. If he had been quick thinking, he might have been able to run me out. But like Anderson a few minutes earlier, he was horrified. 'Jesus Christ,' he said, 'I hope he doesn't get a hundred.'

Those were haunting words. Lara went on to set a record of 501* which is unlikely to be beaten in our lifetime. The previous first-class record, 499 by Hanif Mohammad at Karachi in 1959, had stood for thirty-five years. On that occasion the Pakistan batsman scored 64.63% of the runs, compared to

Lara's 61.85%. W.G. Grace was the distinguished record holder from 1876 when he scored 344 against Kent on the sloping ground at Canterbury; Archie MacLaren took over the baton in 1895 with 424 at Taunton (he was the only one of the record holders to hit a six, until Lara's innings, when ten were struck; Lara stands out as the only one who was confident enough to take the aerial route regularly); Bill Ponsford edged the record higher to 429 at Melbourne in 1923 and four years later he improved it to 437, also at Melbourne; Don Bradman's 452*, scored at Sydney in 1930, remained unchallenged until Hanif Mohammad beat it.

The sportsman who says he doesn't believe in luck is a liar. Lara is a firm believer in luck and he admitted:

> The period before tea was one of my sketchiest at the crease in my first year with Warwickshire. My feet simply wouldn't go to the right places. Having quick feet is essential to a top-class batsman but like a dancer they have to be in time to the music or in this case, the bowling.

As tea was called, the players trooped in to the low-level dressing-rooms and a minute later Lara emerged from the Warwickshire room accompanied by Keith Piper, the number seven batsman. Piper threw him a few balls and then they went to the Indoor School for more throw-downs. Lara said, 'I believe I can put things right with some co-ordinated practice and it works. Bob Woolmer believed videos were the answer. That's not a method I prefer. After ten minutes of work with Keith I felt happier.' Very few top-class players copy Lara's approach, if any. They want to rest and have some refreshment in the tea interval. Gladstone Small recalled memories of Lara's net sessions on other occasions:

> He didn't spend a lot of time in the nets full stop. But if he had to sort something out he go to the nets, take out the off stump and place it further to the right, about eight inches away. Then I had to bowl at him. He usually took middle and leg and when the ball pitched outside of the line of the moved stump he would pad up and let the ball go. But if it was pitching in that eight inches he would absolutely flay the ball. I only got him out once, and I hit the wide stump.

On the Friday night he had set the first of his many records when he became the first batsman in history to score seven hundreds in eight innings, beating the seven in nine by C.B. Fry (1901), Ernest Tydesley (1926) and Bradman, who did it four times. His unbeaten 111 off 143 balls brought his aggregate of runs to 1,161 in only forty-seven days. On the Monday he undertook a fifteen-minute knock-up in the nets, short for him. Roger Twose, who now lives and works in New Zealand, was the joker in the side and before play started he said to Lara: 'You're just a glam fast-century flashpot. Why don't you set out your stall for the really big jobs like I do? Bet you can't beat my 277 today then?' Lara smiled. He recalled: 'Right from the first ball from Simon Brown which I worked away for two, I felt very comfortable. The ball was hitting the middle of the bat. My timing was good. It was sweet.' The boundaries started flowing and the crowd started building up. Over at Trent Bridge, Jack Bannister was told about Lara's exploits and the canny reporter knew he had to get over there. A world record might be looming. Other journalists made arrangements to join the exodus.

After the records were counted and the full credit was given to Lara, some critics raised the issue of the standard of the opposing side's bowling. One said, 'He benefited from facing some pretty ordinary bowling.' But Lara himself said, 'Brown and Anderson didn't bowl badly. They compared favourably with many opening bowlers around the counties.' Simon John Emmerson Brown, born at Cleadon village, Sunderland, and known as 'Chubby,' had been picked for the Youth World Cup in Australia in 1987/88 along with Mike Atherton, Nasser Hussain, Mark Ramprakash and Martin Bicknell and was looked on as a potential England fast bowler. Lara played in the same competition, which was never repeated (unfortunately, as it helped the players mature quickly). In 1994 Brown topped Durham's averages and was voted the county's Player of the Year.

The injured Graveney bowled only seven overs before he retired and his role was filled by the twenty-two-year-old David Cox, a bespectacled slow left-arm spinner from Southall who was making his debut. Early on, Cox found Lara's edge, a rare mistake from the batsman, and Graveney, sitting in the front row of the away dressing-room, said, 'The more runs Lara scores, the more ice I am going to put on my leg!' Cox took much of the Lara bombardment and failed to take a wicket, not just in this match but for the whole of the season. Later in the year he found solace in marrying his girlfriend Hazel.

Dominic Ostler fell for eight and Twose for 51 but Lara careered on like a one-day cricketer playing in the final over of the innings. The back-up bowling was indifferent, with opening batsman Wayne 'Ned' Larkins bowling five overs and and number three batsman John Morris also bowling five, including the final, decisive over. Between the start and lunch, 'The Prince' scored 174 runs in 135 minutes, six short of the Championship record, 180 by K.S. Ranjitsinhji in 150 minutes for Sussex against Surrey in 1902.

Alex Davis, the excited Warwickshire scorer, showed that Lara had scored more boundaries – 32: 25 fours and seven sixes – than Trevor Penney had scored runs (27), and the third wicket eventually brought 314 runs of which Penney's share was just 44. Penney was one of the fastest runners of his time and he said, 'Brian is a fantastic runner himself and his judgement on how to run has always been excellent.'

At 238 another powerful drive flashed past Cummins and it wasn't even a half-chance. Lara passed Twose's 277, the club's record, set thirty-seven days earlier and as he came in for tea on 285 the other players were talking about Hanif's record. Keith Piper unstrapped the pads of the perspiring champion who called for the lightest possible lunch: a half-filled plate of mashed potato and a pint of blackcurrant juice. Alex Davis came over to confirm that his total of runs between the start of play and the lunch interval fell just six runs short of Ranji's record. 'Archie MacLaren's 424 is the next target,' he said. Lara asked skipper Reeve, 'You aren't going to declare are you?' In his book Reeve wrote: 'I was curious why he said it and he replied that he wanted to go for Hanif's record. I thought, "This guy's a confident character – he's still got to get another 200-odd before the close."' It was pointless to declare because Bainbridge wasn't interested in a deal to bring a result. 'As long as you are there, I won't declare,' Reeve said.

On the terraces, and also in the Press box, the spaces were being filled rapidly and if it was slaughter before, it was literally genocide now. Bainbridge, a thirty-six-year-old all-rounder born in Stoke-on-Trent, formerly with Gloucestershire, was looking vainly round for volunteers to bowl. He brought himself on and packed the boundaries to restrict Lara to ones. Often Lara ran two. Once he ran four to reach 400 and hardly showed any discomfort. The late John Thicknesse, the *Evening Standard* cricket correspondent who chauffeured Bannister to Edgbaston from Trent Bridge, an hour's fast ride, recalled: 'We saw him score his final 130 runs and one amazing aspect of his play was his fitness. Tiring, was he, after six hours at the crease? Pigs might fly!' Graeme Hick's 405, the top score of the twentieth century in English county cricket, sailed into oblivion. Penney and Paul Smith had departed earlier and Piper, who came in with a confident air at 448 for four, batted like an authentic batsman, as though some of the magic of Lara had rubbed on him. Lara kept repeating to him, 'Make sure you get a big one.'

Reeve admitted: 'When they got back out there I watched open mouthed as Lara kept hitting boundaries. It was an amazing feat physically because he had to concentrate for such a long time.' Records were falling like coconuts in a Caribbean typhoon. At 286 he became the highest scorer at the ground, beating Peter May's 285* in the 1957 Test against the West Indies; at 306 he passed Frank Foster's 305* record for the county, set at Dudley in 1914; at 325 his 1,000 runs for the season, from seven innings, equalled Bradman's feat of 1938; at 376 he had made the highest score by a West Indian; and at tea, when he was 386, he had passed the world record score for a left-hander, made by Bert Sutcliffe at Christchurch in 1952/53.

At the interval he was on 418, frustratingly short of MacLaren's 424. He'd scored 133 in the afternoon session and at 411 he became the nineteenth player in history to score 300 runs in a day. Those who make an obsession in keeping records must have been dizzy. Two runs later he made one of his rare mistakes, skewing a pull shot high into the air in the direction of mid-wicket. Mike Burns, the substitute fielder, looked up to see which fielder had the best chance of taking it. The others hesitated and Burns went for it, just failing to reach it.

On 423 his 274 from boundaries (nine sixes and 55 fours) beat the Championship record of 272 (68 fours) set by Percival Perrin of Essex against Derbyshire at Chesterfield in 1904. The prolific Perrin finished up as chairman of the England selectors in Hutton's day. Two more runs and MacLaren's 424 had been bettered. Lara played an amazing, one-handed straight drive to pass Bradman's 452*. And then he passed C.G. Macartney's 458, the highest individual score in a single day.

Piper, who now coaches Warwickshire's second team, said in the 1995 edition of *Wisden*:

> I'm not one for records but he told me that 424 was his first target. Then when he went past that score, he said that 500 was next. He didn't say a lot, just told me to keep concentrating. All through the season he kept on that if he batted an hour, then he shouldn't get out and he expected a hundred. Yet he was so relaxed about everything that I felt none of the pressure I expected batting with someone who finally scored 390 that day.

Piper reached his first century and Lara said, 'No one deserved a century more.' As a reward, the England selectors picked him for the England 'A' tour of India. He had the qualities to make the senior England team but afterwards he failed to make the progress needed. He could have been a Test star. There was an hour remaining and with 60 runs required Lara felt sure he would pass 500. He was easing through the 460s and the 470s and then the 480s, up past 490, but for some odd reason no one informed him that play would cease on the dot of 5.30 p.m. owing to the fact that there was no chance of a result. If there had been a chance, the match could have continued. Durham captain Bainbridge knew the laws, and knew that if Lara failed to score in the 136th and final over of the innings, he would be stranded on 497, two runs short of Hanif's record.

Most of the fans thought it would be a doddle, especially as John Morris, an occasional bowler whose seven first-class wickets up to that point had cost 128 runs apiece, was set to bowl the final, decisive over. Known to his teammates as 'Animal', the thirty-year-old Crewe-born Morris is a likeable character. He became a minor celebrity on England's tour of Australia in 1990/91 when he joined in with David Gower's joyride in a light aircraft during a match. Both Gower and he were fined by shocked officials. He played three Tests and was a fine, aggressive batsman with Derbyshire and Durham but he wasn't much of a bowler. Lara faced his bowling at the start of the last over and he proceeded to block the first three deliveries, all slow medium-paced dobbers. It was an odd way to go about it. This heightened the tension and Morris, matching the mood, surprised Lara with a bouncer which struck him on his helmet. Everyone laughed and Morris said, 'I've found your weakness.' Lara said later:

> I had intended to glance it down to fine leg and it was just as well that I missed it because we would have run one, which would have left me on 498 with Keith facing the final two deliveries. The pressure would have been on him to get a single from the fifth ball.

Piper came down the pitch to inquire about his health. 'You've only got two balls,' he told him. Lara said, 'Are you sure?' 'Yes,' said Piper, 'I've checked with [umpire] Peter Wight.' Lara went to resume. In came Morris and bowled another non-testing delivery, just on off stump. Lara came down the pitch and with a high swing of the bat drove exquisitely through the short extra cover boundary for four. 'I felt relieved, happy and tired all the same time,' he said. There was no chance of bending down and kissing the pitch like when he scored his 375 in Antigua. He might not have managed to get up again unaided. As he raised his arms aloft he was engulfed by a flood of teammates, photographers and ecstatic supporters. His colleagues formed a guard of honour as he went off. In the dressing-room he was presented with a bottle of champagne for being voted Warwickshire's Player of the Month for May. Much of it was poured on to his head. Lara rarely

Scorecard from the match.

drinks champagne, except for special occasions – but this was certainly one. A second bottle was opened and he raised his glass to Piper for scoring 116 in Warwickshire's 810 for four. His mobile phone started ringing and one of the callers was Hanif Mohammed, who said, 'I am not sad at losing my record. Records are there to be broken and I congratulate you. It is good for cricket.' Hanif's brother Mushtaq lives in Birmingham and he had arranged the phone link-up.

Tom Graveney said, 'I can't believe it. If he goes on like this they will have to change the laws.' Ian Botham said, 'He's convinced me I retired at exactly the right time. Bloody good luck to him. He is great for cricket.' Peter Johnson, the cricket correspondent of the *Daily Mail*, wrote:

> Once the pain of their repeated thrashings has subsided, the cricketers of England will be grateful to Brian Lara. Until this smiling, energetic young man burst into world cricket, the accumulation of masses of runs – of even a solitary Test century – had become too grim a ritual. To do it, you seemed to need the self-denial of a monk. No more. Not the least of Lara's astonishing gifts is the obvious, almost boyish enjoyment he pours into virtually every innings.

He was right. Lara just loves batting and he is still in love with the game of cricket.

Alan Smith, formerly chief executive of Warwickshire, failed to share the euphoria:

> I'm afraid his 501* left me cold. So what if he gets another record – what about trying to win the match? He tends to play for records and I always think going for the result is best for the team. He has an immense talent but failed to carry it out. He's a bit like George Best, who wasted his talent. Lara needed a wife like Kathy Botham. Kathy would have straightened him out.

The dressing-room celebrations were cut short as the television and radio people insisted on interviewing Lara. He rubbed a towel around his head and emerged to talk fluently and modestly for more than forty minutes, his theme being 'it doesn't make me a great player, I've still got a lot to do to achieve that.' The written media men wanted their interviews as well and he sat in the players' dining room for a further half an hour answering questions on a number of topics. 'I've let my team down in one-day matches,' he said. 'And I want to make it up to them. In one-day cricket you tend to be looser and it is easier to get out. I've got to concentrate more.' He also spoke about his father Bunty:

> He would be a very proud man tonight. He was an agricultural manager in the village where I grew up in Santa Cruz and though it was a struggle to bring up a family of eleven, we weren't poor. He would always make the necessary sacrifices to buy my cricket equipment.

The following week, he revealed that he hoped to slip into Port of Spain undetected, 'but I don't think that will be possible.'

So it proved. David Manasseh rang the company who had produced thousands of T-shirts and baseball caps bearing the words 'Brian Lara the legend – 375' to order them to stop production. 'We've got to change it to "Brian Lara the legend – 501",' he said. Bob Woolmer claimed that he was the only man to see Hanif's 499 and Lara's 501. He told a journalist employed by *Wisden*:

> It was a freak that I saw the Hanif innings. I was at prep school at Tonbridge and my father was working in Karachi and I was flown out on a BOAC Comet. I was eleven and I was very scared because our aircraft was forced to

land by fighters in Baghdad. When I eventually got there my Dad dropped me off and left me and came back when Hanif was closing on the record. There was a big crowd, there was a matting pitch, a very rough outfield and a bloke was getting out. My Dad asked me what happened and I said, 'Well, someone got 499.' As for Brian's 501 he was so single-minded, it was always inevitable, almost mystical.

ten

A Comedy-Drama in Five Acts

Act I: A Mobile Phone Call to First Slip

The circus moved on to Taunton. I arrived an hour and a half late on the final day of a county match which was heading for a meaningless draw. The Lara effect was influencing my way of life! As I parked in the small car park under the ramshackle Press box I bumped into Ted Blackbrow, my *Daily Mail* photographer who was covering the match with me. 'Did you see Lara making a call on his mobile phone when the innings started?' he asked. 'I've only just arrived,' I said. 'You're not serious, are you?' He pulled out his shots. One was Lara holding his phone up to his ear while standing at first slip as the Somerset innings was about to start. 'Did anyone else get it?' I asked. Ted, one of the most competitive photographers on the circuit, said, 'No, and I'm not going to share it round.'

Up to then only one call had been made to someone on the field in English cricket. Ian Botham was the culprit. Allan Lamb brought the phone out onto the field and asked Dickie Bird to look after it. When it rang, Bird panicked before realising it was a joke. This was the second instance and the umpires Ray Julian and Kevin Lyons, although amused by it, had to reprimand Lara. 'We don't allow mobile phones out here,' said Julian. 'We'll see you in our room later and we'll have a quiet word.'

Dermot Reeve had been missing when the match started, on duty with the England one-day squad, and Tim Munton was filling in as captain. Somerset had scored 355 for nine and Warwickshire were 57 for no wicket at the end of the second day. The third day was washed out and Lara had spent most of his time either speaking on his phone or taking naps. The weather was still bad on the last day and both sides had been ready to pack up and go home until the rain stopped. Andy Hayhurst, the Somerset skipper, met Munton and they did a deal, leaving Warwickshire to chase 321, initially in 95 overs, in murky light.

Warwickshire declared on their 57 for 0 and Somerset came out to bat for fifteen minutes to satisfy the conditions. As the innings was about to start Lara, stationed at first slip, was startled to hear his mobile ringing. He took it out of his pocket and answered it shamefacedly and heard the voice of Reeve, who had since arrived at the ground, saying, 'Brian, I think you are standing a bit close to Keith [Piper the wicketkeeper].' Some of the Warwickshire second-team players were laughing on the balcony and waving to him, intimating that he should put his mobile away. Reeve said later:

> It wasn't the done thing but the atmosphere was going to be light-hearted for the first few overs as we gave them some cheap runs. Just for a laugh I agreed with some of the other lads that I'd phone Brian before the first ball was delivered. Afterwards Brian was very sniffy with me. He didn't realise that it was a gentle bit of leg pulling. He kept saying that he was just one of the boys but I realised that he would laugh at himself if the joke or quip was from the others in the team, but not me.

Warwickshire were 87 for one when Lara, wearing three sweaters, came in. The light was bad enough to worry Dickie Bird but with no fast bowler in the home side the match was allowed to continue. Lara soon started rattling up boundaries – Taunton was one of the smallest county grounds – and he reached his century in 72 balls, the fastest hundred of the season. Early on Graham Rose, Somerset's medium fast bowler, bowled a beamer at his head and he had to take evasive action. 'It slipped,' said Rose. The outfield was wet and it was difficult to keep the ball dry. Rose bowled another beamer and Lara thought it might not have slipped. He was very angry. He yanked his head out of the way, cricking his neck. The physiotherapist had to come to treat him. Paul Smith, who batted at four, said, 'Brian watched both of these deliveries all the way. Most players would have ducked.' Jack Bannister's book *Brian Lara: The Story of a Record Breaking Year* quoted Smith as saying:

> [Lara] doesn't chat much while you are batting with him. He is easily the best player I have ever seen because he is so watchful and plays so straight. He is not a great timekeeper as far as turning up is concerned but I've got no problem with that because he has showed the rest of us what can be achieved. He has mixed well with us and when we are away, he always comes out with us. He is quiet and patient.

At tea I came round to the pavilion to leave a message for him, telling the dressing-room attendant to ring my number once he was out because I had to write his column before 6.30 p.m. Alex Davis, the Warwickshire scorer, told the journalists next to the scorers' box, 'I asked Brian what he intended to do now and he said, "Some crash, some bang and definitely plenty of wallop."' Back out in the middle, he kept his word and Bannister said, 'What followed was brutal and spectacular beyond belief.' Mushtaq Ahmed was conceding ten an over before he bowled him for 136 off only 94 balls. On a sodden outfield and with the light dismal, Lara played a remarkable innings even by his standards and Warwickshire won by six wickets. Tim Munton said, 'They had everyone round the boundary and he was still beating them. It was an amazing performance.' It was his fifth consecutive first-class hundred in the sequence begun in the Antigua Test and equalled a record set by Sir Everton Weekes. Lara was generous about Mushtaq Ahmed. 'I rate him a better leg-spin bowler than Shane Warne because of his greater subtlety and range of spin,' he said.

It was well past five o'clock, and allowing half an hour for a shower and a rub-down, I came back to the pavilion and knocked at the door. The attendant answered it and said, 'He's in the shower. I gave him your message.' Another anxious ten minutes passed. Surely his shower had been completed. I knocked again. The attendant appeared. 'He's just driven off,' he said. 'How long ago?' I asked. 'About five minutes,' he replied. I rushed out to the car park at the other side of the pavilion and was relieved to see him signing autographs. He never ducks out of that. I congratulated him and said, 'I've got to write a column. Can I sit with you in the car for a minute or two in a quiet spot somewhere?' 'I'm sorry,' he said. 'I've got to get back to Edgbaston for treatment on my neck. We're playing tomorrow.' Suddenly half a dozen reporters appeared, asking questions about his marvellous innings and his mysterious injury. I realised it would be impossible to bring up the subject of his mobile phone call because the other journalists, who didn't know about it, would jump on it and ruin our *Daily Mail* scoop. Lara turned and started to get into his car. 'Just one thing,' I said. 'What about your phone call out there?' He sat down in the driver's seat, smiled and said, 'Yes, I shouldn't have done that. I apologised to the umpires.' The other reporters had turned to leave and none of them heard what he said. The scoop was safe.

Unfortunately the sports editor of that time, the thirteenth I had worked under, failed to recognise the value of the story. He turned my story round, starting with Lara's innings and only recording the facts of the phone call near the end. But Ted Blackbrow's picture was displayed on the back page. Julian said years later:

The ECB wanted a report on it but Brian didn't come to see me afterwards and we heard no more. He's a lovely man, so friendly, and he always had time for me. I once gave him out lbw on 95 and we used to joke about it. I've given a few big ones out in the nineties! Another time he tried to chat up my daughter and I asked him to sign a card and he wrote, 'To your lovely daughter.' He's a real gentleman and he is totally devoted to cricket. He's almost in the same class as Don Bradman, not far off.

Act II: 'You're Turning Into a Prima Donna!'

Thursday 23 June 1994 saw one of the great cricketing battles of all time: Curtly Ambrose, the fearsome West Indian fast bowler playing for Northamptonshire against Brian Lara. The Press billed it as the world's best bowler against the world's number one batsman and Lara wasn't happy about it. 'It put extra pressure on me,' he said. I had arranged to meet him at 9.30 a.m. at the County Ground to discuss our weekly column, plus the coaching strip, and it was 10.40 a.m. when he finally arrived following a brief break on a barge at Stratford on Avon. He looked a little grumpy. 'I got lost in the one-way system,' he said. Sir Richard Hadlee, the New Zealand all-rounder, now retired, was also waiting in the car park next to the dressing-rooms. He had half a dozen bats in his hand and came up to him saying, 'Good to see you Brian. Can you please sign these? I would appreciate it.' Lara shook hands and smiled. 'Certainly,' he said. When Sir Richard thanked him and departed it was 10.50, just ten minutes from the start of play. 'Obviously we can't have a chat now,' I said, 'but if you're out, can I pop round? Or if you're still there, at lunch? Deadlines are looming.' It was the first intimation to him that Warwickshire were batting. 'Okay,' he said. There must have been pandemonium in the dressing-room: Where's our number three superstar? Woolmer, speaking twelve years later, said, 'You could say that but fortunately Andy Moles and Roger Twose put on 71 for the first wicket; even then Brian went out to face Ambrose without his helmet. It like like a red rag to a bull.' Lara explained, 'I wasn't being arrrogant. The helmet I brought with me was slightly suspect and you can't take chances. I asked the twelfth man to bring out another one.' He needed it. Early in his innings a bouncer from Ambrose reared up and smacked into the helmet. Lara staggered backwards and the physiotherapist came on. Ambrose looked uninterested. Lara took off his headwear, felt his head and discovered there was a small swelling. His head was spinning as though it was crashing about in a tumble drier. 'I got a headache but I decided to bat on,' he said afterwards.

1. Lara's parents, Bunty and Pearl, on their wedding day.

2. Young Brian with one of his early trophies – almost as big as him! Bunty was rarely seen smiling on these occasions.

3. Lara's first trip, as a fifteen-year-old, to India.

4. Flanked by Curtly Ambrose and Gordon Greenidge on his first senior overseas tour to Pakistan. He made his Test debut against Waqar Younis and Wasim Akram.

5. Rising like a ballet dancer as he executes a classic off drive on the back foot.

6. Celebrating with Curtly Ambrose.

7. The pull to leg that beat the world record of 375 set by Sir Garfield Sobers. Lara's right pad brushed against the wicket, almost knocking a bail off.

8. The chaotic scene in the middle, as seen from the stand.

9. A guard of honour for the new world record holder.

10 & 11. The moment when Lara, fielding at first slip in a championship game at Taunton during his first spell at Warwickshire, achieved the unusual distinction of being the first Test player to take a call on a mobile phone while the game was going on.

12. *Left*: On his way to 501* against Durham.

13. *Opposite:* Celebrating his first-class world-record innings of 501*. Wayne Larkins is on the right.

14. Thanks to the Lord… and not forgetting his much-loved father Bunty.

15. *Left*: Arriving at the Excelsior Hotel, Heathrow for talks to end the players' strike of November 1998.

16. *Above*: Happier times after the strike. Lara is pictured with Steve Camacho (left), the former secretary of the West Indies Board, and Pat Rousseau, the president.

17. *Below*: Lara with Revd Wes Hall at a press conference.

18. Lara plays golf right-handed and according to some experts he could have been a professional.

19. *Above left*: Trying out his football skills before the second Test at Edgbaston in 2000.

20. *Above right*: The barbecue king.

21. 'Liming' with some of his friends.

22. The inseparable friends: Dwight Yorke, born in Tobago on 3 November 1971, and Brian Lara, born in Trinidad on 2 May 1969.

23. *Left*: Proud to be given an honorary doctorate by the University of Sheffield.

24. *Below*: With his mother Pearl and some of his trophies in 1994.

25. Lara's chocolate box-style mansion overlooking the Savannah in Port of Spain. The land was given to him by an admiring government.

26. *Right*: Lara is generally available to sign autographs, especially for youngsters. The dreadlocked man at the right of the group is his friend David Rudder, the calypso singer.

27. *Below*: Returning to the classroom at his school, Fatima College, in 1994.

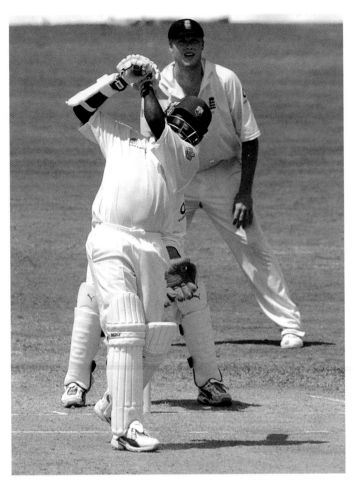

28. *Left*: Slightly pudgier than when he first took the world record ten years earlier, Lara drives another boundary straight down the pitch on his way to his 400, watched by an anxious Andrew Flintoff.

29. *Below*: Turning for yet another run on his way to the record.

30. The sweep to fine leg that took him past Matthew Hayden's record, putting him on 384.

31. A ceremonial kiss for the St John's Recreation Ground pitch, now gone.

32. Brian Lara leaves the field after losing his wicket in the 2007 World Cup match against Sri Lanka. Despite starting the tournament with a good win over Pakistan, West Indies were ultimately unsuccessful.

Curtly, a man of few words and much menace, rocked Lara on a number of occasions when he resumed but the batsman courageously held on. Whether by clever design or accident, Lara faced only 45 deliveries from Ambrose and every one was lethal. Lara took a mere 12 runs off him and hit just one boundary in his eventual tally of 197, which brought him level with another Bradman record of eight centuries in 11 first-class innings, set in 1938/39.

Ambrose's figures were 1-37 in 25 overs. The wicket he took was Lara's near the close of a memorable day which tingled with unremitting excitement. Ambrose, who hadn't got him out in nine meetings, bowled short, Lara hooked towards long on and Mal Loye pulled down the catch above his head, right on the line. When asked for a few words after the close, he said, 'I can't come out to speak. My head is throbbing. I've got to lie down.'

The previous week Reeve had called a meeting of the senior players to discuss Lara's lateness and his complaints about his knee, which he thought were an excuse to avoid fielding throughout each day. He said Dennis Amiss was reluctant to take action, calling for a softly-softly approach. He wanted his star man out there even if he missed practice. They agreed to ask Gladstone Small to speak to Lara because he was a good friend. On the second morning Lara took his place at slip without any sign of animation but when Rob Bailey, on 50, nicked the ball towards Piper and the keeper appealed for a catch, and umpire Allan Jones turned it down, he made remarks which caused the final split between the superstar and the hyperactive captain. In his book *Winning Ways* Reeve said:

> Jones said firmly, 'I saw the ball bounce – not out.' 'You must have f——ing good eyesight then,' said Lara. The umpire's reply was instant. 'There was nothing wrong with my eyesight when I gave you not out first ball yesterday – you concentrate on your fielding and I'll do the umpiring.'

Reeve tried to calm Lara down, unavailingly. Lara shouted, 'We've got him out once, let's do it again.' Four runs later Bailey edged another delivery to Piper and was given out. Reeve recalled: 'I simply said, "Brian – don't" and that led to the torrent of abuse and four-letter words at me in front of the team. After Brian had told me to f—— off seven times, I said, "Brian, you're turning into a prima donna."'

In his autobiography Lara dismissed the incident as a minor one. 'There was no attempt to abuse the umpire,' he said. 'It was the kind of incident that happens occasionally and everyone forgets about it by the next interval.' Reeve describes that as 'nonsense'. At the time he called for disciplinary action to be taken, but again the club's executive failed to respond.

At the end of the over Lara pointed to his knee, said to Jones 'sore knee' and walked off, upsetting his captain again. On the third day he spent most of the day sleeping under the treatment table. Dennis Amiss told the Press that Lara went off feeling dizzy.

On the Sunday there was further drama. When Lara turned up, late, for the AXA Equity and Law League match between the same teams on the same ground, he was approached by Jonathan Agnew, the BBC cricket correspondent, for an interview and said, 'I don't think I am fit enough to play. My knee is troubling me.' Reeve announced the XI, with no Lara. Woolmer wanted a sixth successive win and he said later: 'The ground was full. It was the first time that happened and they were expecting to see Brian out there. There could have been ructions.' Amiss said to Reeve, 'Brian has to play, the TV cameras are there.' Reluctantly, Lara decided to play and a furious Reeve had to tell Trevor Penney that he wasn't playing twenty minutes before the start. Lara went in to bat to loud applause but miscued a sweep and the ball struck him close to the eye. He hit the next ball for six and was caught for 34 in the deep. Warwickshire duly won and Amiss, Woolmer, Tim Munton, Lara and Reeve held a meeting and Amiss laid out the official policy, saying: 'We have to sweep this under the carpet. The official line is that Brian is suffering from the after-effects of a blow to the head.' The knee of Lara was no longer sore... or was it?

Lara rested on the final day of the championship game, which Warwickshire won by four wickets, and the sports pages carried damaging stories about the Northampton affair. They said a 'showdown meeting' had been called for but it turned out to be a friendly round of golf between Amiss and Lara. Amiss said he was fixing Lara up with a secretary to handle his postbag and if he wanted to play for the county in 1996 – the West Indies were touring in 1995 – they would like to have him back. Reeve's position was considerably weakened. Though most of the players backed him, the executive didn't. One anonymous player said, 'I'd string him up on a hook in the dressing-room if there was any more nonsense from him.' Reeve wasn't having a good season, he missed half the summer and he felt isolated. Then Amiss told him he must apologise to Lara for calling him a prima donna. Reeve was staggered. 'We mustn't upset Brian,' Amiss explained. Reeve claimed he never swore in the exchange while Lara used the f-word seven times. 'Lara should apologise, not me,' he said. Then Reeve backed off – because he was due a benefit the following year. So he rang

Lara (it must have taken some time to get through!) and said, 'Brian, I don't like to insinuate that anyone is behaving like a prima donna or turning into one. I'm sorry about the incident and we have to get a working relationship going for the sake of the team. If doesn't matter if we are not mates.' Lara responded, 'You're right, I'm sorry it happened too but you never wanted me in the first place.' Reeve was stunned, deflated. Looking back, Bob Woolmer said of the row, 'It was a mighty clash of egos and Brian won hands down.' Amiss, a respected and amiable man who played in 50 Tests with an average of 46.30, was chief executive between 1994 and 2005 when he retired to become a consultant. He was a fine cricketer and an able diplomat – and he needed to be.

Reeve admitted that he experienced the worst fortnight of his life at that time. His wife left him and went to Australia, taking their daughter Emily with her and it was a traumatic time. The following year, in his benefit year, his leadership was highly praised as the Bears won two trophies, the County Championship and the NatWest Trophy. His benefit was reckoned to have brought in up to £500,000, which would have been a record, although no figure was officially disclosed for tax reasons. By keeping quiet after the Lara controversies, he had made a considerable sum.

According to Woolmer, a worse row took place between Lara and his captain on 7 August when Worcestershire beat Warwickshire by three runs in front of 10,500 spectators, the biggest audience for Sunday cricket at Edgbaston since they last won the title in 1980. He said:

> Dominic Ostler and Neil Smith put on 105 for the first wicket in 14 overs facing a target of 183 but we lost a couple of wickets and Brian decided to block it out against Richard Illingworth, their slow left-hander. Illingworth's eight overs cost only 25 runs and Reeve was furious. When the teams came off, he locked the dressing-room and I asked Brian for an explanation. There were raised voices for an hour and we finally agreed that Reeve should concentrate on playing in one-day matches because of his hip and Brian would play in the championship matches.

Ten years later the two protagonists met at a Warwickshire reunion dinner at the Botanical Gardens and they sat furthest apart on the long table. 'They exchanged a few brief words when they met but it was a tense moment,' said Woolmer.

Reeve threatened to resign in June 1994 because he felt he wasn't being given the full backing of some players, including Lara, or the management.

'Lara did wonders for our performances but he was a pain to captain,' he said. Reeve stayed on and eventually left at the end of the following season because of his chronic hip condition. In February he was very upset to learn that Lara, not Allan Donald, would be the club's overseas player for 1996. Lara was about to sign a three-year contract. Reeve said:

> Surely the captain ought to have had some say, especially as our relationship had been rocky for most of the previous season? It was terribly hard for Allan, a true professional. Lara didn't give English domestic cricket much respect. He saw it as a chore, it was too easy for him.

Realising what he had undertaken, Lara finally decided to not to accept the three-year deal.

Now a more contented and forgiving man, Reeve is establishing a new life in New Zealand. He said:

> No matter how talented you are, and Brian remains the most gifted player I have seen, peace within is so difficult to find. He has given so much pleasure to others who have watched him yet I do not believe satisfaction from his efforts has tamed some inner torment. Most of us have some inner demons to control and I am busy dealing with mine constantly. Brian seems at peace when distracted by the cricket ball but a huge test will follow when he retires. Positive thoughts are how I wish to approach my life now and I wish Brian all the best. I will attempt only to remember my cricket days with happiness as this is better than regret. You can only give 100% effort but rarely is a sportsman satisfied with the outcome and perhaps Brian has regrets.

Act III: The Hero Suddenly Returns Home

The morning of 30 June I was standing in another car park waiting for Lara. It was 9.20 a.m. and he had said he would be there by 9.30. At 9.45 he turned up for a photographic shoot for the coaching strips in his normal clothes. 'Is it all right to wear this?' he said pointing to his black sports shirt and dark flannels. I had to be firm. 'No,' I said. 'It's got to be in your cricket gear.' He pondered for a while. 'I've got to see Bob Woolmer,' he said. 'It won't take much time.'

The night before I had managed to reach him on his mobile and, struggling for an idea for his column, I went back to a favourite question which almost every batsman is asked at least once in his career: 'Who is the most hostile bowler you've played against?' 'Wasim Akram,' he said without any hesitation. 'He's caused me a few problems,' he said. 'He's got a quick arm, he's quick, bowls both sides of the wicket, swings it both ways, varies his pace and bowls several types of bouncer.' This was before the phrase 'reverse swing' became well known. Wasim was one of the pioneers of it.

I was keen to write the Lara column about Wasim from his own words but a few minutes after our encounter a local photographer hired to take the coaching pictures walked swiftly up to me on the outfield and said, 'I've just seen Lara drive off!' I went to Woolmer's office and asked if this rather disturbing news was correct. 'Yes,' he said. 'He brought in a certificate from a doctor in Berkshire, or Hertfordshire, I'm not sure, saying that his knee ligaments have been slightly damaged and he advised him against playing in this match. He's now driving down the M1 to Heathrow and is off to Port of Spain.'

I tried to ring his number and there was no reply. Jason Ratcliffe took his place in the side and he took a bit of a battering from Wasim Akram while scoring 69. Someone suggested that Lara ducked out from facing Wasim on a bouncier pitch than usual at Edgbaston but others disagreed. 'He just fancies a short holiday,' one said.

Keith Piper was nearby and it occurred to me that, with him being the same colour and height as Lara, with a helmet on and a few brushes on the prints we might just get away with using him as Brian's 'double'. Keith was reluctant when I approached him with the idea. 'What about twenty-five quid?' I asked. 'Okay,' he said. He duly returned from the dressing-room in his flannels and was enjoying the limelight. I managed to enlarge the couple of sentences from Lara on Akram to 500 words for his column and left reasonably contented. However, later in the day the chief sub editor at the *Mail* called and said, 'We've just had a close look at those pictures and they don't look like Lara. Who was it?' I had to confess. And the strip was left out. But Piper kept his £25. Today a famous sportsman in a similar position would want thousands of pounds, or rather, his agent would.

Five days later I got through to Lara, back in England, and we talked about our next column. He never mentioned his walk-out. Not wishing to upset him, I didn't mention it either. After Warwickshire's semi-final win over Surrey in the Benson & Hedges I accompanied him on one of his frequent trips back home and it was another hair-raising event. Lara was booked on the next day's BWIA flight to Port of Spain, part of his concession of TT$375,000 worth (around £32,000). Thirty-seven media writers and photographers were also booked, three of them in club class, the rest in economy. My seat was in the row next to club class, strategically placed to see where he and David Manasseh were sitting. Half an hour before departure there was no sign of the pair. As the minutes ticked by, the media men, and one lady, Anne Barrowclough of the *Daily Mail*, were thinking that Lara was not on the aircraft and their trip would be in vain. Three minutes from departure time, with the last calls long gone, Lara and Manasseh rushed in. Lara told me later, 'I needed to do some shopping at Selfridges. Unfortunately the traffic was heavy coming out of London and we had to sprint for it. Just made it!'

Sitting in club class was Viv Richards, whose award of the OBE was to be announced in the Queen's Birthday List the next day and he had a long chat with Lara. He told the journalists:

> It makes me so proud that this boy has become a man so quickly. This boy, whom I kept back a little because I knew he was so special and I wanted him to grow in his own space, in his own era, has set himself the greatest standards any cricketer has ever achieved. I am a religious man and when people told me cricket was dying, I said, man, a Moses will come to deliver us. Well Moses has come. His name is Brian Lara. I am only surprised he has done so much, so quickly. What it tells us is that he can become the greatest batsman who has ever lived.

The plane landed at Antigua and more media people came on for the final leg to Port of Spain. I spoke to Manasseh about handling the Press and suggested that the others should be allowed one day's access and no more. He agreed and so did Lara. The *Mail* had exclusive rights and could have blocked their rivals but it would have caused immense problems for Lara and his family. A parade of vehicles, headed by the local hero, his agent and the *Mail* trio wound its way to Cantaro, his birthplace, in Santa Cruz, an agricultural area of Trinidad. The other media men were allowed to meet his mother Pearl, a stately, upright lady who was both welcoming and caring for the guests. After the photo shoot and interviews, our trio accompanied Lara on a visit to Fatima College, his old grammar school. All 911 children were allowed time off to see him and our photographer arranged them outside in a huge group with Lara in the middle. The picture was about to be taken from a second-floor window when the photographer spotted a female journalist from the *Evening Standard* close to Lara. Her presence would ruin his picture and he shouted angrily, 'If you don't f——ing get out of there I'll come down and whack you.' She prudently withdrew.

Miss Barrowclough managed to get one of the better lines from Lara. She quoted him as saying:

> People say to kids to stay away from drugs and violence but to be honest, if I didn't have strict parents who made sure I was straight, I think I might have gone down the wrong road. I have a lot of friends, guys I grew up with, who are now wasted, who have made a shambles of their lives and have gone into drugs and violent crime. As soon as your friends became more influential than your parents, you will go down with them.

And she quoted his mother Pearl as saying:

> He was never going to be a bad boy but sometimes he was in little pranks. He would break a window with a ball sometimes. I prayed very hard for him and I knew that he would be a success. To God to the glory, I am not happy for myself. I am happy for Brian. He always wanted to be a cricketer, to do all the things he is doing and I thank God he is doing it. I am not responsible for what he is doing. God is. I was used as the instrument to bring him into the world.

Lara wanted to stay on over the weekend as there was no championship match but he was required to play in a country house game for John Paul Getty's team against E. W. Swanton's Arabs CC at Shenley, near Radlett on the Sunday. Everyone wanted a piece of him and being an obliging young man he agreed. We were sitting in the departure lounge talking to his girl-friend Leasel Rovedas, a former bank clerk, who found it difficult to cope with all the attention, when a member of staff came up and said the aircraft was delayed. 'Someone has rung up to say there is a bomb on the plane,' they said. There were no sniffer dogs available so it took three hours for the aircraft to be given clearance. The next hurdle was that the captain would be running out of time in his shift so the decision was made to abandon the stop in Barbados and fly straight to Heathrow. There were 126 passengers waiting in Barbados and they were flown to Port of Spain to catch the Heathrow-bound aircraft. Rather oddly, their plane landed at 9.52 p.m., two minutes after Lara's aircraft flew off. The next day there were nasty headlines about a plane overflying Barbados just to please the organisers of a charity cricket match featuring Brian Lara. BWIA offered profuse apologies and compensated the 126 passengers.

Act IV: 'Can I Miss This One? My Girlfriend is Coming'

In one match Brian Lara shouted out, 'I've got to go and make a telephone call to Trinidad,' and walked off the field. Dermot Reeve was incensed but he said, 'I bit my tongue and my hands were tied.' He said in his book:

> I was worried about this preferential treatment. I was having to work at getting him on to the field on Sundays. He clearly didn't fancy the helter-skelter style of the Sunday League, he wasn't making runs in these games and was trying hard to get a day off. He was complaining about his knee and I had to compromise, putting him in certain positions that wouldn't tax his knee. Yet when he really had to, he fielded like a gazelle and still put in some tremendous sprints between the wickets when he was pushed. So I was taking all his protestations with a pinch of salt, trying to keep the lid on the whole situation for the good of the team, and trying to ignore the fact that the star player didn't like or rate his captain.

On the eve of the NatWest game against Bedfordshire at Edgbaston in June Lara went to Reeve and said, 'Can I miss this one? My girlfriend is arriving from Trinidad. It's only a Minor County, you'll beat them.' Warwickshire were the holders and Reeve wanted his services 'because we could be on a hiding to nothing'. As it turned out, Warwickshire could have done without Lara as they won by a massive 197 runs. Leasel Rovedas, Lara's girlfriend, was supposed to be arriving at Heathrow at 9 a.m. and he said he would get to the ground by 10.30, the starting time. The roads were busier than usual as there was a rail strike on, and even Michael Schumacher would have struggled. Lara turned up at midday and, fortunately for him, Dominic Ostler and Roger Twose were in the middle of adding 156 runs for the first wicket. He was able to come in at his usual three but showed little animation and Matthew White, a trainee architect, bowled him for 23. Reeve said it was acutely embarrassing for the club and some journalists found out that Lara was late and were ready to write damning stories. 'I had to bend the truth a bit,' he said.

Jack Bannister, the former Warwickshire bowler who is one of the longest serving and most dedicated of cricket journalists, published a list of Lara's absences off the field in his newspaper and it provoked an angry reaction. Jonathan Barnett rang Dennis Amiss and requested him to ban Bannister from covering Warwickshire matches. That was one request that Amiss rejected.

Act V: The Book

When I eventually tracked Lara down for his interviewing sessions to complete his autobiography, he spoke intelligently and interestingly about the game which he obviously loved very much. David Manasseh tried to get him to appear on time and by the end of the summer he was losing the fight. I told David, 'I've got a week at the end of the cricket season free and I see he has a clear week as well, so can you arrange a daily get-together? Otherwise this book won't come out.' There were three chapters to go, about 8,000 words. Assembling 1,000 words a day shouldn't have been a problem. David promised me that he would be there. Alas, he wasn't. So I wrote the words from other conversations with him, with copious additions from my own knowledge.

Someone recommended a piece written by the distinguished Trinidadian author V.S. Naipaul and we had approval to use it. Naipaul wrote:

> Cricket has always been more than a game in Trinidad. In a society which demanded no skills and offered no rewards to merit, cricket was the only activity which permitted a man to grow to his full stature and to be measured against international standards. Alone on a field, beyond obscuring intrigue, the cricketer's worth could be seen by all. His education, wealth did not matter. We had no scientists, engineers, explorers, soldiers or poets. The cricketer was our only hero figure. That is why cricket is played in the West Indies with such panache.

It was very appropriate, I felt. The book was published on time and sold reasonably well, although it is fair to question whether a young sporting hero of twenty-five years of age really merits an autobiography at that stage of his career. When Lara's book came out, the publicist employed by Transworld arranged a series of book signings for him. The biggest was at a bookshop close to London's Liverpool Street Station. He was supposed to have arrived at 5 p.m. There were around 200 people queueing outside and the hero hadn't arrived. Twenty minutes later, he still hadn't arrived. There was a message: 'He'll be there in five minutes.' He finally turned up at 5.40 p.m. and his first words to me were 'I'll only be available for fifteen minutes. I've got another appointment.' I said 'If you can sign 200-odd books in fifteen minutes you'll beat the world record – but you won't. If you leave early, there could be a riot!' He decided to stay on and signed the whole lot with a smile and friendly comment for every customer. His record-breaking summer had started in chaos and it ended the same way.

eleven

They Shoot Horses, Don't They?

Brian Lara's mad summer of 1994 was summed up by what happened in the twenty-four hours following his unbeaten innings of 501. After a long shower he dressed and, after facing the Press, he came out to take on scores of autograph-hunters and well-wishers. It was some time before he was allowed to depart. In any normal sport a great performance of shattering proportions would have earned a few days off for the champion. Not in cricket. Around 9 p.m., Lara was talking to Keith Piper about whether he was going to be fit to drive to London for the next day's Benson & Hedges semi-final at The Oval. He felt completely drained and he asked Piper, 'Can you drive?' Piper was happy to do it and they eventually set off. Coming into North London he got lost and it was 2 a.m. before the two tired sportsmen arrived at the then-named Tower Hotel next to Tower Bridge.

Lara recalled: 'When I woke next morning, I didn't feel much like playing in a high-pressure game. My head was buzzing.' Without eating much in the way of breakfast, he and Piper travelled the two-mile journey in heavy traffic and when they arrived in the dressing-room, they were upset to learn that Surrey had won the toss. It was a hot and humid day and Lara's head was still spinning after three and a half hours in the field. 'I can't focus on the ball,' he said. So he moved to the boundary but a few overs later he said, 'I can't see properly.' He asked to come off and the umpires, David Constant and Barry Dudleston, agreed. A doctor was called and recommended an ice pack to be placed on the back of his head. Bob Woolmer told him, 'You can't stay off much longer, otherwise you will have to bat down the order. You've got to go back out there.' Lara was off the field for forty-six minutes and when the Surrey fielders came off they discovered that he was fast asleep. Gladstone Small said, 'They tried to wake him and they shook him but he couldn't wake up. Bob Woolmer said, "Leave him" but later when wickets were falling, he had to be woken up.'

There was an American film about poor people in the southern states in the early 1930s who entered non-stop dance contests where the prize would go to the last pair still on their feet. It was based on a true story. Lara must have felt the same way. The forty-minute delay meant he had to wait and go in at number six, with the Warwickshire total 120 for four. The target was 148 in 30 overs and having scored 267 for seven in their 55 overs, Surrey thought they had a good chance of winning now with Lara groggy and bleary-eyed. The packed crowd, particularly the members, rose to their feet to clap him in. He came in at 5.30 p.m. and, realising that Warwickshire needed a result, he proceeded to play a Test match-style innings, playing himself in with caution before opening up. 'I was desperately tired but was seeing the ball well,' he said. He struck nine effortless boundaries and his knock of 70 was a considerable performance, especially as it came from only 73 deliveries following a slow start. That 70 off 73 balls equalled Ted Dexter's performance in the drawn 'Greatest Test of All' between England and the West Indies at Lord's in 1963, when he played one of the greatest innings of all time. Lara and Reeve added 93 runs in 20 overs and when Lara had a stump knocked back by Adam Hollioake only 16 runs were needed. Warwickshire won by four wickets with four balls remaining.

Nick Knight said:

> I don't know how it he did it, the day after he'd scored 501. It was incredible. But he knew the side needed an innings from him and he did it. He still has that appetite and desire to win matches and he's still getting double hundreds. I remember when I first played against him, for Essex at Edgbaston. It was the last over before lunch and John Stephenson was skipper and he put me at silly point. I think Peter Such was bowling and most batsmen would bat the over out. Not him. He ran down the pitch to the last ball and drove it nearly out of the ground. He showed absolute disdain. I thought to myself, 'That's what a really great player does.'

After the semi-final win at The Oval the champagne was poured again but Lara didn't feel like celebrating. He stayed overnight in London and the next morning he flew to Port of Spain for a short break. Thirty-two days later Warwickshire won the Benson & Hedges Cup for the first time, by six wickets with 10.4 overs in hand. Another capacity crowd turned up at Lord's to watch him but he was caught by Graeme Hick for only eight. He wasn't really needed. By this time Lara was complaining about his workload. 'I don't want to finish up with a walking stick,' he said. Warwickshire's medical experts saw little evidence that the supposedly troublesome knee was swollen enough to keep him out of the side. Amiss and Woolmer wanted him to be in action as often as possible but they recognised that his brief breaks would be beneficial.

When Lara wasn't playing cricket, he still played a round or two of golf. In mid-summer he played a round with Sir Gary Sobers and said in his column:

> It was a most enjoyable day. When Gary joined Nottinghamshire in 1968, when the ban on foreign players was lifted, he scored 1,570 runs for an average of 44.85 and took 83 wickets at 22.67 each. He bowled 773 overs in a 28-match championship and must have ended up a very tired man. The year before he arrived at Trent Bridge they were fifteenth. They were fourth in 1968.

Sobers' knee was irretrievably damaged by wear and tear and Lara often brought it up as a reason for not playing pressure cricket on an almost daily basis. His impact at Warwickshire was arguably greater than the contribution of Sobers in 1968, certainly in terms of trophies. He inspired his colleagues to win a first treble: the championship, the Sunday League and the B&H.

Sobers is one of the few sportsmen to play left and right-handed in golf. Playing left-handed, he brought his handicap down to two, and switching to the right he played at four for a while. He still plays but his handicap has risen considerably. He loves it. Gladstone Small said:

> Brian took every opportunity to drive over to the Belfry to play golf and in that summer he reduced his handicap down from eighteen to eight. He played right-handed because he said, 'If I played left-handed it would ruin my cricket.' But one day he borrowed Roger Twose's set of left-handed clubs and played a round left-handed and shot a low ninety.

Woolmer thought Lara's finest batting achievement was on a green top at Chesterfield at the end of July. 'His hundred came off 94 balls and he made 142 out of 280,' said Woolmer. 'No one looked comfortable out there, except Brian.' Gladstone Small said: 'That was one of his greatest innings. Devon Malcolm smacked him in the head early on and that woke him up!'

Against Nottinghamshire, Lara had to field 166 overs and he batted at seven in the first innings, being lbw for 15. In the second innings, restored to three, he was bowled first ball by fellow West Indian and later West Indies captain Jimmy Adams for his first duck of the season in first-class cricket. Adams was never a threatening bowler and overconfidence may well have been the reason Lara lost his wicket: he tried to cut the first ball he faced and was bowled by a delivery which kept low. The whole Nottinghamshire side mobbed Adams. Lara's average fell to under a hundred.

There was now talk that Lara's success had 'gone to his head'. One eminent critic said, 'It's proved too much for him. He's not used to being chased about by autograph hunters, agents and photographers. And he's starting to believe his own publicity.' Lara's explanation was simple. 'I'm not fit,' he said. 'My left knee was swollen and the right knee started playing up.' At Scarborough he had to play and insisted on having a runner, the first time he had used one at any level of cricket. Sixteen-stone Andy Moles was his runner and it provided much laughter and ribaldry in front of a large crowd. Lara dropped out of the Sunday game, which was watched by a near-capacity crowd but carried out the duties of twelfth man. It showed that he wasn't an egomaniac and he said 'I had no worries about that. Someone had to do the job.'

Paul Smith, the Warwickshire all-rounder, said, 'Edgbaston was like Las Vegas when Brian was in his first year with us.' That was an unfortunate comparison: Lara does have a flutter, particularly on horses, just as Gary Sobers does, but he didn't spend time in casinos. Smith went on:

> You couldn't move and what astounded me was how many people wanted a little piece of him. An autograph. A phone call. A bit of his time in the evening. For someone in that position, there must come a time when you think, 'I'm not living my own life, I'm living for other people.'

Lara was in a similar position to a pop star of the stature of Elton John or Madonna. These people are protected by minders, agents and PR people and they rarely meet the public. Lara must have felt he needed the same kind of support. Unfortunately for him, he didn't have the wealth to maintain backup staff. Mark Nicholas wrote a piece in the *Daily Telegraph* quoting Bob Woolmer about Lara's travails and this is what the sensitively intelligent Warwickshire coach said:

> The trouble with Brian was twofold. We never knew where he was and he never allowed us to get close enough to know him any better so that we could help. The media pressure which surrounded him was absurd. I've never

seen the like and none of us knew how to handle it. Actually, Brian is a lovely guy with a perceptive cricket brain but his overall behaviour and his daily views were very set. They were all-or-nothing views which made him awkward to handle.

He clashed with Dermot because they both needed to be top dog. He wasn't flexible within a team framework and always accused us of thinking only of Warwickshire and rarely of Lara. I wondered whether it was him or us getting it right. Communication was a permanent problem. We did talk to his agent about it because if he turned up at Edgbaston ten minutes before the start of play, as he did quite often, we wanted to know why and to know where he had been. We had a team to pick, after all. After six months with him and even a private round of golf with him at The Belfry, I still didn't know him any better. It's sad in a way. One last thing, he never let us down on the field, you know, never.

The rift between Lara and Reeve deepened at the summer wore on and at one team meeting Lara suggested that his captain wasn't worth a place in the first team because of his injury. 'What he said was fully justified,' said Paul Smith. 'He said Dermot hadn't scored many runs and hardly took a wicket for two months.' Lara's apology to the rest of the squad was delivered on the morning of the B&H final at Lord's. Smith said:

It was a pretty emotional thing. He levelled with us and the result was that everyone went into the match psyched up to win. Brian is a strong man. I can think of several people who in the same circumstances wouldn't have been able to bring themselves to apologise.

Reeve and Amiss agreed that the captain should play only one-day matches and forsake county matches for a while, with the very able Tim Munton taking over as skipper. Amiss said, 'Brian's apology was brilliant. Basically he is a good bloke and I think he handled the pressure pretty well. When I see him now he always comes up and has a chat and a laugh.' Late in the season Lara told Alan Fraser of the *Daily Mail*:

I was really worried when I read that my teammates were wondering what was happening to Brian, getting too big for his boots and stuff like that. I did not get that feeling in the dressing-room, yet it was said in the dressing-room. The guys assured me they were quite happy with the way things were going. Before April I was just a cricketer trying to establish myself, trying to get recognised on the international scene. I didn't have a county contract and wouldn't have had one but for the injury to Prabhakar. I was trying to get in there, get as many runs as possible and get people to notice me. Within two months I was propelled into a situation where you are compared ridiculously with people that have done the business over ten to fifteen years and become great players. It is something you cannot get caught up in because you have got a whole career ahead of you.

I don't think it turned my head because I personally thought it was nice to get the scores, nice to be up there. But if you look at my average, it is not even close to Sir Don Bradman's. I have not played as many matches at Sir Gary Sobers and scored as many centuries as he did. So it is nothing to get carried away with. It is just 501 and 375. World records, yes, but if from now on you get carried away with it and your cricket suffers, you are going to be considered no more than a one-season wonder.

Thankfully for the game of cricket, he wasn't a one-season wonder! There was an amusing incident at the Hove ground when Lara arrived for his championship match against Sussex. Someone showed him a cutting from the *Sunday Mirror*, an article by David Smith, the former Sussex, Surrey and England left-handed opening batsman. Smith was renowned for his physical strength – he was once selected by England for a tour of the West Indies because of his fearlessness against the West Indian fast bowlers – and the gist of his article was 'quit moaning about the demands of county cricket and get on with it'. When Lara stepped out of his car one of the first people he spotted was the 6ft 4in, sixteen-stone Smith. The 5ft 8ins, eleven-stone Lara confronted him and said, 'What do you mean, writing that?' Smith was acutely embarrassed. 'I wasn't having a go at you,' he said.

Sussex picked two England spin bowlers, Eddie Hemmings who had just signed up from Nottinghamshire, and Ian Salisbury, and the reason for that was the state of the pitch. In the middle, it was grassy and green looking but the ends were bare to suit spin. 'I learned a lot from all these different pitches in England,' said Lara. The then Test and County Cricket Board later banned the two-tone pitch. Lara spent much of the Sussex game in the treatment room and three days later he declared himself fit to take on Hampshire at Edgbaston. Warwickshire needed to win to claim their first championship since 1972 and they wanted a big innings from him. Lara forsook his helmet for much of the time and hit 191 off 222 balls. It gave his side time to bowl Hampshire out again in an innings-and-95-run defeat. It was his ninth century of the season, equalling Alvin Kallicharran's record for

Warwickshire, and he became the first player to pass 2,000 runs. His tally of 2,066 first-class runs came off 2,262 balls and he scored twice as fast as the average county batsman. His average was 89.82, a figure bettered by only eight players since the Second World War. They were Denis Compton with 90.85 from 3,816 runs in 1947; Don Bradman, 89.92 in 1948; Bill Johnson, 102.00 from 102 runs in 1953; Geoff Boycott, 100.12 in 1971; Boycott again, 102.53 in 1979; Glenn Turner, 90.07 in 1982; Graham Gooch, 101.70 in 1990; Carl Hooper, 93.81 in 1991; Gooch again, 91.75 in 1993; and, surprisingly, John Carr 90.76 in 1994. Carr, son of the Derbyshire and England captain who was long-serving secretary of the TCCB, had a cack-handed style of playing and everything went his way. But everyone knew that Lara had towered over the 1994 season, not John Carr.

Lara earned around £15,000 in bonuses on top of his £45,000 salary from Warwickshire that season – a total of £60,000, which is what many of today's Premiership footballers earn per week. The bounty for winning the title was £48,500 and there were bonuses of £6,600 for winning eleven matches. The money was shared by the squad. Talking about the achievement, Lara made no mention of his own contribution, saying, 'Our greatest asset was team spirit and the way the players played for each other.'

Someone left a crate of champagne in the dressing-room but it wasn't opened. Warwickshire's players had to leave early because they were playing against Worcestershire in the final of the NatWest Trophy at Lord's the next day, a repeat of the B&H final which the Bears had won easily. Lara had been invited by the Cricket Writers' Club to accept the Peter Smith Award for making an outstanding contribution to English cricket. The prize was an engraved edition of the 1994 *Wisden*, later to be exchanged for the 1995 edition, which was the one he really treasured. He told an audience of 350 members and their guests, 'I am very proud to accept this award on behalf of my team.' It was presented by Mrs Joan Smith, wife of the much-lamented Peter Smith, the popular press officer of the TCCB. Lara didn't stay on for the celebrations; he had to rejoin the team at their hotel.

Next morning, the omens weren't good. The weather forecast was poor and when Dermot Reeve lost the toss, Lara felt that there was a sense of panic in the Warwickshire dressing-room. Not known as a funny man, he tried to lift the mood by telling a few stories. Phil Newport and Tom Moody, who bowled his twelve overs for 17, moved the ball both ways and Lara took 26 deliveries to get off the mark after Warwickshire struggled to 17 for two. There were several raucous appeals against Lara. One came from wicketkeeper Steve Rhodes, later the coach of Worcestershire, for a catch down the leg side; it was turned down. Rhodes made an insulting remark to Lara, who raised a placatory arm. Umpire Nigel Plews was unmoved by his decision, which was supported by television replays. To add to Rhodes's anguish, the umpire called the delivery wide and the keeper showed his anger.

Lara survived another appeal, this time for lbw and there was further uproar. David Shepherd, the senior umpire, strode over purposefully to Rhodes at the end of the over and told him to calm down or else he would be in trouble. Rhodes spread his arms wide, gesturing his innocence but Shepherd refused to back down. It was an unseemly incident but Lara handled it superbly. He battled his way to 36 before rain ended the proceedings, with his side 88 for three. The next day the conditions were unchanged as the innings restarted and Lara had to be restrained against the swinging ball. He advanced to 81 when he clipped a nondescript delivery from medium-pacer Gavin Haynes straight to Graeme Hick on the mid-wicket boundary. This was the same shot from which he had been dismissed in the B&H final and he was livid when he arrived back at the dressing-room. He has a flawless memory of his mistakes and to make two on the same stage was, for him, unforgivable. Later he said it was one of the finest one-day innings he had played, but a total of 223 wasn't enough after the pitch dried out and as the clouds lifted. Gladstone Small said: 'That 70 he scored against Surrey and this innings were the two great knocks by Lara and I rated his 81 as a greater innings than his 501. The ball was moving all over the place. No one middled it, except him.'

For the first time that summer, Warwickshire had a sudden puncture and their assault plan in that match failed to get back on the road. After tea, Roger Twose was hit for twelve and the over-excited Paul Smith was taken out of the attack after conceding 54 runs in seven overs. Hick plundered 93 off 101 balls in typical style and Moody's contribution was 88 in 112 balls in Worcestershire's eight-wicket win with 65 balls remaining. In his autobiography, Lara dismissed both men as 'short of the very highest level of Test cricket', which was true. He also criticised the authorities for staging a 60-overs final at the end of the season. He called for 50 overs a side with the venue switched to The Oval. 'There is always moisture at Lord's at the end of the season and the side winning the toss always have a great chance of winning,' he said. Except for the administrators at The Oval, no one supported the change of ground. Lara showed that he has positive views about the game and if he doesn't want to be a coach or a manager, his future could be as an administrator... or a politician.

He was in trouble on Sunday 18 September when Warwickshire played their final AXA Equity and Law League match of the season at Gloucestershire's unique ground in Bristol. *The Times* reported that he was late. He turned up at midday for a 1 p.m. start but excused himself, saying, 'When I am feeling in good form I try not to do too much.' Courtney Walsh, the home side's captain, won the toss and asked Warwickshire to bat first. They failed to score a run off the bat in the opening six overs while losing the pinch hitter Neil Smith, Dominic Ostler and Roger Twose. It was down to Lara again and he played circumspectly until he cracked a shot just over the head of Bobby Dawson at square leg. Trevor Penney, who helped him put on a match-winning stand of 68, spooned a simple catch to Walsh at mid-wicket and it was spilled. Luck had gone Warwickshire's way. When he was on 38, Lara wasn't quite in the right place to drive an extra cover shot and the ball came off the top edge high into the air, plummeting towards the third man boundary. Mike Smith, not the fastest mover in the side, ran in and dived, claiming the catch. Lara recalled in his book:

> I had no reason to doubt that it was a fair catch and left the crease. Later, some of the players told me on the replay it looked as though the ball had bounced first. The BBC experts said there was a lot of doubt about it. I didn't worry too much about it. My policy is to leave it to the fielder. If he claims a catch then I accept his word. I don't believe fielders cheat on something like that and often the fielder is the only person who can definitely say whether it was a clean catch or not. Even with the increased rewards in top cricket, I don't think anyone would risk the dishonour that would follow.

Not many top players take the opinion of the fielder. Almost invariably they wait for the verdict of the television replay. Smith was a much-respected cricketer and Lara cleared up what might well have been a moment of lingering controversy by his ingrained sportsmanship. Warwickshire's 183 for eight off 39 overs proved enough and Gloucestershire fell 46 runs short. Most of the crowd were from Birmingham and they rushed out to the middle to congratulate the Bears. Lara was one of the first to leave the field. 'I felt I hadn't contributed much to a historic Treble,' he said. But the crowd chanted, 'There's only one Brian Lara.' Warwickshire's prize money was £36,062.50 and their aggregate total from three competitions was £139,337.50. Again, it was shared out equally among the players. Lara pointed out that a golfer often wins £139,000 in a single tournament and said, 'We are the poor relations but we have to accept it. Still, it is a good life and to us, especially West Indians, the emphasis is not so much on money but on pride, recognition and love of the game.' He sounds portentous but that is Brian Lara.

twelve

A Stressful Tour of India

If Brian Lara was hoping for a quiet winding-down period after his exertions in England, his hopes were soon dashed. In October he was selected for the West Indies' tour of India which started badly and rapidly became worse. An outbreak of pneumonic plague in the western state of Gujarat raised doubts about whether the tour would take place and Lara must have been hoping it would be called off. But after a week's delay, the team assembled at the Piarco Airport in Port of Spain and flew off to London before enduring two more flights to Chandigarh without their main attraction. 'There was a misunderstanding,' he explained. 'I showed up only to discover that the ticket I was expecting wasn't there. It meant I had to wait until the next day's flight and I arrived late.' Richie Richardson, the captain, was unable to go – he was suffering from exhaustion. Lara should have offered the same excuse. Courtney Walsh, a man of firm convictions, took over the captaincy and the West Indies Board of Control fined Lara US$1,000.

'I wasn't in the best shape for an arduous tour,' Lara said. 'I was pretty tired after my season in England and put myself under a lot of pressure both on and off the field. Everyone wanted to see what I could do but the pitches were slow and I felt they weren't proper Test pitches.' Nagpur is not the most desirable of cities. He said, 'It's pretty tough out there.' Monkeys, cows, dogs, cats and other animals parade up and down the unrepaired roads and a pall of stench hangs in the air, most of it coming from excreta from the animals. Unlike in the royal parks of London, the locals don't pick it up and put it in bins. The West Indians were unhappy to be whisked around the country, crossing from one side to the other and back in elderly aircraft and there were few laughs. They were also dogged by loose bowels.

Lara's top score in the five one-day internationals – which India won 4-1 – was 89, and he showed little appetite for these matches played at Faridabad, Bombay, Vishakhapatnam, Cuttack and Jaipur. Only Bombay and

Jaipur are on the tourists' list. In the Jaipur match, he took over as captain for the first time in place of the injured Walsh; he lost the toss and dropped a catch as the Indians reached 259 for five with Sachin Tendulkar making 105. He was out for 47 to a shooter and the West Indies lost by five runs. In the three-match Test series, ill fortune kept following the West Indians. At the Wankhede Stadium in Bombay, a ghastly, concrete mausoleum, they had India 11 for three at the end of the second day but the next morning, the fidgety Dickie Bird, umpiring for the first time in India after the introduction of neutral ICC umpires, ruled that the foot holes were dangerous and the start was delayed for forty-five minutes. Instead of bowling on a flier for a short time, the West Indians found themselves on a slow-turning pitch and India managed to win by 96 runs. Lara recorded a rare duck following his 14 in the first innings.

He batted patiently in the second Test at Nagpur, which was drawn, scoring a slow 50, and in the third, on a good batting pitch at Mohali, a suburb of the relatively new northern city of Chandragarh, they won to square the series 1-1. Lara managed to avoid stomach problems and Courtney Walsh asked him to open the batting in the second innings in place of Stuart Williams, one of the players in the sickbay of the team's luxury hotel. It was the first time he had opened in a Test and his partner Phil Simmons said, 'He batted beautifully. He was more relaxed and he was on 91 at about one a ball when he walked. I didn't hear the snick but he walked off. I don't think many players would do that.' Lara said, 'I tried to steer Venkatapathy Raju through the slips and got a faint edge to Mongia, the wicketkeeper. Realising I was out I left the crease before the umpire had made his mind up.' Raman Subba Row was the ICC referee and he said, 'That was typical of Brian. He's done it a few times in Tests and his average would be higher if he hadn't done it.'

There was an ironic moment on the final day – the turning point, when Manoj Prabhakar, the man Dermot Reeve chose over Lara as the Warwickshire overseas player in 1994, was struck in the face by a bouncer from Courtney Walsh and had to quit having scored no runs. The ball crashed through his visor and he needed five stitches to his nose. During that tour, the Wills World Series three-country tournament was sandwiched in the middle and more controversy followed Lara and Subba Row. In the match at Goa, Lara was given out, stumped by New Zealand wicketkeeper Adam Parore for 32, and he protested vehemently against the decision. The umpire, a newcomer named Mohali, told him to leave. Lara asked him to look at the replay because he was sure that his foot was over the line before the bails were removed. R. Mohan, the distinguished Indian cricket writer, said, 'Lara showed some truculence when Mohali refused.' The replay was indecisive and so Lara might have been reprieved. But Raman Subba Row suspended him for one match and fined him half his match fee. 'Apparently I was only the second player to be suspended by the ICC,' said Lara. Aqib Javed, the Pakistan fast bowler who was later banned for life for being involved in illegal betting, was the first. David Holford, the West Indies manager, said the tour was the worst he had known. Lara agreed.

Raman Subba Row is now retired from the ICC panel and years later he recalled:

> I found Brian rather difficult to handle. In some ways he was a nice, decent fellow but in others he could be awkward. I don't say he was devious, just not easy to handle. He came from a large family and it wasn't easy to make his way in the world without a lot of loving support from his parents and that affected him. Geoff Boycott was similar: he was difficult when he was younger. I had to take disciplinary action against Brian and it wasn't a big deal but he resented it. I had the impression he didn't like to be treated like that. On the other hand, he has a fine reputation for sportsmanship and is one of the few players who walk. He is an exception and that counts a lot.

When the team travelled to the airport for the trip home, thousands of excited Indians turned up to say goodbye. There was pandemonium and on the plane Lara asked Bryan Davis, who was travelling with the team as a journalist, 'Can anyone play this game after the age of thirty?' Davis said, 'I just made it. I retired from playing from Glamorgan when I was thirty and going on one tour of India was enough for me. I didn't play in a Test but they never let you go. They're always wanting to touch you or ask for your autograph.' Years later, Davis recalled, 'I think Brian was feeling the pressure. He was worried that he couldn't last the distance but he's still there at the top. That says a lot for him.'

Lara asked Davis to check the proofs for *Beating the Field*, his autobiography which was soon to be published. Davis said:

> I went through it and made a few changes. He told me, 'I'll let you have a copy when it comes out.' I'm still waiting for his copy. We have the same birthday, May 2, and he used to ring me on that date to congratulate me. After that the calls failed to materialise and I wasn't going to call him. I felt he had changed, for the worse. Then a few years later he rang again. He wanted to

ask for the telephone number of my daughter. He wanted to take her out. I think she spoke to him and said 'you are spoilt and selfish' and that brought the conversation to an end!'

After the unhappy tour to India, Lara managed to catch the right plane to take part in a charity match at Bowral, the birthplace of Sir Don Bradman, to raise money for the trust fund to maintain the Bradman Museum. He batted for a while with Graeme Pollock, one of his heroes, before he was caught behind off the bowling of Zoe Cross, the Australian women's cricketer. He was sad that Sir Don wasn't fit enough to attend in person. On the way back he stopped in the USA to play some golf. Late in January 1995, he flew to Auckland for a short tour of New Zealand as vice-captain under Walsh and the West Indies won the Test series 1-0 and all three one-day internationals. Lara was dismissed twice in the two Tests by the charismatic New Zealand pace bowler Danny Morrison's so-called 'soft pie' (his slower delivery). Morrison, now living in Australia, said:

> In the first Test at Christchurch I said to Ken Rutherford, the skipper, 'I'm going to bowl one to him,' and he said, 'Are you mad?' He seemed to indicate that I should just do my job and dish out a few bouncers and yorkers and leave the slow stuff to the spinners. As it turned out it wasn't a bad ball, a slow outswinger, in-ducker to Lara, and he chopped the ball on to the stumps. I said to Ken, 'There you go skipper, it's your shout for dinner!'
>
> Then I got him in the second Test as well but he had scored 147 by then. I always enjoyed taking on the challenge, bowling to such a gifted and unique player. He was at his peak in 1994-1996 and to get him out twice was fabulous fun. I didn't really get to know him as a man. I found him rather quiet and laconic.

Lara made only two at Christchurch but in the Wellington Test he played a truly memorable innings. He was lbw for 147 and New Zealand journalist Terry Power said, 'It came from 181 balls and he upheld his reputation with a glorious range of strokes all around the wicket before he was fooled by a slowey from Danny Morrison.'

thirteen

'I Quit'

With four independent countries and up to fourteen variously governed islands in the Leewards and Windwards supplying cricketers to the West Indies team, there has always turmoil and strife in West Indian cricket. Famous players like Andy Roberts, Rohan Kanhai and Clive Lloyd have spoken about 'the attitude of some of our players' but since the emergence of Brian Lara as the region's superstar, the problems have mounted. He has walked out of the squad several times, he threatened to quit in protest at being disciplined in the 1995 tour of England and said he wouldn't tour Australia the following winter. Four years later, with his career madly yo-yoing up and down, he played a major part in a players' strike at Heathrow in 1998 before a personal plea from Nelson Mandela persuaded the strikers to undertake a tour in South Africa which turned out to be one of the most shameful tours ever engaged by a West Indian side.

In an editorial in the *Trinidad Express* early in December 1996, when the West Indies Board was about to come to a decision over the Lara affair, a leading writer wrote, 'Is Lara a spoiled brat or a victim of incompetent officialdom? A genius on a self-destruct course or a proud individual making a stand against the mismanagement of the West Indies Board? Is he Brian Wrong, or Brian Wronged?' Unlike India, the richest of the cricketing nations where the money comes more from television than gate receipts, and the other two wealthy countries, Australia and England, the West Indies never had much money. Their governments financed the rebuilding of their grounds for the 2007 World Cup and most of the workers came from China and Taiwan. Famous former cricketers have governed their cricket, mostly part-time and unpaid, in tandem with business people who love cricket. Up until recently, there was a dire absence of professionalism with four changes in the presidency of the West Indies Board in six years and with people coming and going. There has always been mismanagement in West Indies cricket and the simmering revolt was kept in check for many years when their best players, like Sir Learie Constantine, Sir Clyde Walcott, Sir Frank Worrell, Sir Gary Sobers and others, earned the majority of their income in England. These men inspired the next generation but the seam of talent was wearing out and today's young players have been too long on the losing side. Like Lara, their guiding mentor, they wanted reform.

With power swinging towards the Caribbean between 1975 and 1995, firstly under Clive Lloyd, yet to be knighted, and then under Sir Viv Richards, the players wanted higher rewards and for a while their salaries matched those of other countries' stars. Lloyd departed, then Richards, and a new generation of players, perhaps less dedicated, wanted better rights and conditions. Lara was thrust to the forefront because he was dedicated, cherished cricket and wanted to see things changed. He has strong principles and took the part-time administrators on, refusing to compromise. He is a very proud man. The bosses found themselves in an impossible situation. They wanted tougher discipline in the ranks but they didn't want to upset the Prince. The *Trinidad Guardian* said:

> This is the best possible moment for a challenge from Lara. The West Indies now has a player with the stature to stand up to the authorities and we have a gut feeling that he could carry other disenchanted players with him. The Board has no choice but to select him for the World Cup: the population wouldn't allow them to leave him out. Lara is not bigger than the game, but he is bigger than the Board. There can only be one winner!

Eventually, Lara did win but the crisis in 1995 was due, in part, to overwork. After a chaotic summer in England the year before, the West Indies played in nine Tests and eighteen one-day internationals in India, New Zealand and the Caribbean, and arrived in England only five days after they were beaten by Steve Waugh's side in Kingston. It was a chastening time for West Indian cricket. After fifteen years and twenty-nine series, their colours were lowered, losing 2-1. The abrasive Steve Waugh virtually won the series himself, although Mark Taylor, who lost all four tosses, was skipper. Showing immense courage, Waugh scored 429 runs with an average of 107.25, a third of the total, and he outdid Lara, who topped the home averages with 308 runs at a modest 44.00. Importantly, he out-psyched Lara from the outset, ruffling him with provocative comments.

On the first day of the first Test in Bridgetown, Lara was given out, caught by him at gully for 65 when the television showed that the ball had hit the ground. It was a ferocious hit and Waugh juggled with it four times before the ball fell under his body. Waugh said later:

> I could never have imagined what a profound effect the outcome of one delivery would have on my career. When my right arm hit the ground, the ball bounced off my wrist at the same time as I grabbed hold of it, clumsily but safely. Lara rightly waited for confirmation from me and the surrounding fieldsmen that the catch had been completed before leaving.

Lara's view was different. He lingered before departing. On television, Michael Holding slated Waugh and Viv Richards called him a cheat in his newspaper column. The West Indies went on to collapse and lost by ten wickets.

Lara was on his way to a century in the second Test at St John's, Antigua, when David Boon stuck out a hand to hold a sizzling catch off the bowling of Steve Waugh. He'd reached 88 from 101 balls and the game petered out in a draw. On the eve of the third Test in Port of Spain, Waugh was woken by a caller who said, 'Don't go out at night, man. If I see you on the street, you're dead man!' Waugh took the advice and he and his players lost a little of their bravado in the rest of the match, losing by nine wickets. In the deciding game at Kingston, Waugh found himself booed and hissed instead of listening to applause when he scored 200 to win the match. There was a lot of nastiness on the field, and plenty more off it. If that disputed catch had been ruled out, Lara might well have been appointed captain of the tour to England instead of Richie Richardson, who scored 229 runs at 32.71.

After the inconsistent performances of the West Indies in England, Tony Cozier wrote in *Wisden*, 'Richardson was always a captain under pressure. A calm, undemonstrative individual, he often let the game take its course and seemed out of touch with his players.' The underlying feeling was that the Board had appointed the wrong leader. The tour began with farce. The tourists arrived for the opening match against Lavinia, Duchess of Norfolk's XI at Arundel without their scorebook and flag. For some reason, Lara was allowed to return to Port of Spain 'for business reasons'. Rejoining the team at Northampton, where he had such bad memories from the previous year, he was bowled second ball for a duck. Later, he recorded a first pair at Canterbury and the bowler who got him out for nought on each occasion wasn't even a county regular – South African born Dr Julian Thompson, a P.G. Wodehouse fan who was working as a house surgeon at the Royal Berkshire Hospital in Reading.

But he enjoyed himself in the first Test at Leeds – his first innings 53 and 48* off 40 balls in the second brought a nine-wicket win for his side. After scoring 91 off 90 balls at Durham, a defeat at Lord's in the second Test was followed by the first signs of serious misconduct among the players. The manager, Revd Wes Hall, a former Bajan government minister, sent Winston Keithroy Matthew Benjamin home on 'disciplinary and fitness grounds'. The moody Benjamin, born in St John's, close to where Lara made his 375, played six seasons with Leicestershire and in 1993 he was replaced by Phil Simmons. Two years earlier he was injured in a shooting incident at the Leewards team hotel in Barbados.

A hat-trick by Dominic Cork at Old Trafford enabled England to square the rubber at 2-2 – England's batting collapsed to 89 in the previous Test at Birmingham where they lost by an innings and 64 runs – and most of the resistance came from Lara, who suddenly returned to form. But for his 87 and 145 the West Indians would have been annihilated. Team spirit was evaporating with the players bickering and blaming each other. At an excitable team meeting, Lara complained about the attitudes of some of his colleagues, including Curtly Ambrose and Kenny Charlie Griffith Benjamin (yes, his father named him after the Barbadian fast bowler and he hated it). The Benjamins went to the same school but they were not related. It was significant that Richardson, from Five Island Village, Ambrose and the Benjamins all came from Antigua.

As voices were raised, Lara said to skipper Richardson, 'You are always with the team, on and off the field, and you are doing nothing to change the behaviour of the team.' Richardson countered, 'I've known you a long time and you have your own agenda and own ambitions.' In his report to the West Indies Board, Richardson wrote:

> Brian personally accused me for the indiscipline that had developed in the team. He went on to say he knew other players felt the same way. I responded by saying that if the players felt that way and were not happy with my captaincy, I would resign, but I would not be pushed by anyone who got an ambitious agenda. He got up in anger and said a number of things including, his life being destroyed, money did not mean anything to him and that he was resigning. He then walked out of the meeting.

Richardson also wrote critically of Lara's treatment of Wes Hall when the manager gave him permission to return home early on the tour, saying, 'On the day he was leaving, in the presence of myself, Andy Roberts and Courtney Walsh, his behaviour and conduct to the manager were abominable. Wes Hall is one of the most respected Caribbean personalities and the way Brian spoke to him left me in shock.'

At the stormy team meeting following the Old Trafford defeat, Lara was in a foul mood. He rose to his feet and said, 'If you think I have hidden motives for what I said, then I am going to retire from cricket.' He then proceeded to leave the room. Wes Hall rang his bedroom and persuaded him to reconsider his decision and come back with an answer in the morning. In his report to the Board, subsequently leaked to a Trinidad newspaper, Hall wrote:

> The commercial demands on Lara are like an albatross on his neck. He kept saying it was ruining his life and he staggered me when he said that he had received an offer of £3m from a bat manufacturer company and one condition was that he had to continue playing Test cricket and he was prepared to refuse it because of his decision to retire. I advised him to sleep on it and the next morning he hadn't changed his mind. I hugged him and wished him goodbye.

Lara packed and then drove to the home of Dwight Yorke. If he had kept to his word, and later refused to join the West Indians in Australia for the World Series, his career could have been over. He wouldn't have been captain of his country and he wouldn't be the current holder of the individual Test record. But one of the nicest, and most rational, administrators from the West Indies, the extravagantly moustachioed Captain Peter Short, OBE, SCM, JP, who lives in Barbados, intervened and saved him. The long-time secretary of the Board, and current president, had just arrived in England nursing his wife Anne. He is of English stock and served in the Royal Artillery in the Malaysian Emergency after the Second World War. He visits London most years. He knows almost everyone in world cricket and he was in London for another reason: to have a heart bypass operation. He was fit enough to ring Lara and ask him to return for the sake of West Indian cricket and himself. After a short conversation, Lara agreed to meet him in Taunton where the team was staying for a match against Somerset. Wes Hall, Richardson and members of the tour committee came along as well. Short said:

> You know what it means if you quit Brian, you'll be bringing West Indian cricket into disrepute. You are under contract and if you continue like this the Board will throw the book at you. Your reputation is based on cricket and it would be the greatest mistake of your life. If you do this everything would go down the drain. You can't take a break when you feel like it.

The official Board report stated: 'Lara's demeanour changed alarmingly and he said, "What are you going to do with me? Please be lenient with me. Cricket has ruined my life."' Short recalled later:

> Brian was rather emotional. He felt some of the players who supported him failed to speak up for him and also I think his agent was giving certain advice which we felt was wrong. Suddenly he caved in and apologised. I said to him the manager and the Tour Committee would deal with this matter and the Board would almost certainly sanction their decision. One good thing was that nothing came out in the Press. No one knew he had walked out.
>
> Afterwards, there was a bit of buck passing and the tour committee didn't come to a decision. In his end of tour report to the Board, Wes Hall mentioned Lara's walk-out and someone leaked it to the newspapers. The Board met and decided to charge the players, Brian as well as the three other players [Ambrose, Kenneth Benjamin and Carl Hooper, who also left the tour party] and that upset him. I was very sad about what happened. I have always been a good supporter of Brian. He's good for the game and for West Indies.

Dwight Yorke proved to be another saviour, telling Lara not to quit. Yorke is a friendly man with a ready smile and has the same relaxed attitude to life as Lara. He was run over by a car when he was two and a half years old and his mother Grace was told that he had died in hospital. Three months later he was discharged with no after-effects and his mother said, 'God spared him for great things.'

One of the troublemakers on the tour of England was Winston Benjamin who had received a six-month suspension for abusing a parking attendant. Curtly Ambrose didn't actually do anything wrong, but his boisterous approach, especially on the team coach, attracted criticism. He played a leading role in the inquest after the Old Trafford Test. He said to Lara, 'It seems to me that you didn't bat long again. Where is the hunger, will and determination?' On another occasion, Ambrose was himself reprimanded for his behaviour at an official West Indies Board dinner when he rudely snatched his medal which was being presented to him by Sir Clyde Walcott. He apologised and the Board 'censured him in the strongest possible manner', advising him that 'any repeat would be severely dealt with'.

In his report, Hall spoke about the indiscipline of some players who brought drinks onto the team coach and caused too much noise. Ambrose, in particular, was singled out for refusing to sign autographs for Cornhill, the Test sponsors. There were also instances of lateness and swearing and complaints about the lack of hot meals. Lara was angry that he was censured for abusing Keith Arthurton when Ambrose, who did the same thing, wasn't censured. It all seemed rather petty and a strong captain would have sorted it out himself. Five days later, Lara reappeared at Bristol and scored 30 and 0 in a victory against Gloucestershire. At the final Test at the Oval he entertained a full house with a peerless 152 off 182 balls with 28 fours and the series and the match were drawn.

Late in November, a disciplinary committee of the West Indies Board found Hooper, Ambrose, Kenny Benjamin and Lara guilty of misconduct. Lara's offence was leaving the team without permission. The others were penalised for general behaviour. They were all fined ten per cent of their tour fees – around £2,000. Lara was livid. Joey Carew, who has been a surrogate father to him, said, 'Tears came in his eyes when he saw the headline in the paper "Four rebels fined". He couldn't come to terms with the fact that he was being branded with men he had been complaining about.' There was a differing view from Alloy Lequay, the veteran Trinidad Board president:

> I think the man in the street is behind Brian but there are those who now believe he is too big for his cap, that he is beyond discipline. Brian might have overreacted in England but the Board has to think about its own concepts of management. West Indies cricket cannot do without Lara. There is something of a parallel in our history. In the late forties, Frank Worrell asked to be paid to go to India. The Board refused and Worrell decided not to go. Worrell was neither a rebel nor a spoilt brat. Genius is rare and must be treated differently. And I think Brian Lara will become a folk hero just as Sir Frank did.

Lara's first reaction was to resign from the West Indian party soon to be bound for Australia for a World Series warm-up competition prior to the World Cup in 1996. He wrote to the Board saying, 'This has damaged my character and self-confidence. It is with this in mind, I now write to request that you release me from my obligation to travel with the team to Australia.' Andrew Sealey, secretary of the West Indies Board, said, 'A lot has happened to him in a short time and I don't think it's helped him to maintain his stability.' Warwickshire's Paul Smith, whose career ended prematurely through a serious knee injury, said, 'Everyone needs a break and the only thing I can compare his life to is the life of an an international pop star. He and Ian Botham are the only cricketers who have been through that.' And his then agent Jonathan Barnett said, 'He hasn't had a proper rest since he started

breaking records, more than eighteen months ago. He took a stand on prin-
ciple. There are no deep dark currents here. He just wants them to see his
point of view.'

Joey Carew failed to persuade Lara to change his mind and he said, 'Brian
is very emotionally and physically tired. A lot of people would say he is a
spoilt brat but that is not the case.' Wes Hall, one of the most decent and
respected men in Barbados, was blamed by Barnett for the rift and Barnett
described Hall as 'rude and arrogant'. Hall responded:

> I will not dignify that remark with comment except to say I am a Christian
> gentleman and the last time I was rude was when I was two. Brian has decided
> not to go to Australia and there is no joy in our camp at the moment, only
> sadness. We have to give Brian as much help as we can. We are engaged in a
> build up before the World Cup and are going without the world's best player.
> It's a tragedy.

Short summed it up, saying, 'We lurch from crisis to crisis.'

Without telling Hall, the Board called up Roland Holder from Barbados
as Lara's replacement. Hall and Andy Roberts, the coach, both resigned
and Richardson made his decision to quit after the World Cup, held in Sri
Lanka, India and Pakistan in 1996. The Board set up a disciplinary committee to decide Lara's fate and they took the only decision they could possibly
make after the way he dropped out of the squad while under contract, to
reprimand him and warn him about his future conduct. Steve Camacho, the
long-time secretary of the West Indies Board, now a consultant, said:

> Julian Hunte, the St Lucia representative to the United Nations in the pre-
> vious Government, was the chairman, along with Teddy Griffith and Peter
> Short. We met Brian at the Hilton in Barbados and he turned up dressed
> in a beautiful suit. Then he started to cry. Butter was melting in his mouth.
> Everyone felt sorry for him and he got off with it.

Lara decided to change his mind and was duly chosen for the World Cup
squad but the ramifications lingered on and the West Indies endured its
greatest cricketing humiliation when the semi-amateurs of Kenya beat them
by 73 runs in Pune. Kenya's modest 166 proved far too much and only Shiv
Chanderpaul and Roger Harper reached double figures. Lara was caught by
the portly, fumble-gloved wicketkeeper Tariq Iqbal for eight. Four days later,
in Jaipur, Richardson's side rose from the funeral pyre and beat Australia by

four wickets with the skipper scoring an unbeaten 93 and Lara whistling up 60 off 70 deliveries. *Wisden* reported, 'Richardson didn't seem to notice as he accepted the emotional embraces of his team-mates.'

Lara, now restored to hero status again, was chiefly instrumental for the quarter-final defeat of favourites South Africa, scoring 111 in 94 balls, his customary ODI scoring rate. Earlier, he had put away his repertoire of sweep shots. But this time he played too early as he tried to play the ball backward of square and was caught. More trouble emerged: he allegedly made comments about some of the all-white South African cricketers and a newspaper called his views racist. He vehemently denied this before eventually apologising.

In the semi-final at Mohali, the West Indies virtually only had to stay on their feet to go through to the final, despite Lara being bowled by Steve Waugh for 45. But, as *Wisden* aptly wrote, 'West Indies pulled off an extraordinary defeat, losing eight wickets in the final fifty minutes.' Two short visits by New Zealand and Sri Lanka under new leadership followed but it was too soon for Lara to be forgiven. The selectors awarded the captaincy to Courtney Walsh and Clive Lloyd took over as manager, both safety-net appointments. Lara, appointed vice-captain, played a typical hometown innings of 146 off 134 in the third ODI in Port of Spain and in the fifth, at the Arnos Vale ground at St Vincent, he scored 104 in 103 balls.

Lloyd soon won the confidence of the players at the first meeting and he said later of his new vice-captain:

> I am stirred by his relentless quest for excellence and his desire for a leadership role. As he matures, he will lead West Indies into the 21st century. He has redefined the art of batting and I am proud of his West Indian pedigree and panache.

It was Lloyd's way of raising Lara's morale after a thoroughly depressing year. The Prince had the winter off at home and he had to digest two more letters from Camacho about his conduct. The first one was about 'incidents' during the World Cup. He was overheard making remarks of a racist nature after the West Indies' defeat at the hands of Kenya which were picked up on a tape recorder.

He said, 'It wasn't too bad losing to you guys. You are black. Know what I mean? Now a team like South Africa is a different matter altogether. You know this white thing comes into the picture. We can't stand losing to them.' He explained to Wes Hall, 'What I said was that the defeat of Kenya was not as humiliating as when we lost to South Africa in the last World Cup. At the time, South Africa had just come out of apartheid.'

On 16 May 1996, the West Indies Board reported:

> Brian Lara has been repimanded for making unsatisfactory reports, firstly after the Kenya game and secondly, for remarks made by him to Dennis Waight on a journey from Bombay in London, on March 16, 1996. Waight withdrew his complaint immediately before the Board meeting after an unqualified apology from Lara. In doing so, it took into account Lara's written and verbal apologies during the tour as well as his later letter to the Board apologising to them, the team and all West Indians for his role in these incidents and giving an assurance that that there would not be a repetition. The Board stipulated that any future breach of conduct will attract the strongest condemnation.

Another letter soon followed, informing him he was being fined ten per cent of his match fee for turning up late prior to the first Test against Sri Lanka in June. The Board was getting tough. Lara rejected Warwickshire's offer of a three-year contract, pleading overwork, and Shaun Pollock was named as the club's new overseas star the following summer. After his winter break, he was now ready for another tilt at the Australians on their home ground.

Lara's walk-out in the 1995 tour of England was nearly replicated four years later. The first Cornhill Test, the 1,500th Test to be played, was over in three days at Edgbaston with the West Indies winning by an innings and 93 runs, a triumph for the line-and-length quick bowling of veterans Courtney Walsh and Curtly Ambrose operating in very amenable bowling conditions. That night, Ricky Skerrett, the West Indies' manager, revealed to the author that Lara was threatening to retire from cricket. He had seen reports implicating him in betting coups in India and was extremely upset. He said:

> I've been trying to talk him round in his room but he hasn't changed his mind. But I intend to talk to him again and make him see sense. He feels persecuted and thinks there is a plot against him to bring him down. He was twenty-three when this was supposed to have happened and only just coming into Test cricket. He said he had remembered speaking to a particular guy but there was nothing about him breaking the rules. He denies that strenuously and I accept his word. Brian doesn't need all this. He has worked very hard to get back with the team.

The betting allegations had appeared in a South African newspaper five days previously. A businessman from Cape Town claimed he handed over £4,500 to Lara as winnings following matches in the Total Triangular series in 1993. Pat Rousseau, the West Indies' president, said he was arranging an investigation and Lara responded: 'I never placed any bets nor did I give any information to a bookmaker. I can categorically deny all the allegations against me. They are absolute and total rubbish. My teammates and management are disgusted by this attempt to discredit me.'

By the following morning, following talks with Skerrett that had gone on until 3 a.m., Lara had agreed to carry on. Lara was quoted saying, 'My conscience is clear and I intend to make an important contribution to the tour and the future plans of West Indies cricket.' The international betting saga dragged on for some years with detectives interviewing Bombay bookies and various players and the all clear was only sounded at the end of 2002 when Barbadian attorney Elliott Mottley said that no evidence could be found to support allegations against Lara by the Bureau of Criminal Investigations in 2000. There were allegations that Lara received money for underperforming in two one-day internationals in India in 1994 but no proof was forthcoming. Lara was innocent and everyone suspected that he was framed, but it was a worrying time for him.

One of the people who helped Lara's mental state at this time was Dr Rudi Webster, the Barbadian fast bowler who played for Scotland and Warwickshire in the 1960s. He said:

> Brian was very, very close to quitting the game. He felt like a soldier who simply couldn't stomach the battle anymore. In battle conditions, concentration goes and soldiers get tired and stressed. They cannot sleep properly and start doing irrational things. Eventually they crack. They have to be taken out of the front line and allowed rest to recharge. That was happening to Brian. His mother was ill as well and that didn't help.
>
> He had an illness and he felt 95% of the people were at his throat. He didn't think he had a future any more. He needed assistance but I am afraid in the West Indies there is a lack of proper counselling which can turn things round. He was confused and felt alone. Sir Gary and Sir Viv weren't under the same pressure Brian experienced. Expectations were so high and he was constantly dissected by the public and the Press. He was severely criticised after the defeats in New Zealand and South Africa and the paparazzi were following him all the time and he had no privacy. Fortunately he came through and I think he will play on and break more records to leave a greater legacy.

These rare superstars have to be aided and now he has more support, mainly from within the team, Brian knows he has friends he can turn to. Tiger Woods is one of the few sporting geniuses who has been handled properly and he was lucky. Brian has suffered but he's come through.

fourteen

Captain at Last, But Not a Good Year

Brian Lara finally became captain of the West Indies on 27 March 1997 at Bridgetown in the third Test against India almost seven years after he was first capped. But it was only a stop-gap appointment. Courtney Walsh, the injured skipper, was fit to resume in the fourth Test and he was back in the ranks again. His temporary appointment was halfway through a twelve-month period which was the worst of his life. It started Down Under with rows with the Australian players – when his manager Clive Lloyd had to reprimand him and write to the Australian Board of Control to apologise – and ended in an humiliating 3-0 defeat in Pakistan which Tony Cozier called 'an unqualfied disaster'.

There were constant reports that he had fallen out with Walsh and team spirit had disintegrated. After reaching the top of cricket's roller coaster and staying there for two decades, West Indies had crashed down to the lowest point. The last of their great fast bowlers, Ambrose and Walsh, were wearing out at a rapid pace and there were no replacements coming along behind them. The supply of great batsmen had also dried up… with one exception. Brian Lara was carrying the load on his small frame and it was too much.

The Sir Frank Worrell Trophy was snatched back by the Australians and the margin of 3-2 exaggerated what actually happened on the pitch. Lara failed to record a century until his penultimate innings of the tour. Sydney, his favourite ground in Australia, was the scene of his nemesis. The home side had some plenty of sharp sledgers – Steve Waugh, Ian Healy, Shane Warne and Glenn McGrath in particular – and the obvious targets were Lara and his younger players. They didn't risk upsetting the skipper Walsh and his moody compatriot Ambrose.

When Lara came in, wicketkeeper Healy was the first to come up with a few chippy comments and soon appealed for a catch. Lara thought the ball had bounced first but he was given out. Waugh said later:

Tempers and emotion boiled over on a regular basis and that was the first flashpoint. The video replays showed the ball bubbling out of Healy's gloves for a second but no one else gave the out decision much thought at the time. Still in his whites, Lara made a beeline through the members' bar before belting on our door. A disbelieving Geoff Marsh [the team coach] took his succinct message: 'Tell Healy he is not welcome in our dressing room.'

In Australian cricket, not allowing the opposition in for a drink at the close of play is contrary to their code of fair play. A rather strange habit, one would think, but perhaps it still happens in the bar of the House of Commons. Lloyd had wanted good relations from the outset and had met Marsh early in the tour where they agreed on a kind of friendly pact, so it was tantamount of a declaration of war by his star player when Lara demanded the exclusion of the popular Healy. Waugh said:

> Once Lara overstepped the boundaries by putting his personal grievances ahead of the teams' goodwill, the mood changed dramatically.
>
> The animosity was at its sharpest during the fifth Test in Perth when Lara went into bat belatedly to support one of his young batsmen, Robert Samuels, who was in his first year as a Test player and was experiencing the customary testing-out period at the top level. I didn't believe we were over the top with our chatter but Lara was keen to make a lasting impression within his ranks and went directly to the Press, accusing us of unfair tactics. At the same time, he tried to absolve himself of any blame, even though at the end of the Windies' first innings he had returned as a runner for the injured Walsh and immediately tried to cause trouble. He was doing a Ranatunga – giving as good as he got on the field, but divulging only half of the information to the media afterwards.

Umpires David Shepherd and Darrell Hair intervened and lectured both captains, Walsh and Mark Taylor, neither of whom was responsible for any of the misbehaviour. In his press conference afterwards, Taylor had to stick up for his team, calling Lara 'a provocateur in the style of Sri Lanka's captain Arjuna Ranatunga'. When Lara is really upset on the field he usually comes up with a big innings and that happened in this match. Greg Baum, the Australian journalist, wrote of his 132: 'He came in at 43-2 and for him, the cracks on the pitch closed up and the bounce evened out, or so it seemed. His innings grew like a symphony, two hours for his first fifty, just over an hour for the second and then a crescendo as he hit Warne for 26 in 14 balls.'

Lara also earned praise for his captaincy while the injured Walsh was off. Lloyd said, 'He used his fast bowlers in one-over spells in the 43°C heat and when Walsh came out on the final day and saw what was happening, he bowled twenty overs on the trot to take five wickets to win the game.' Lloyd defended Lara's actions which had angered most of the Australians:

> People think he is soft but he isn't. He is not an angel but he is a strong personality who has strong principles and if something is wrong he will stand up for his players and that is what he did. Robert Samuels was a young player and he wanted to protect him.
>
> I had to speak to Brian and tell him it wasn't his responsibility to take up these matters with the Australians. It was mine. I am responsible for discipline and he accepted that. I wrote to the Australian Board and they accepted my apology and there wasn't any more animosity.

Temporarily, Lara lost his number one rating in the West Indies batting and finished fourth in the Test averages with 32.88, behind Carl Hooper, 45.25, Shiv Chanderpaul, 38.22, and Samuels, 33.00, and later in the series Walsh demoted him to four, with Chanderpaul moving up to first wicket in his place.

A month later, the Indians visited the West Indies and it was a similar story. Lara came second to Chanderpaul in the averages with figures of 48.87 from 391 runs to Chanderpauls's 73.83 from 443 runs. The battle between Lara and Tendulkar ended with no advantage to either side. Tendulkar failed to score a Test century and was second in the Indian averages with 72.00 from 289 runs. The two men have always had a good relationship and they have similar views about the way the game is played. When Shane Warne announced he was retiring from Test cricket, they were among the first to send him messages of congratulation. And significantly, Warne repeated an earlier comment: 'These two guys played me better than anyone I ever faced.'

Lara's disenchantment continued in 1997 when he turned up late for the first Test against Sri Lanka at St John's, Antigua, and was fined half of his match fee by his team manager. Bruce Yardley, the Australian coach of the Sri Lankan side, described the pitch as 'crap', somewhat different to the 1994 one. Lara made little contribution, being given out for a duck, when he felt he wasn't out, to a catch by Kaluwitharana and in the second innings he virtually threw his wicket away to Muralitharan's second delivery. The second and last Test was played at the picturesque ground of Arnos Vale in St Vincent, the seventy-eighth and latest Test ground, and he was out for one. After acquiring just five runs from three innings, there were questions about his commitment, even in his native Trinidad. 'Is his halo slipping?' asked a correspondent. Craig Cozier, son of Tony, wrote in *Wisden*, 'When he put his mind to it, at the last time of asking, he scored a crucial hundred, 115, and when he reached 111 he raised his bat to acknowledge the applause for reaching 4,000 Test runs.'

Lara's performance in Pakistan in a three-match series in November was woeful: he mustered only 129 runs from six innings, averaging 21. The selectors wanted him to be captain but the Board overruled them and gave the job to Walsh. There was continual speculation in Pakistan and the Caribbean about the supposed row between him and Walsh, who had come to leadership at the age of thirty-four. The West Indies Board fuelled it by refusing to appoint Lara as vice-captain after he held the position on previous tours. Lloyd called the unabated gossip 'a calculated ploy to unsettle my team'. The West Indies lost the Test series 3-0, lost the ODIs 3-0 and failed to win a first-class match; their only victory was in a non-first-class fixture. No previous West Indian side had ever taken part in such an unsuccessful tour. Lloyd said:

> Yes, it was bad, we really had a drubbing but the Pakistan side was a very good one and the series was played on excellent pitches. Our ageing bowlers were close to the end of their careers and the younger ones didn't look as though they were good enough to take over their roles. It was an inexperienced squad and perhaps other players could have been selected. I didn't play any part in the selection.

The great Bajan fast bowler Malcolm Marshall, who was working under Lloyd as coach, said, 'I didn't think Brian's lack of runs in Pakistan was anything technical, he just needed to occupy the crease longer. It was a difficult time for him, he knows so much is expected and he was very disappointed.' Like Lloyd, Malcolm denied that there was friction between Lara and Walsh:

> It was a close relationship. The stories weren't true but it was difficult for Brian when he got home. In the Caribbean you have the rivalry between the islands and players get abuse from different crowds and he might find it a problem in Jamaica. We were disappointed with the stuff coming out of the Caribbean tarnishing Brian as a person. When you become a great player they say these things, like he wants Courtney's job. Of course he wanted to captain his nation.

fifteen

A Winning Captain at Last

Down but not out, Brian Lara soon found himself riding back up to the top of the roller coaster and four months later, after the Pakistan disaster, he led the West Indies to a 3-1 Test win over Mike Atherton's England side in the Caribbean. Nearly all of his detractors, who were many, were won over. He was a hero again. At twenty-eight, it was his time to take the mantle and if he failed, his hopes of captaincy would disappear.

He realised this, accepted some sensible advice and proceeded to undergo a personality change. He was more open and friendly, smiled more and was more eager to help his teammates, particularly the younger ones. Tony Cozier wrote in *The Independent* after the transformation:

No West Indies captain has been more diligently groomed for the post, more actively promoted for it or more openly coveted. No one came to it by a longer or more contentious route. The simple answer is that he won. As Mike Atherton, his beleaguered counterpart, and Richie Richardson and Courtney Walsh, Lara's predecessors, have painfully discovered, it is one criterion by which all captains are ultimately judged, winning. In Lara's case, his instant success, by a 3-1 advantage, was more critical.

Clive Lloyd, the former revered captain, spoke of a lack of pride and commitment in the team. There were snide suggestions that Walsh and Lara were at loggerheads and that Lara did not pull his weight. Lara's disciplinary record was such that there were serious doubts that he was temperamentally capable of handling the responsibility. His publicised tantrums had put him under the microscope and he knew it. In the past two and a half months he has not put a foot wrong off the field and not much on the field either. A smile has seldom been far from his handsome face and he has been co-operative with the media and clearly at ease with his players.

Both Lara and Atherton were under severe pressure at the start of that series. Atherton had lost his enthusiasm for leadership and in his book *Opening Up*, one of the best self-written cricket books, he said, 'I was becoming Captain Grumpy in private. I couldn't switch off and the people closest to me started to worry. I needed sleeping tablets and it was time to get my life back.' As the Australians were on their way to winning the fifth Test at Trent Bridge to retain the Ashes, he was seen playing with a yo-yo on the dressing-room balcony while Graham Thorpe, who scored 82, failed to shield the tail-enders. Atherton should have sent a message out to Thorpe. At that time, hardly any of the leading journalists got on well with Atherton because he had a policy of saying little and refusing to cooperate.

The most successful captains have also been outstanding PR agents, for example Richie Benaud, Sir Frank Worrell, Mike Brearley and Ray Illingworth. The worst English captains in terms of PR – which is a vital part of the job – have been Douglas Jardine, Peter May (who was too sensitive, although a good captain) and Atherton. Lara might have followed that route if he had not undergone his metamorphosis.

Lord MacLaurin, the chairman of the ECB, tried to talk Atherton into staying on after the defeat at The Oval. After hiding away fishing in Cumbria, Atherton reluctantly decided to keep the job. 'I should have been strong, it was a bad decision,' he said later. He was never motivated by money – he never asked for a rise in the whole of his reign. In the other camp, Lara had to repair any damage to his somewhat strained relationship with Courtney Walsh, who was smouldering after being stripped of the captaincy. Atherton's will to fight on was almost broken because of the criticism. Now Lara was subjected to similar criticism and, though apprehensive about what might happen, he did have the will to face up to it. Then Richie Richardson put his oar in:

> There doesn't seem to be too much support for Lara as captain. Even in his home island they have doubts about it. West Indies cricket is in a bad way and people are questioning whether the captaincy should be given to someone so controversial, someone the Board is not completely happy with. My opinion is that Courtney should have kept the job. He bowled his heart out in Pakistan and always gives his best. The feeling here was that not everyone was doing that.

Walsh was threatening to quit but in the end he decided to play on after he and Ambrose attended a peace meeting with Lara. 'Brian has my full support and I hope he does all the things people want him to,' said Walsh. Pat Rousseau, the Board president, told Lara, 'the future of West Indies depends on you.' A contrite Lara said, 'I know I will have to start setting a better example. You learn from your mistakes and make sure you handle things differently next time.' Radio stations and newspapers were stoking up anger over the Walsh issue, but when Lara led the team out for the first Test at Sabina Park Walsh was alongside him. A less enthusiastic than usual starting crowd of 4,000 were there to cheer them on. The Jamaican Board, concerned about the lack of pace at Sabina Park, had decided to relay the whole of the square using clay from the Appleton sugar estate. When Atherton and Hussain, who had made his Test debut at Sabina Park, inspected the pitch three days before the start, they were aghast. 'It looked like a corrugated iron roof,' said Hussain. Atherton, a betting man, said, 'It has more undulations than Epsom Downs on Derby Day.'

Realising the pitch would rapidly deteriorate, Atherton opted to bat. John Crawley, next man to come in at 17 for three, had smoked his way through a packet of cigarettes in the dressing-room and shouted, 'Jesus, someone's going to get killed out there.' Phil Tufnell was starting a panic attack although he was number eleven. The match lasted fifty-six minutes, there were six interruptions for England physiotherapist Wayne Morton to come on and treat the wounded and Matthew Engel described Alec Stewart's innings as 'the bravest 9 ever scored'. Atherton had asked Lara what he thought about the pitch and, according to him, Lara said, 'It is not fit.'

The next day, the *Gleaner* quoted him as saying:

We would have definitely have carried on. If the West Indies batted first we would have seen it as the sort of situation where you have to fight it out as cricketers. It was dangerous I agree but a lot of our guys said it would be tough to call off the match because we have experienced pitches such as this before in the West Indies. I was going to bowl if we won the toss.

Atherton was very surprised to read Lara's comments and at a cocktail party that night he asked him why he had changed his mind. Atherton later reported: 'He said he had to be careful in Jamaica because he had just replaced a local legend in Courtney Walsh and wanted to say something to boost his popularity on the island.' Colin Croft, the former West Indies Test player and commentator, the man who asks the pertinent questions in press interviews in the Caribbean, said: 'The abandonment has shamed West Indies cricket. The pitch should be now dug up and those directly responsible for this travesty of a pitch should be buried in the same hole.' In their inquiry later, the Jamaican Board put the blame on a defective roller. There were 500 British supporters at the ground and to placate them, the Jamaican Prime Minister arranged a party for them. Quickly, a substitute Test was staged in Port of Spain, back to back with the second Test, and Lara finished up winning his first Test as captain. He was helped by an injudicious remark by the talkative Andrew Caddick who said in a local newspaper that he had the measure of him. Foolish man! In favourable conditions, Caddick bowled thirty overs, failed to take a wicket and never troubled the Prince.

Clive Lloyd thinks Lara is a good, imaginative captain but at that stage he was still learning the art. In the second innings, he decided to open the bowling with Kenny Benjamin and Nixon McLean instead of Walsh and Ambrose. Three days later, Lara was throwing up the coin again and this time he was on the losing side. Gus Fraser exploited the Glenn McGrath strategy – bowling an off stump line just short of a length – and using a high seam ball brought by England, he captured twenty wickets in those two Tests. It was a throbbing, noisy time and on his home territory, Lara looked relaxed and in command whereas Atherton was increasingly fraught.

All successful generals have luck in their knapsacks and Lara was no exception in this campaign. He was able to win the toss at Georgetown when Guyana was in the middle of the worst drought in living memory and England went down to defeat by 242 runs as the pitch turned to dust. Luck went with him again in the next Test at Kensington Oval when he decided to put England in on an excellent pitch, which was seen by the locals as a bad mistake. The twinkling feet of Mark Ramprakash helped him to his first Test century, 154, and with a total of 403 and the West Indies only managing 231, Atherton set a target of 375 in four sessions, encouraging the view that England might win. There had been a drought lasting five months but on the last day a thunderstorm erupted turning the ground into a shallow lake. If someone had located the Barbados Cricket Association's motorised whale, a machine to help the drying up process, England could still have had time to win but it was discovered too late. The draw enabled the West Indies to retain the Wisden Trophy and Lara and his players paraded it around the St John's Recreation Ground in the final Test.

While that was going on, Atherton was choking out a short statement to the Press, announcing his resignation after five years in charge. In Barbados he gave the V sign to Philo Wallace as the Barbadian batsman departed for the pavilion but despite pictures of the incident being published in the

Sunday newspapers, ICC referee Barry Jarman took no action. Everything caved in for Atherton and the final ignominy was when he stayed on for the one-day series, without being picked, and had to call for a taxi at the team hotel when he saw his car being driven off by the ODI skipper Adam Holioake. Lara won that series by 4-1 and he scored the most runs in the Tests – 417, average 52.12. And he held an incredibly high number of catches too – 13.

sixteen

No Way Back at Edgbaston

In the spring of 1998, Derek Pringle made a very astute observation: 'Even Brian Lara is only as good as his last innings – even if it was 500.' Less than a week after the final ODI in Port of Spain, when he was raising his bat in triumph after a scintillating 93, the Atlantic BWIA commuter was scheduled to fly to London to take over the post as captain of Warwickshire. Four years previously, his career had been at its zenith and Birmingham's cricket lovers were prepared to excuse any excess, any lateness. But things had changed: they were now less tolerant of his aberrations. They wanted the same magic without the embarrassments.

He was around the age that George Best had been when he quit top-class football. Best couldn't stand the pressure; he squandered his immense talent and had to live by selling stories about his undisciplined life to the tabloid newspapers. They wanted to know whether Lara would go the same way. That gentle, devout Catholic Sir Matt Busby failed to convince Best that he had to be more restrained. Countless admirers offered the same kind of advice to Lara and though there were welcome signs that he was beginning to mature as a leader, his off-field behaviour was being put on trust by Warwickshire's committee. Some had reservations about signing him on a basic salary of around £100,000, which could have been doubled had he repeated his 1994 glories. They wanted the reliable and popular Tim Munton.

Amiss had to send out a letter to the members explaining the controversial decision. 'It couldn't be certain about Tim's fitness after his back injury,' he said. 'Since the announcement that Brian was appointed, six members have resigned and 325 have joined.' Amiss desperately wanted him back to revive a club which was fading fast. He had tried to get him back before but Lara wanted rest and recuperation, not the daily grind of county cricket. 'He was still a phenomenal cricketer at his peak and we thought he would be a success as skipper,' he said. 'I did tell him he had to toe the line and he accepted that with a big smile. You could forgive him a lot but I said "now you're skipper you've got to take more responsibility.""

Lara's passionate love for his sport was much deeper than Best's love for football, so those close to him knew that he would play as long as his body could take it. He has already out-distanced all the other naughty-but-nice lads like Shane Warne, Denis Compton, Keith Miller and Ian Botham. But his new odyssey got off to an awful start. Piarco International Airport in Port of Spain wasn't the smartest or the most glamorous airport in the world at that time – now it has been elegantly rebuilt – and for some reason Lara rarely got there on time. He had been due to fly into Heathrow for his unveiling at Edgbaston. Television cameramen had been alerted and chairs were set out for a press conference for the great man, a flashback to 1994. Then Lara telephoned to say he had failed to catch the flight. Enter an unruffled Amiss who announced, 'Brian couldn't make the scheduled flight because he was unwell.' There were groans all around. In a short space of time, Lara had managed to cadge a ticket from his mate Phil Simmons who was setting out on his way to play for Leicestershire. Simmons surrendered his seat because he didn't have a championship match until that weekend and Lara said, 'If it hadn't been for Phil I couldn't have made it until the next day.' The genial Simmons said:

> It wasn't a great deal. I live close by and it wasn't a hassle. But Brian has a thing about planes. They used to hold the plane up a few minutes when he used to fly back but now with the current security arrangements it's going to be tough for him in future.

By coincidence, Warwickshire's first opponents were Durham, the youngest county, who had been lashed by Lara four years earlier in his monolithic 501. The bristling David Boon, Durham's captain, inserted Warwickshire and Lara came in first wicket down at nought, survived eight deliveries and was caught by wicketkeeper Martin Speight for a duck. Speight is an interesting character – he's a professional artist, has thirteen 'O' Levels and a bachelors degree in Archaeology and Ancient History. The happy bowler was sixteen-stone John Wood from Wakefield who came out with an immortal quote: 'He's just like a batsman like everybody else.' The Speight–Wood combination also dismissed Lara in the second innings for 13.

At the Oval, Warwickshire went down to an innings' defeat and though Lara accumulated 95 runs in his two innings, he was twice dismissed by the slow, dobby bowling of Mark Butcher. While the Prince had run up hundreds in his first conquest of county cricket, his second attempt was turning into a disaster. Jack Bannister wrote, 'the tinkling of alarm bells was now reaching a crescendo.' At the end of May, things became nasty. Lara was given permission to go back to Port of Spain for four days on one of his free air miles trips and was due back on 30 May ready to drive to Taunton for an AXA League game. Again, he failed to make the flight and when he flew back the next day, he arrived at the County Ground at 1.45 p.m. for a 2.10 p.m. start expecting to play. In 1994, Warwickshire would have let him play but not now. Amiss was upset and he said:

> Phil Neale, our director of coaching, took the decision along with vice-captain Nick Knight to leave him out of the side. Brian expressed his regret for this and has apologised. We heard a full account from him of the problems he experienced and accepted there were some mitigating circumstances. I am sure it was a one-off and Brian said it will not happen again. I think he is much more mature than he was when he was here before. He is much more of a team man.

To make matters worse, Warwickshire were bowled out for 96 and lost. Amiss convened a disciplinary hearing four days later and announced that Lara was to be fined £2,000 – less than half a week's salary.

In another setback, early on, Lara dropped Somerset's number five left-handed batsman Simon Ecclestone – who went on to score 94 – and also missed another catch off the number seven batsman Marcus Trescothick, who reached 98 as Somerset won easily. In his first innings he carved five fours in quick succession before going for a sixth and was dismissed for 21. Second time out, he batted 114 minutes for 21. These were sure signs that his confidence was being affected.

Unlike professional football, cricket abounds with highly intelligent young men and Ecclestone, who went to Durham and Oxford Universities, would have got on well with Lara. In the copious notes for his entry in the *Cricketers' Who's Who*, he wrote, 'The culture in county cricket is defensive and suspicious. Left as it is, the system will continue to inhibit players on the pitch.' Lara tried to change this at Edgbaston, encouraging a more positive style of play. Nick Knight shared his view. He said, 'He was always trying to try different things and his summing-up of other players was amazing.'

Amiss said, 'It was a pretty wet season and pitches weren't as good. He was never going to score another 2,000 runs.' Late in June, Warwickshire lost to Lancashire in a contrived declaration match and it was their fifth defeat of the season. In 1994, Lara had spoken out against Reeve's contrived declaration matches saying they were 'not cricket' but here he was opening the bowling and conceding 24 runs with his lollipop bowling off two overs to let Lancashire declare on 39 for no wicket and rattle up a winning 338 for six. A month later, Lara and his players were booed at the end of another defeat by Essex. Lara's exaggerated foot movements were costing him his wicket and the late Neil Williams had him lbw for a duck. His county batting average tumbled to a depressing 22.

There was some relief early in August when he suddenly returned to form at Lord's after fourteen months and 39 first innings without a century. It was a big one, 226 from 281 balls, but the match against Middlesex was drawn. Bill Day, the veteran *Mail on Sunday* cricket writer, told an extraordinary story about Lara's next match at Northampton:

> I had to see him to interview him and I fixed it up through Phil Neale. Brian played a fantastic innings of 158 off 154 balls, including five sixes and 18 fours and when he was out Phil told me that Brian needed treatment on his knee. It went on a long time and I was standing on the first floor landing next to the dressing room and I could see he had an ice pack on his knee. Brian came over and said a few curt words and turned his back saying, 'I can't say any more now.' I was very upset about it. He was treating me like a piece of dirt. I am an experienced journalist and that wasn't the way to treat me.
>
> I had another word with Phil and some time later, with my deadline rapidly approaching, Lara emerged and was most apologetic. There was an empty room nearby and he said, 'Come in, we won't be disturbed.' His mood had changed completely. He spoke extremely well and was very polite and helpful until he suddenly started getting emotional. 'These Press people are ruining my life,' he said, forgetting that I am a member of the same group. Then he burst into tears. I felt a bit sorry for him. Then he composed himself and he explained why he had scored his runs so quickly to win the match by four wickets. 'I had to get away early to drive up to Newcastle to see my friend Dwight Yorke playing for Aston Villa,' he said. Actually Villa won the match 1-0 but Yorke didn't score the goal. It showed that if he wanted to bat a certain way to win a match, he could. What a genius he is!

Moving westwards to Worcester, Lara piled up 144 in three hours, passing his 1,000 runs at the end of the month. This burst of 586 runs from five innings was followed by another alarming slump. In both innings against Leicestershire, he padded up and was lbw for low scores. With no prospect of any success in the one-day competitions, he opted out from playing in the final two county matches and quit by mutual consent. He was fourth in the averages with 1,033 runs, average 39.73. He was human after all.

seventeen

Strike at Heathrow

There have been scores of industrial strikes at Heathrow but none was more strange than that which took place at the Excelsior Hotel, one of several posh hotels on the A4 next to the airport's runways, starting on 4 November 1998. Brian Lara was one of the leaders who declined to go on the West Indies tour to South Africa – it was cricket's first strike. It lasted a week before the players surrendered and accepted the Board's promise of 'taking all practical steps to improve players' pay and conditions'. Nelson Mandela was the peacemaker. He appealed to Lara and his colleagues to allow the tour to go ahead and that helped enormously.

For weeks the West Indies Players' Association were trying to seek new terms from the West Indies Cricket Board for their players but no agreement had been reached when the tour of South Africa was about to start. Being forced to play three one-day internationals in four days in the baking hot temperature of 40°C in Dhaka between 29 October and 1 November didn't help the black mood of the players. The ICC wanted to raise money to help cricket's development in the Third World, including Bangladesh, a very worthy cause, and the crammed tournament produced £10 million. All nine Test-playing nations were ordered to take part. England fielded a second XI, lost to South Africa and went home. Their one-day skipper and Man of the Match Adam Hollioake became disoriented in the heat and needed to consume twenty large bottles of water and a dozen glucose drinks in a short space of time. He also ate five Mars bars, three bowls of noodles and a pile of naan bread. As he came off the field he described his state as being 'as though I'd smoked ten joints', causing concern for the English authorities. Another sufferer was Jack Russell, who announced his retirement from international cricket.

Lara might also have been disorientated after leading his side to a 30-run victory over a Pakistan side racked by the aftermath of the bribe inquiry.

The West Indies beat India by six wickets two days later and went down in a four-wicket defeat to South Africa in the final twenty-four hours later. Lara and vice-captain Carl Hooper, plus Courtney Walsh and six other players, flew from Dhaka to Bangkok and instead of following the tour programme and flying to Johannesburg, they changed planes and went to London. Seven other players were already in Johannesburg. Lara's mobile phone, always busy, was working overtime as he fielded calls from representatives of the Board and his teammates. The Board officials told him that he and his colleagues were in breach of their contracts but the rebels countered saying that they hadn't agreed a contract for the South African tour although they were under contract for the trip to Bangladesh. The manager, Clive Lloyd, said:

> That's where it went wrong. The contracts should have been sorted out a long time before. I'd spent thirty hours flying from Dhaka to Hong Kong and on to Johannesburg and then I was told to get to London. I was dog tired, I tell you. I told these guys, 'You're making a big mistake. If you want to make a stand you should do it in South Africa, not there.' I said to the Board they should cancel the tour and pick another team for a tour starting a month later. But it wasn't easy to do that because we had a West Indies 'A' tour start-ing in Bangladesh.

Flying on the plane from Johannesburg to London was Dr Ali Bacher, the South African Board managing director. He had sixteen copies of a four-page letter signed by Nelson Mandela to hand to each of the sixteen tour members as soon as he arrived at the Excelsior.

Meanwhile, the West Indies Board met and decided to sack Lara and Hooper as captain and vice-captain and told the others that they would be docked ten per cent from their tour fee, if they subsequently went to South Africa, with younger players losing five per cent of their fees. The Board had already approved the players' pay scales, ranging from around £15,000 for the three-month tour for younger players up to £35,000 for senior players. For most, that was below the going rate for Australian, South African and England players, who were on a basic of £35,000 due to better sponsorship. Barrie Gill, the agent who was hired by the West Indies Players' Association, was able to fill in some details:

> They are concerned about principles as much as money. One point is guaran-teeing the security in Johannesburg after two Pakistan players were mugged

on tour last year. They claim they were offered less than the sum they received in Australia two years ago. They also wanted more money for ODIs, and better allowances for meals.

Pat Rousseau, the peppery Jamaican President, was the man taking a tough stance. He wanted Lara and Hooper to fly to Kingston to meet him but the WIPA said in a statement:

> We have requested an emergency meeting with the Board in London to be attended by Brian Lara, Carl Hooper, Courtney Walsh and James Adams. This request was denied by the West Indies Board. Messrs Lara and Hooper, the vice-president and players' representative of WIPA, subsequently flew to London to meet the WIPA president Courtney Walsh and other members of the team. Therefore, statements to the effect that Messrs Lara and Hooper have abandoned the tour to South Africa are unfounded and untrue.

Rousseau said, 'The strike has dealt a serious blow to West Indies cricket.' He said he wasn't available until the following Monday and asked Joel Garner, the 6ft 7ins tall former Barbados and West Indian fast bowler, to represent him.

Garner arrived the next morning and the players' delegation told him that unless he was empowered to take decisions they would not talk to him, only Rousseau. 'We will sit it out as long as it takes,' said one. But the WIPA £30,000 annual subsidy from the Board was running out fast after paying £150 for each room. Bacher spent most of his time sitting in the hotel lobby, taking calls on his mobile at a rate of one every minute and a half, as frequently as the planes were landing outside. He kept saying, 'There's no news, ring me later.' Courtney Walsh, the elder statesman, took over as spokesman. He said, 'This is not about money. It is to do with generalised conditions, the future of West Indies cricket and safeguarding the younger guys who are coming in.' And he walked off.

Bacher sent up a message saying he would like to see him to discuss Nelson Mandela's letter and it took an hour before he re-emerged to accept the letter, mobbed by newsmen. Walsh soon disappeared again and Bacher said, 'It will be lunacy if this tour does not go ahead. It means so much to our country and the young black population in particular. It should be possible to reach an agreement. There are no contingency plans. We have to find an answer.' The WIPA delegation hired a lawyer, Alan Burdon-Cooper, to advise them and after a change of mind, Rousseau flew in to Heathrow on 7 November along with three of his colleagues. They went straight into talks with the players' group and it broke up at 4 a.m. without agreement.

The squad was scheduled to fly to Johannesburg sixteen hours later. Further talks lasted until late afternoon before there was a deal. It took nineteen hours of frank talking. Lara and Hooper were reinstated and the Board offered a share in their marketing activities and promised extra cash on retainer contracts, one of the points WIPA wanted. Gill recalled, 'Brian wasn't happy at all and that's why he kept out away from the microphones.' Jimmy Adams said, 'No side has won.' Clive Lloyd said, 'That's right, it was a waste of time in my view. I am relieved it's ended but deeply sad that it happened in the first place. I can forgive them but I don't forget.' Rousseau said the dismissal of Lara and Hooper 'was a misunderstanding. Clive hadn't understood the reason why they wanted to go to London, to attend a WIPA meeting, and he refused permission.'

Bacher told the real story. 'There is a real lack of trust on both sides,' he said. 'A lot of intransigence and a lot of mistrust. When we get playing cricket and they go into the townships, where they are so needed, the trouble will be forgotten. But it would be easy to envisage it breaking out again.' Gill said, 'Both sides are very suspicious of each other. And the players still believe they are in a master-slave situation.' Smartly dressed in their maroon blazers and ties, Lara's team got on to the bus taking them to the airport terminal. Walsh and Ambrose actually missed the flight.

The next day, Lara appeared in a press conference and said, 'The players are pretty sorry at this time for any offence but we are here to win the Test series and that is our aim.' Cricket's first strike had ended but the friction intensified. Up to then, the West Indies had handed out three 5–0 whitewashes, one to India and two to England when David Gower was the captain, but now they were on the receiving end themselves. Lara said it was the worst tour he had been on and Clive Lloyd said, 'We got walloped and we deserved it.' None of their batsmen reached a century and Lara's top score was 79 with a dismal average of 31. In the first Test he had his middle stump cartwheeling away for 11 and, despite fitness problems, Allan Donald dismissed him five times in the eight innings. In his book *White Lightning*, Donald said:

> He was too loose, too keen on dominating rather than toughing it out and I lost a lot of respect for him. He made little apparent effort to rally his demoralised players. He lacked the dynamism and professionalism to pull them around and the younger players looked out of their depth. They were desperate for

strong leadership. I've known him since 1992 and I was saddened at the change. Even though he had been preferred to me as Warwickshire's overseas player for the 1996 season [Lara decided not to accept their contract] I had nothing personal against him.

I don't know whether his drive had been sapped by all the money he made but his attitude was in total contrast to Sachin Tendulkar who is in a different class as a professional cricketer. I found it very hard to have a conversation with him on that tour. He gave the impression that he felt superior to me.

After the West Indies lost the one-day series 6-1, Donald went to the dressing-room to ask Lara to sign a pair of batting gloves for his imminent benefit. According to Donald, Lara declined and told him to 'F— off'. Later, Lara relented and threw him a pair. It wasn't surprising that Lara was unco-operative after the sledging he had endured in the final Test at Centurion Park. Lara took six fours off Donald's bowling in the space of twelve balls and the South African told him he had no discipline and set a bad example in a bid to upset his rhythm. Lara complained and the bowler responded saying, 'It's part of a tough game.'

Lara admitted at the end of the Test series, 'We were not together as a team.' That was evident from the start. Geoffrey Dean, wrote in *Wisden*:

> His public criticism of Nixon McLean and Mervyn Dillon after the second Test capitulation seemed to sap their confidence and neither bowled consist-ently all tour. He failed to get the best not only from them but also several other unproven Test players.

According to Donald, Lara reduced Rawle Lewis to tears in the second Test.

But Lara has an outstanding record of visiting townships in South Africa, not just on that tour but on previous trips. His former agent Jonathan Barnett said, 'He loves doing that and he feels it is really worthwhile.' Bryan Davis, a critic, said, 'Brian is an enigma and he displays the best of himself and the worst. Being one of the leaders put him into a powerful position and that really started the decline of West Indies cricket.'

eighteen

Reincarnation at Sabina Park

After his depressing exit from Edgbaston, the Prince had reached new depths with the strike at Heathrow, the first industrial dispute in the history of cricket, followed by the shattering 5-0 whitewash in South Africa, and the admiration of many Caribbean cricket lovers turned to anger. Even in Trinidad, more and more people despised him. They thought he had let them down with his self-indulgence and indiscipline. Michael Holding called him 'a spoilt brat' and countless others used that phrase as well.

Clive Lloyd said at that time:

> He's at the crossroads. He has got to try and pull things round. When you are captain of the West Indies cricket team, you are probably the most important man in the West Indies. The top man. Because throughout all the Caribbean it is the only cohesive unit that we have. You are more important than any of the Prime Ministers. The Prime Minister of Trinidad and Tobago can make decisions only for his own island. The West Indies captain is making decisions for five million people. People don't understand that. It is entirely up to him now to prove that he is going to grasp the nettle and get back. I think he has the capabilities to do it but he has to listen to people around him.

The Board gave him that chance and he took it on Sunday 13 March 1999 at Sabina Park when he scored a double century which Tony Cozier described 'the greatest ever scored by a West Indian'. *Wisden* recorded:

> Only Lara could have changed the course of the series after Trinidad and he did so by defying the odds and circumstances that would have crushed most men. On one fantastic, sunny, windy Sunday, he seduced the people of a bankrupt nation, resurrected his career as a batsman of rare gifts which enabled his side to reach an imposing total of 431.

He scored 213, almost half the total number of runs scored. Ken Mahood, the long-serving sports cartoonist at the *Daily Mail*, produced a cartoon of a caped and helmeted Lara, his bat held high in one hand and a stump in the other, soaring out of a grave marked 'West Indies Cricket'. That was exactly how it seemed.

Five days earlier the West Indies had been bowled out for 51, their lowest ever score in Test cricket, and the Australians had won by a margin of 312 runs in the first Test at Port of Spain. The critics called for Lara's head and a lesser man would have resigned on the spot. It was the worst possible start for him. When he arrived at the ground, he was concerned about the conditions, particularly the nets, and he criticised the practice facilities in the Press, upsetting Bryan Davis, the man in charge of the ground, who said:

> I was very upset about the way he used the Press in that way and not speaking to me first. Brian was a member of the Queen's Park Cricket Club and he shouldn't have castigated his own club. He even said 'they're always bad' which wasn't true. The Australians practised out in the middle and he could have done that as well. It rained in the previous days and it was difficult to roll the practice nets which is why we suggested the change. After that I told him you go your way and I'll go mine.

A local wit reckoned that the onset of rain attracted a profusion of ducks – there were eleven ducks in the match, equalling a Test record. Seven Tests have now produced this number of ducks, the sixth being West Indies *v.* England at Georgetown in 1997/98.

Lara thought the Port of Spain pitch was a result pitch and he was soon proved right. Australia's 269 was a reasonable total in the circumstances and Lara smacked eleven boundaries in his 62 out of his side's 167. He wanted to gain a psychological advantage over Shane Warne, whose style of bowling was suited to the Port of Spain pitch. Warne failed to take a wicket and wasn't needed in the second innings as Glenn McGrath, with 5-28, and Jason Gillespie, 4-18, bowled out the West Indies for 51 in 19.1 overs. Gillespie had Lara caught by Mark Waugh for three off the second ball he faced and only Ridley Jacobs, with 19, reached doubled figures. The last seventeen West Indian wickets went down for 69 and their players, particularly Lara, were ridiculed. 'The prime target for the vitriol was captain Lara,' said *Wisden*, 'even doting followers in his native Trinidad showed signs of disaffection, if not anger and when the match ended after lunch on the fourth day, there were renewed loud calls for his head.'

When he flew into Kingston he was jeered. Team morale? There wasn't any. Some of the players were less than cordial when senior officials were told that Lara had been spotted in a nightclub in the early hours. As the *Daily Mail*'s Alan Fraser wrote:

> It was exquisitely named 'The Asylum'. It seemed to sum up what was happening to the state of West Indies cricket which had ruled the world for so long. Steve Waugh recalled 'one of the strangest sensations of my whole career when I walked out to toss with Lara, he was being booed all the way to the middle and back. As we parted ways after I called correctly, we shook hands and I said, "Play well". He replied, "This is the last time I'm gonna have to put up with this shit."'

Back in the dressing-room, Waugh said to Justin Langer, 'This guy's fragile and ready to offload the captaincy.' Waugh obviously thought Lara was a quitter. He was wrong.

'Then a miracle happened,' said Revd Wes Hall. And luck was certainly with Lara. Mark Waugh dropped him on 44 and at 99. Many people, not just the Australians, thought he was run out when Greg Blewett knocked down the wicket going for a risky run. The overjoyed crowd were on their feet and some of them raced out to the middle, repeating the scenes from when he had scored his 375. Police and security officials tried to force them back and he had to retire to the boundary rope to await the third umpire's decision. There was only one camera available and the evidence was unclear. Roars from all around the ground greeted the sight of the flashing green light.

Lara's second hundred was close to perfection and when he passed the 200 mark a man charged out to the middle holding a baby. Another man, only wearing a bandana, joined in the stampede. Lara had to be escorted to the pavilion before order was restored. When the magical run was scored he looked up to the heavens, with his arms raised high. His bat was held in his left hand, the stronger one, and his right forearm was swaddled in protective white material. His forehead was furrowed and bore no smile. It was as though he was thanking the Lord for giving him one last chance. If Bradman had toured the West Indies, would he have provoked such emotional scenes? Or has any other cricketer come close to it? One doubts it. Renowned for their mental strength, Waugh's Australians, who included those two all-time great bowlers Shane Warne and Glenn McGrath, capitulated, losing by ten wickets.

B.C. Pires, one of the most respected Trinidadian cricket writers, a caring man, was one of the critics who thought that the Board would cede to Lara because:

> Ian Bishop and Jimmy Adams, the men identified for the job as captain by Tony Cozier, are unlikely to make the team. Chanderpaul is injured and at twenty-four he is considered by many to be callow. Not even this Board could bring Courtney Walsh back after tossing him aside to make way for the Prince. But even if there were someone who could take over the job, this Board lacks the moral authority to do virtually anything and can do nothing at all to Lara, with whom they injudiciously locked horns last September at Heathrow Airport.

However, president Rousseau and his much-derided Board members came up with a good solution, threatening to take the guillotine to Lara if he didn't improve his behaviour and putting him on probation. After long discussions with him, Lara admitted that he had made mistakes and they appointed him as captain for the first two Tests. If he failed to carry out his promises, he would be out. They wanted him to spend more time with his players off the field, work to eradicate the current disunity of the players, travel to matches with them on the same bus and maintain certain standards. Rousseau said:

> We recognise the tremendous cricketing ability of Lara but he must improve on certain aspects of his captaincy as we are not prepared to wait indefinitely. Our investigations pointed clearly to weakness in leadership that contributed to the poor performance of the team. The captain himself reported difficulty in achieving unity. We have told him he needs to make significant improvements in his leadership skills. We believe he has it within him to fulfil his potential but we are not prepared to wait forever. We have set up a sub-committee to ensure that he understands clearly these rigorous demands.

If Warwickshire had used similar tactics in 1994, Lara's cricketing life might have been very different, and much more successful. He could have developed into one of the greatest captains of all time as well as being one of the greatest batsmen. But coping with a suddenly emerging superstar it was understandable that they were too tolerant with him. Before the agreement was confirmed, there was plenty of opposition from leading players who thought that Lara wasn't deserving of another chance and the sternest critic was Michael Holding. He told Peter Hayter of the *Mail on Sunday*:

I have marked down February 22, the day Lara was reappointed as captain, as the saddest day in the history of West Indies cricket. It was a shocking decision and those responsible should resign immediately. The job needs a big man and Brian Lara isn't. He has been spoilt throughout his cricketing life by his adoring fans in Trinidad and he now thinks he can do whatever he wants.

With all those faults which the Board has talked about, how can they reappoint him? By doing so they are condoning his action. Lara is not a leader of men. He thinks of himself as numero uno and the rest of the players as a few rungs below him. I really believe he needs psychiatric help. He needs to learn the part he has to play in real life, not in the world that he has in his head.

Lara was shocked by the ferocity of the great fast bowler's attack on him and he responded with some verve: 'Michael Holding is paid to come out with such things. I just ignore all that rubbish. You can respond to your critics and prove them wrong but they always find a way to stick it up you. So I am not getting involved.'

On several occasions in his controversial life Lara has been big enough to say sorry and this was another one. It is one of the reasons why he has stayed so long at the top. Clive Pantin was the first person to advise him to say sorry after his misdemeanours in 1994/95 and he said:

He was horrible at his most gifted years. He was selfish and inconsiderate and let his fame go to his head. He listened to the wrong people. But underneath it all, he is a very decent person and came from a highly respected family. He is very generous. I heard one true story about him concerning a plane trip he made back from a trip to Pakistan. Someone told him that a man who had just had a serious operation had difficulty in sitting in his seat in economy. Brian was told about the man's predicament and he volunteered to give up his business class seat in exchange and the man was delighted. What changed him? It was his daughter Sydney. He adores her. She has brought love and goodness into his life.

After the victory in Barbados, which turned out to be another brilliantly staged triumph with the Prince playing the key role, Holding said:

He is a very proud man. I know he always wanted to captain the West Indies and hated the thought of giving it up. I was very critical of Brian after the defeat in South Africa but he is now looking a completely different man. What we have seen here, even when we lost in Trinidad, is a Brian Lara who means business. He doesn't have to score a century every time. All we want is for him to talk to his players, to gee them up and that has been happening. I don't know why he has changed. Perhaps the criticism got to him.

Viv Richards has been a supporter of Lara and in his autobiography *Sir Vivian* he said:

> His knocks in that series were some of the greatest I have seen. At other times he can look a bit inferior and maybe even casual. But greatness goes with the individual who looks lethargic one day and rips you apart the next. When I speak with him, I find him a mature kid who can hold his own in any company.

Was the third Test at the Kensington Oval, won by the West Indies by one wicket after they had been 105 for five, when Lara scored 153* out of 311 for nine, the greatest Test of all? 'I haven't seen a better one,' said Waugh, who became the fifth man to be dismissed on 199. 'It was Lara's cool head and presence under pressure that guided his team home by the barest of margins.' Peter Roebuck wrote:

> Brian Lara has played one of the greatest innings of the history of the game. Certainly his match-winning and mouth-watering 153 was the best of its type it has been my privilege to watch. Perhaps it was the best of any sort. Throughout a long, hot fifth day, played in a frenzied atmosphere against fierce opponents and before a packed and expectant crowd, the Trinidadian kept his head and his wicket. He showed impeccable judgement and remarkable calm as he took his team to a famous victory in the most exciting and draining Test I have seen. Lara's efforts surpassed his magnificent 213 at Sabina Park since this time the Australians were on their toes – besides which it was a fifth day pitch and there was a match to win.

Roebuck made similar comments about Lara's 182 in Adelaide eighteen months later and said:

> He stood out like a strawberry on a plate of plums. Nowadays he seems to produce his best when his fortunes are at their lowest. Last year in the Caribbean he was about to lose the captaincy and his dignity, and promptly saved both with a string of innings that combined the power of Sanath, the mastery of Sachin and the grit of Steve Waugh. And then he went back into his shell. He was reluctant to tour England and flopped badly. Perhaps it works

this way. He must summon immense willpower to produce a great performance. No longer do runs appear like water through a tap. Moreover, his mind
has distracted and tired as his life has widened. He needs a long period of rest
and some particular motivation to produce those scintillating innings that
win matches and delight spectators.

Lara made the right comments after his 153, saying modestly, 'It was a team
effort.' Clive Lloyd said, 'It was an innings I'll remember for the best of my
life.' Raman Subba Row, the ubiquitous ICC referee, agreed. One of the
chief appeals of Test cricket is the way fortunes swing one way and then the
other, and the finest matches are those when the result is in doubt to the
very end, as was the case here, with last man Courtney Walsh blocking away
with his exaggerated, jerky style of batting and Lara hitting the winning run
with a shot through extra cover. Many of his memorable big-score innings
have finished with a flourishing, trademark drive in that area. With players
like him and the current Australian batsmen leading the way and scoring
4-5 an over, there are fewer draws and Test cricket has made a startling and
entertaining comeback. The pop version, the ODIs, are often over when
the team batting second have no chance of winning. The ICC and their
member countries could do worse than to hire Lara when he retires to plug
the line that Test cricket is proper cricket, the rest is just a spicy aperitif.

Once again, the Prince had luck in his knapsack at the Kensington Oval
on his way to 153. Warne, not fully fit, dropped a hard return when he was
101 and seven runs from victory. Wicketkeeper Ian Healy, who had a dreadful tour, missed him. Several experts claimed that Warne was finished after
he was dropped from that match. Waugh and coach Geoff Marsh agreed to
leave him out but chairman of selectors Allan Border wanted him to stay.
Warne came in to see them to plead for clemency before their decision was
confirmed, with Border rebuffed. Only Warney would have done that – ask
for another chance. McGrath, who had to bowl 77 overs in 88°F heat for
his 9-220, lost his temper when one of his short deliveries hit Lara in the
helmet and his frustration brought on a nasty altercation which Subba Row
decided wasn't worthy of a penalty.

Most of the Australian players became extremely drunk that evening and
Waugh said in his book that 'wasting opportunities and talent is a sportsper-
son's greatest crime.' He introduced a curfew for a while, until he realised
that it was impossible to impose it. Lara may have faults but he has never
allowed himself to be seen in public in a paralytic state. He recorded a third
century in as many weeks, scoring 100 off only 82 balls, including three

sixes and 15 fours but his patience failed him and the determined Australians won by 176 runs, squaring the rubber 2–2. McGrath, his greatest antagonist, ended up with 30 wickets at what was an amazingly low average of 16.93 on these lightning-fast grounds.

Lara played an insignificant part in the 3–3 tie in the seven-match ODI competition and he handed over the captaincy to Jimmy Adams when he missed the final three through a wrist injury. That saved him more controversy as the fifth and seventh games ended in riots. There have always been crowd disturbances in West Indian cricket and the problem has never been tackled properly. Some of the new Chinese-built stadia for the 2007 World Cup should improve crowd control and perhaps the discipline of the Chinese might quieten these excitable characters in future!

The game at Georgetown was shortened to 30 overs and with Steve Waugh batting with Warne, the Australians only needed six runs from the last over. Keith Arthurton, not a regular bowler, pinned Waugh down on an unbeaten 67 with yorkers and bouncers and the Australian skipper needed three to tie. Without proper fences, hundreds of supporters were lining the boundary ready to charge on. Waugh smote the ball into mid-wicket as they stormed on, and one tried to seize his bat. Two runs had been made but the stumps had disappeared as the batsman turned in an abortive attempt to complete a third run.

Police horses were brought out in to clear the pitch eventually as the captains, umpires, officials, police officers and the unfortunate Subba Row had to decide what to do. As a thoroughly decent man, Subba Row plumped for a tie but Clive Lloyd was furious. 'The stumps had been already broken by us before the crowd came on,' he said. 'We should have been awarded the game and we would have won the series. We showed a great sense of sportsmanship but it still hurt.' Lara was party to that compromise.

There was more trouble in the last match at Bridgetown when the crowd erupted after Sherwin Campbell had been run out for 52 and was left spread-eagled on the ground following a collision with Brendon Julian. Eddie Nicholls, the umpire, ruled that Campbell was out but bottles started flying on to the ground, one just missing Steve Waugh. The Australians retreated to their dressing-room and play was held up for forty-five minutes before the police announced that unless they went back, they couldn't guarantee their safety. Another embarrassing compromise was set up: the Australians withdrew their appeal and Campbell, a local player, was reinstated. All these unseemly events took the gloss off Lara's reincarnation, which was sad. But his sullied reputation had been gilded and he was ready to take on the world in the World Cup.

nineteen

Troubled Times

The Prince had carried the West Indies to outdo the Australians and it was too much to expect that he would lead them to victory in the World Cup in England two weeks later. He wasn't fully fit, his troops were weary and none of his batsmen offered much in terms of scoring. His highest score in the tournament was 36 against New Zealand and his other scores were 11 against Pakistan, 25 against Bangladesh, 25* against Scotland and nine against the eventual winners Australia.

He was booed in the final match against Australia by a frustrated 21,238 crowd at Old Trafford after being accused of collusion with his opponents. At the time, the cricket betting scandal was on the front pages and one match in particular – Bangladesh v. Pakistan, in which Bangladesh beat the favourites Pakistan by 62 runs at Northampton – was later investigated but no prosecutions followed. Glenn McGrath, Lara's perpetual antagonist, bowled him with a purler in his 5-14, the fourth best analysis in World Cup history, and the West Indies were dismissed for 110 off 46.4 overs.

Ambrose ripped out Adam Gilchrist, Mark Waugh and Darren Lehmann but at 53 for three Steve Waugh ordered the block, dawdling over the final twenty overs as the captain and Michael Bevan accumulated the same number of runs. Angry Lancastrians started walking out, protesting that it was a fiddle. Einstein would have been needed to understand the complicated rules. The crowd couldn't understand them but Steve Waugh had done his research and he worked out that he only needed to qualify for the next stage, the Super Six, on net run rate, while enabling the West Indies to improve their own side of the equation against New Zealand. But in the end the West Indies missed out by 0.07 on net run rate and they were on their way back home. Waugh said, 'I copped some blasts but I was steadfast, if not a little hot headed, when I said "we are not here to win friends, just win the World Cup."' They did, routing the disorganised Pakistanis by eight wickets and bowling them out for 132 by 4.32 p.m. in a very unsatisfactory final which seemed tainted. There were claims that some of their younger players had a late night and one or two of them appeared not to be in prime condition. Shoaib Akhtar's four overs cost 37 runs and some of the bowling was just as kamikaze as the batting.

But there was plenty of humour three days later at Buckingham Palace when the teams were presented to the Queen on her birthday. Murray Goodwin, the former Zimbabwe Test player now playing for Sussex, found himself in the West Indies group as they were introduced to Prince Philip and the Queen, and the Prince, who played a few matches as an off-spinner in his younger days, laughed and said to Murray, 'You don't look much like a West Indian!' Goodwin, a dry character, replied, 'No sir, but I wish I was hung like one!' Courtney Walsh caught his foot in the carpet, stumbled down a couple of steps before regaining his balance, and said to the Queen with an embarrassed smile, 'Ma'am, nice to meet you!' The Australians used to replay the video of the incident on their coach and it always provoked raucous laughter.

There wasn't much joy in Lara's heart immediately after the World Cup. He had just passed the age of thirty, a dangerous age for an unmarried male without strong roots. The health of his mother Pearl was deteriorating and he was constantly on the phone to her. In December 1999 he led the team on a tour to New Zealand which turned out to be more disastrous than the whitewash in South Africa a year earlier. They lost the first Test in Hamilton after being 282 for one at the end of the first day's play and then contrived to be bowled out for 97 in the second innings. In the second, at Wellington, their bowling collapsed in the strong crosswinds and they lost by an innings and 105 runs despite Lara top-scoring with 67 and 75, totting up forty-five per cent of his side's runs.

Sir Viv Richards had taken over as coach in place of the sick Malcolm Marshall and he said:

> We had a good rapport. I liked his attitude and he is seriously concerned about the future of West Indies cricket. He desperately wants to turn things around as captain. He was very willing to learn and we had a dialogue every day. The others also responded and despite the reverses I felt we had a good relationship.

They might have been good mates, mentor and eager pupil, but disillusionment soon set in as the Kiwis won the ODIs 5-0. Again, Lara was unable to control events. His scores were poor − 76, 2, 30, 5 and 37. 'Everyone is hurt,' he said. 'But there is no one to blame except ourselves. It is a greater hurt than in South Africa because it is a year later and you expect to make a difference.'

Realising that there wasn't much more he could do, he told the Board that he no longer wanted to stay on as captain. Clive Lloyd also made way and the Australian physiotherapist Dennis Waight, who had been a popular member of the team for the previous twenty years, resigned as well. Waight's departure was hastened by an incident on a flight when he had a nasty argument with Lara, who subsequently apologised.

The Board members thought that Richards wasn't quite the man they needed as coach – he didn't have the full coaching qualifications – and advertised his job before they told him he was surplus to requirements. The news that he was out was passed on to him by a junior member of staff. In St John's, Antigua, not far from where Lara scored his 375, windows were smashed as angry pro-Richards demonstrators marched to the Board's offices carrying placards saying 'The Board Must Go', 'No Board, No Viv' and 'Love Viv, Hate the Board'. The West Indies move their headquarters between different islands and they must have thought their decision to choose Antigua had been an unwise one. The Guyanan Roger Harper, a calm individual, was appointed as coach in place of Richards. Lloyd, upset at being excluded from the selection process, said, 'These are traumatic times for West Indies cricket and there are a lot of things wrong.'

The English cricket writer Geoffrey Dean, who covered that tour, said, 'Lara was mentally stale and he needed a break.' Lara soon took one, writing to the Board saying he wasn't available for the visits of Zimbabwe and Pakistan and thanked them for their support 'at a difficult time'. He writes a tasteful letter and this one contained these words: 'After two years the moderate success and devastating failure that has engulfed West Indian cricket has brought me to the realisation that there is a need for me to withdraw from my present leadership position.' Marshall, who sadly died from cancer, never played on the losing side in a Test series. Lara, by contrast, had found it difficult to be in a winning side, with the West Indies losing nine out of his 15 Tests.

He was one of twenty players who were asked to attend a nine-day training camp in Jamaica before the Zimbabwe and Pakistan series and his late withdrawal upset Rousseau who said, 'Brian told me he was going to be there so I announced the news. Then he told me he wouldn't be coming for various reasons and that was it. I am very disappointed and I feel let down.' Cynics put the withdrawal down to the fact that Lara was setting up a management company called LLAY with Dwight Yorke and Russell Latapy and he was being featured in a Channel 4 programme which was being filmed in Trinidad at the same time. Tony Francis, the programme maker, said:

Making a TV documentary about Lara and Yorke was always destined to be a white knuckle ride. When Yorke says Tuesday at 10.30 he means Friday at four. But Lara has more sides to him than a dodecahedron. He is your best mate and sternest foe in the same half an hour. In the year it took to make the film, Lara exhausted three agents, numerous girlfriends and the patience of the entire western Hemisphere. And yet you want to help him. Especially when he telephones, as he did at 3 a.m., his time, from New Zealand, to have a chat.

The newspapers in the Caribbean were speculating about whether Lara would be fit to go on the tour to England at the end of May. Earlier in the year he visited a psychologist in New Jersey over five days to talk about his mental state. It was being suggested that he was heading for a nervous breakdown and his career was about to end. Michael Holding had previously told him to see a headshrinker and Lara said:

> It is very tough being an international sportsman if you don't have the right tools. I don't think seeing a psychologist should be considered anything out of the ordinary. In cricket, there isn't enough of it. I thought I needed to look for another route to represent myself. I needed to get away, refocus and get back to do what I wanted to do. People put a lot of hopes on you, especially in the West Indies. I went to see a doctor. It wasn't too strenuous and we had a really nice talk about my future, what I had planned and what I wanted to achieve. It got me back mentally to where I wanted to be. I've got to be more consistent. That is what I am craving for. If I become a liability then I will make way for one of the younger guys, but I would like to think I could carry on past forty, like Clive Lloyd and Viv Richards.

Holding wanted a clearance report from Lara's medical advisors before the selectors chose him for the England tour. He said, 'We haven't heard about that trip or if he is back to normal from whatever was ailing him. But if he comes to England with problems and then he decides it isn't for him, we will have problems again.' Lara hadn't had a bat in his hand since early February, except for a single net, but he was playing plenty of golf. The selectors wanted more than that to assure them that he was ready to go so they asked him to captain the West Indies 'A' side to take on Pakistan at the Kensington Oval starting on 12 May. To their intense annoyance, he rejected their overtures. Darren Ganga, an upright Trinidadian opening batsman, played instead. On the Thursday the *Trinidad Daily Express* trumpeted on its front page 'Goodbye Forever' with Lara's picture.

A friend was quoted as saying, 'He has become disillusioned with cricket. He prefers playing golf, it's more relaxing. If he concentrated on it, he could have been a professional. He's got a great swing. He has been feeling the pressure and wants another challenge.' His handicap once came under ten but he has never equalled Don Bradman's golfing feats. Bradman's handicap came down to scratch for a brief period in the early 1960s. Twenty-four hours later the newspaper carried another story under the headline 'Hello Again'. The story confirmed that Lara was in the tour party, not Ganga. Dwight Yorke, who was in Trinidad at the time playing in a World Cup tie, told Lara he should go and Mike Findlay, the chairman of the selectors, a former Test wicketkeeper who is one of the most rational and sensible people in West Indies cricket, rang Lara himself. He said, 'I told him he should confide in people more and ask for help when you need it. We spoke about his mother, his career and his development as a person and by the end of the conversation I was convinced that he was totally committed to West Indian cricket.'

Findlay passed on the news to the other selectors, Joey Carew and Joel Garner, as well as coach Harper and skipper Jimmy Adams and not all of them agreed straight away. Garner, in particular, was supposed to be sceptical about Lara's mood swings. Another pressing consideration was the expensive promotional ads for the Channel 4 coverage of the series in England. If Lara had withdrawn it could have led to legal action. The *Trinidad Guardian* reported that Lara had been paid extra money to go on the tour and he started legal proceedings. 'This is completely false,' he said.

Four days after the Pakistan series ended, in a victory for Jimmy Adams and his team, Lara was scheduled to fly off from Port of Spain to Barbados to join up with other members of the touring party and that was one flight he didn't miss. Ricky Skerrett, the manager, said the Prince would be able to return home if circumstances demanded. When the nineteen members and officials sat down for the official team picture at Arundel only four had a smile on their faces and the man who wore the most troubled expression was Lara.

The opening match was at Worcester and he was more cheerful as he met the Press on the outfield. Asked who would be his side's biggest run-getter this summer, he said 'Brian Lara'. But his appearance altered slightly later when Glenn McGrath, recruited as the club's overseas, short-term signing filed into the small, wooden pavilion behind him. McGrath told a reporter, 'If he sees me he won't be too cheerful, that's for sure. I've had a few run ins with him.' But McGrath blinked first. He decided not to play and his place was taken by nineteen-year-old Kabir Ali, the young fast medium bowler who later played ODI cricket with England. Ali was in bed that morning when the telephone rang and an official said, 'We need you.' So he drove speedily from Birmingham to New Road in time to open the bowling. When Lara came in, his fourth delivery swung away down the legside and there were hesitant appeals before the batsman turned away and walked towards the pavilion. Kabir said, 'I don't think umpire Jack Hampshire was going to give him out. Brian could easily have batted on and a lot of people were disappointed that he's gone.'

He'd only made one and he also made one in the second innings. Skerrett said, 'We're hoping to get him 80% fit for the first Test but he's very worried about his mother's health.' At Cardiff, the sad-faced Lara was stumped – he is rarely stumped – off the bowling of Robert Croft for nought and in the second innings Croft had him lbw for 11. Moving eastwards to the beautiful ground above Arundel Castle lifted his spirits and against club-class bowling from Zimbabwe his engine spurted into life, scoring 130 runs worth of boundaries in his 163-ball innings of 176.

England's batsmen had a phobia about playing a Test at Edgbaston around that time. It began in 1995 when the first ball of the day bowled by Curtly Ambrose took off, flashing over the helmet of a startled Atherton. Lara shouted, 'I like that Ambi!' This time conditions were wetter and they suited Ambrose and Walsh as England slid to a critically low total of just 179 with local opener Nick Knight making the top score of just 26. Lara looked to be on his way to a big total until Darren Gough got rid of him for 50 in his side's 397. Gough recalled, 'I'd put him on his arse earlier in the same over, and delivered the perfect outswinger which he nudged to Stewie. But there was no support. Caddick wasn't firing.' The match was over in three days with England out for 125. The players were ordered to stay overnight to attend a debriefing which lasted some time.

Whether it was because live reggae music was played for the first time at lunch on a Test match – this was the 100th at Lord's – we will never know but on Friday it was like watching a volcano erupting out in the middle: twenty-one wickets crashed in 75 overs and Lara's men found themselves swept away by the fast-running lava. Their total of 54 followed their 51 in Port of Spain the previous year and was their third lowest Test total. In his book *Dazzler*, Gough says he felt that the music provoked this unparalleled comeback from England's bowlers. He said:

> What really got under our skin wasn't the West Indies opening partnership but the reggae din from the Nursery End as part of Channel 4's 'Caribbean Summer' coverage. We could hardly hear ourselves think as we sat in the dressing room. 'What's this nonsense? Do you think our hosts would put on English music if

we were in the Caribbean?' I went out on the balcony and looked along to the opposition's end of the pavilion. They were jogging and bopping around to the music. It was as if they were celebrating the series, 1-0 up and in a strong position at Lord's and with us in some disarray. When it started they lost two crazy wickets and the general view was 'that's what you get for listening to reggae music.'

Lara was one of the early casualties after stand-in captain Alec Stewart asked the West Indies to bat. Coming in at 162 for two, he was caught by the keeper off Gough for six and the rest of the innings quietly subsided to 267. Walsh and Ambrose soon got to work with their high-speed heart-level bowling and at 50 for five another hiding was on the way. Lara snaffled three catches to contribute to his record of 1.3 catches a Test and England were all out for 134. In the interval, Stewart delivered a General Montgomery-style oration. Gough revealed, 'He told us if we were going to lie down we would be 2-0 down and out of it. So he said let's go out there and fight. And we did.'

Stewart was harshly treated by some critics. They thought he was rather wooden in personality, similar to Bobby Moore, but that was totally false. He had a deep knowledge of the game and its mental side, passed on to him by his father Micky, and he was capable of passion and could inspire, especially when he was keeping. He wasn't given much credit for his keeping by some people but no better wicketkeeping batsman has ever played for England and he had the Barrington spirit, as though the Union Jack was trailing behind as he went out to the middle. He volunteered to open for most of his career and even Adam Gilchrist couldn't do that. But in this series Nasser Hussain wanted him to come in at five. At Lord's, in particular, that was a mistake. Hussain asked Mark Ramprakash to open and he failed twice and was dropped for the last time.

In his typical, immodest style Gough thought the tipping moment of this titanic day's play – Friday 30 June, the anniversary of the day Australians scored 729 for six, the highest Test total at Lord's with Bradman making 254 – came when he caught Sherwin Campbell, hurling himself to the right at an odd position at wide third man. 'It gave us a sniff and Caddy's eyes lit up,' he said. The transformed Caddick had an electric spell of 5-7, dishing out the same punishment the Ambrose–Walsh duo had been serving up and one of his victims was Lara, caught by the inspiring Dominic Cork. The crowd went wild, and the noise was the total opposite of the usual funereal calm. Cork showed the others how to be a winner. In the England dressing-room there is a tradition that if a stand starts up no one is allowed to leave the room. But there were frequent visits to the toilets as England, needing a mountainous 188 in these demanding conditions, lost wickets regularly until the chirpy Gough came in at 160 for eight to help Cork get past the post. It was some day.

The West Indies never recovered, losing the series 3-1. The nation's sporting fans were overcome with pride as the Wisden Trophy was wrested back after twenty-seven years. Lara was absent from the next two county games through a slight hamstring strain but he came back to form in the second innings in the rain-ruined drawn third Test at Old Trafford, scoring 112. His state of mind was intact again. He was 49 not out at lunch and went to have a net instead of a snack.

At Headingley, he was swept away with the rest of the team, capitulating to a two-day defeat by an innings and 39 runs. Both occasions he was lbw, firstly to Craig White and then Gough, without playing a shot, for four and two. Caddick administered the same Lord's medicine – 5-14 including four wickets in an over as the West Indies tumbled to another double-figure total, 61. The interim game before the final Test was played at Taunton, a place where batsmen can play themselves in when they have been failing elsewhere. That didn't apply to the West Indies. They used seven bowlers, all dreadful, as Somerset won by an innings and 269 runs. Lara failed twice on one of his favourite grounds, caught at fine leg hooking and bowled by Jason Kerr, a Lancastrian who missed most of the season with a herniated disc. Lara was the first victim of his hat-trick.

The atmosphere at the Brit Oval for the final Test was similar to Lord's. Thousands were turned away on the final day as England won by 185 runs and *Wisden* said, 'This was sport at its vibrant, colourful best, and it rekindled the public's love for cricket.' In the Caribbean the cricket lovers felt the opposite – was it worth supporting this craven lot who had let us down yet again? Jimmy Adams won the toss and decided to field and though England struggled to 281 on a less-than-perfect Oval pitch, the game was virtually won when the West Indies managed just 125. Lara must have been in despair when he stepped too far across his wicket from a delivery from Craig White and was bowled around his legs for a golden duck, the first of his career. In his second innings, he was finding some rhythm when he was given harshly out lbw for 47. He must have rued his decision to go on the tour. His Test total of runs was a modest 239 and his average was 26.55. For that year, he wasn't cricket's superstar batsman, just an ordinary one.

Floodlit cricket was introduced to ODIs in England that summer and the West Indies might have preferred to switch the lights off. They lost five matches in the NatWest series – one in humiliating circumstances defending a total of 287 for five against Zimbabwe at Chester-le-Street – and won one, with Lara making three half-centuries.

twenty

A Whitewash Down Under

In the autumn of 2000, Brian Lara was having trouble with his eyes and threatened to pull out of the West Indies squad for the brief tour of Kenya. After spending most of his life in glaring sunshine he contracted a minor complaint of the eye which could easily be removed through surgery. By this time he had written articles for the *Mail on Sunday*, the *Daily Mail* and the *Daily Mirror*, which he found very rewarding.

Peter Hayter, the cricket writer for the *Mail on Sunday*, quoted him on 23 September as saying:

> The specialists told me that there is an operation that can cure the condition completely. It involves grafting healthy skin from an unaffected area of the eyeball and the downside is that the recovery period is at least six months. At the moment I am going to carry on using the sunglasses and medication and try to stay out of the bright sunlight if I can. But if the condition gets any worse, I will have to take the advice of the doctors because my aim is to have a long term future in the game. I don't think the condition actually affects my vision as such but on occasions I have had trouble sighting the ball against certain backgrounds and, at its worst, it feels as though there are bits of grit in my eye. In any case, the irritation causes a distraction and that is the last thing you need in the middle of an innings.

He refused to blame his failures in England on his eyes and on medical advice he wore special tinted sunglasses on the field. Most cricketers who play in hot countries experience similar problems and it makes one wonder how the previous generation of cricketers played in such conditions without wearing sunglasses. There were some players who never wore hats or suncream either.

Royce 'Packie' Moore, a pharmacist and friend, said:

He had some problems with pterigium for a while but he never had the operation. He's a great guy but has been a bad boy as well. No one can be in the position he's reached, the top of his profession with so many people hassling him. I was at Barbados in 1994 and asked him if he had any tickets for me. He said, 'Come to the hotel, I'll fix it.' He turned up at nine and had a couple for me and he said with a massive smile, 'I've just signed for Warwickshire.' He was so excited. It was the turning point in his life.

Lara was fit for the twelfth West Indies tour to Australia and it turned out to be the worst with Steve Waugh's men winning all five Tests. There were no excuses. Waugh, now a full-time journalist, wrote scathingly:

> That wasn't how Test cricket is supposed to feel. I hated the lack of spirit by their team, their meek surrender, the scarcity of confrontation. Except for the heart and soul of Courtney Walsh, the talent of Brian Lara and the pluck of Jimmy Adams, they were spineless and not much better than an outfit in Sydney first-grade cricket. It's the way you win – the blood, sweat and tears that go into a hard fought victory that invigorates me, not the demolition of a non-believing foe.

Most observers in the West Indies would agree with that. In the days of the Three Ws, Sobers, Marshall and up to the last days of Walsh and Ambrose, there were players who wanted to make their names as heroes and make sacrifices to achieve their ambitions. But now cultural and economic changes in the islands were producing a generation who had access to all sorts of refineries without having to try too hard to acquire them. Lara was really the only hero left and he hadn't sweated blood like they did because he was a naturally gifted performer. He put the work in in his younger days, his determination and will to win was still there but surrounded by unenthusiastic young men, he was despairing about the future of West Indies cricket which was being run appallingly badly. One couldn't blame him for causing all the ructions and it was to his credit that he was still out there making an effort.

Lara started the tour with just one scoring shot in his first three Test innings, falling each time to Glenn McGrath's cutters. His scores were nought, four and nought and the ogre McGrath followed up his 10-27 match aggregate in the first Test at Brisbane by removing Lara with his hat-trick ball, his 300th Test wicket, at Perth for a duck. Lara has a high percentage of ducks but in this period he was dogged by them – three in the Tests and three in the ODIs. His overall tally of Test ducks is 17 in 232 innings though he has yet to record a pair. The West Indies set a record of 28 ducks in that five-Test series watched by 414,044 spectators. The Australians love a massacre.

Lara suddenly burst into form early in December in Hobart despite complaining about a sore knee. Coming in at 80 for five, he virtually eliminated the quick single by striking 40 fours, a five and two sixes in his 231 off 265 balls. Andy Bichel, a difficult man to score off, conceded 24 runs from one over, all fours. Three days later, Jimmy Adams, soon to be sacked as captain, won the toss on the usual flat Adelaide pitch and Lara followed up with 182 which featured 29 spanking fours and a six. Another blow on his helmet – McGrath was the tormentor yet again – failed to slow him down.

But a total of 391 wasn't enough. A second innings of 141, with Lara top-scoring with 39, gave Australia the Sir Frank Worrell Trophy. He had scored forty-one per cent of his side's runs in another losing cause. Lara was the highest scorer in the series with 321 runs, average 32.10, and his five catches made him the fifteenth Test player to pass the 100 mark. Adams, Sherwin Campbell, who was sacked as vice-captain, Darren Ganga and Ramnaresh Sarwan all averaged under twenty. In the Carlton ODI series, the Australians had a first ever 100 per cent success, winning all ten against the West Indies and Zimbabwe. Lara scored 116 at Sydney off 106 balls and was voted Man of the Series for his 372 runs, average 46.50.

Much of the press attention was focused on his eighteen-year-old girl-friend Lynnsey Ward who joined him in Australia and also the betting scandal which was enveloping him and Mark Waugh. Some of the Australian newspapers called for Lara and Mark Waugh to drop out of the series 'in the interests of the sport'. Lara refused to comment but Waugh was threatened with being left out unless he cooperated with the Criminal Bureau of Investigation. Waugh soon changed tack, turned up and wasn't prosecuted.

Lara sympathisers claimed that the arrival of Miss Ward, a model who was voted Millennium Babe of the Year by a tabloid newspaper, had helped remove some of the worry lines on his forehead. One said, 'Her presence has been very beneficial to deal with these problems.' Others said that having her staying at the team hotel was disruptive and affected team spirit and a campaign went on for some days before the hullabaloo started to die down. Lara has had countless girlfriends, hardly any of them serious relationships because of his incessant travelling, and he was rather taken aback by the Press reaction. You would have thought that the sports-loving men of Australia would respect a man for having a fling with a young beauty rather than abusing him.

Lots of leading West Indian cricketers have had girls in their rooms in the past and it has been a part of cricketing life. Frank Worrell wasn't the only Test captain to have late-night soirees. Not many would want to go through a three-month tour celibate. The ECB spend a fortune on bringing the wives, partners and children of their players, particularly at Christmas time, but they are reviewing their generous policy after the Ashes whitewash of 2006/07 when England were annihilated by Ricky Ponting's side.

Roger Harper, the West Indies coach, said:

> Our policy allows the players to bring their girlfriends and wives on tour providing they have the permission of the team management. The strange thing is that during the first Test I didn't see the Press mention that many of the Australian team had their families in Brisbane. I don't understand why Brian is being singled out.

In recent years a crass celebrity culture has broken out in all strata of the media and cricket's previous code of not talking about girlfriends had eroded. Today, newspapers like the *Sun* appeal to their readers to come up with gossip about famous sportsmen and pay them large sums of money. Cricketers like Ian Botham, Shane Warne and others have been exposed.

Claire Ward, the thirty-three-year-old mother of Lynnsey, was delighted with all the publicity. 'As soon as Brian walked into Durham CCC's ground where Lynnsey was working as a receptionist it blossomed from there,' she said. 'They are really happy together.' But a year later the affair wasn't as lovey-dovey. Miss Ward came to the St Clair police station in Port of Spain to file a complaint claiming that Lara had attacked her on Boxing Day. After being treated for minor injuries at the Port of Spain General Hospital, she was advised to stay at the Hilton Hotel and not return to Lara's opulent home. A few days later, the row was patched up and she said, 'We had a misunderstanding but it was a lovers' tiff, just like a lot of couples have. I feel great being with him. He is my hero. I want to be with him forever. I would like to marry him but not just yet because I want to fulfil my career as a model.'

The affair finally fizzled out a few months later with Miss Ward selling a salacious story to a tabloid newspaper detailing their love-making. She was quoted as saying, 'He had the most incredible stamina and we would do it anytime, anywhere, any place, morning, noon and night. Three times a night was normal, six the record.' Wearing only a necklace, she was photographed for a picture across seven columns under a headline 'A Girl's Sex

Video Battle'. When the affair ended, she said, 'I don't regret not ruining his career. I loved him once but I don't want to be the next Paris Hilton or Pam Anderson.'

Mrs Charisse Rodriguez is a good friend of Lara along with her husband Scott, who played with him in the same school, and she said:

He's very respectful to women, a great, great gentleman. My mother loves him and she hasn't got a single bad word about him. I think most women in Trinidad think the same way. Of course there are some who disagree too. When he's on the losing side they'll 'pong' him [Trinidadian for beating someone down, usually with a humorous comment]. He'll be a great catch. He's looking for a wife and spreads himself around but playing cricket around the world it's very difficult to make a permanent relationship. Motivation is his secret. Right from when we first met him he knew he would make it, and make records and he's put cricket first. He went off the track a bit when he first went to play in England but he's grown up.

twenty-one

Back on High... Briefly

Going to the idyllic but troubled island of Sri Lanka in 2001/02 must have been paradise for Brian Lara. He set three records in quick succession with some of his most dynamic innings. His 688 runs in the three-Test series was the highest aggregate of any West Indian and only Graham Gooch (who scored 752 in 1990) has scored more. His 351 runs from two innings in the third Test played at the Sinhalese Cricket Club ground at Colombo was 53.83 per cent of the total runs scored by the West Indies in the match, beating J.H. Sinclair's record in 1899, and they were the most scored by a batsman on the losing side in a Test. He was back on the peak of the highest mountain, but in character with his turbulent life, he was soon plunged back to the foothills.

On 15 December, playing in an LG Abans Trophy ODI on the beautiful ground of Kandy in the hill region of central Sri Lanka, he was left writhing on the ground in pain with a dislocated left elbow after accidentally colliding with Marvan Atapattu while attempting a quick single. It was a freak accident. At first the local doctor thought it was a normal dislocation without complications. But Lara was in acute agony and had to be airlifted to hospital for X-rays. Ricky Skerritt, the team's highly articulate manager, said:

> We brought in another orthopaedic surgeon at a private hospital because Brian was complaining that his fingers were tingling and seemed somewhat swollen. This was the second opinion that we had planned to have all along anyway. After more X-rays and subsequent examination, a hairline fracture at the elbow joint was diagnosed, which had been dislocated out of position when the collision occurred.

It was a career-threatening injury and he was sent home business class. He spent the next four months out of action. His left arm was two inches short than his right and there were fears that he would never recover. He said:

In some way, I had to start from scratch again I couldn't play the wristy shots the way I wanted to and I had to live with that. Complications in my rehabilitation programme, as well as muscle contraction, caused by having my elbow in plaster, shortened the arm considerably. It was something I had to come to terms with. I was more mature as a person after that.

With regular stretching exercises, the arm went back to its usual length and normal service was eventually resumed.

Lara likes the low-bouncing, easy-paced pitches of Sri Lanka. No one, except a Brett Lee or a Shoaib Akhar, was likely to hit him on his helmet and Tony Cozier wrote in *Wisden* of his epic tour earlier in the year:

> The lasting memory will be of the sublime batting of Lara and especially his duels with the otherwise unstoppable offspinner Muttiah Muralitharan which added fuel to the argument that he was less comfortable bowling to left-handers. Lara had pulled out of the West Indies tour of Zimbabwe in June and his fitness was still in doubt barely a week before the party flew to Sri Lanka. But he said he was determined to raise his Test average, which had dropped below 48, back above 50. It was a monumental task in a short series but he coped with Muralitharan so easily that he achieved it during the final Test when he followed his first innings 221 with 130, carrying his aggregate to 688, an average of nearly 115.

Despite his heroics, Lara and his colleagues were blown away 3-0 and eighteen of them went for ducks. Muralitharan and Chaminda Vaas bowled 358 overs of the 566 which were bowled and captured 50 of the 60 wickets, an astonishing performance in humid, hot conditions. Skerrett and the selectors spent much of their time recruiting new players as Merv Dinnon was sent home for disciplinary reasons, Chanderpaul, Jermaine Lawson, Garrick and Ramnarine were injured or ill, and Wavell Hinds returned for a family funeral.

Barry Richards, recognised as one of the greatest right-handed batsmen in the history of the game, covered that series for television and he said:

> Brian's 221 and 130 were the best innings I saw from him. Murali dominated the first two Tests but when it got to the Third Test, he only took three wickets. Lara totally dominated him and it was awesome. He was coming down the pitch to hit him over extra cover and was never in any trouble. But Sri Lanka won all three Tests so it didn't help West Indies cricket. They were in

a bad state. Twenty years ago they had some great players, strong characters. By this time there was only one, Lara. So they let him run things and I don't think that benefited him or West Indies cricket. I got on well with him but you had others saying that he did this and that and the jury is out on him. But you can't dispute that he was a great player.

In one match in the LG Abans Trophy Lara helped a victory at the Premadasa Stadium with a rapid 60 in 53 deliveries in a day/night match and four days later he was going well on 24 when he collided with Atapattu and his tour was brought to a sad end.

There was pressure on him to play in the series against India in the Caribbean in April and May after missing the Pakistan series and it was billed Lara *v.* Tendulkar for the world crown. Lara had just regained the world number one ranking from Tendulkar after his successes in Sri Lanka but with a stiff elbow and probing Indian bowling he performed well below his usual standards. The same applied to Tendulkar. Lara came sixth in his side's batting averages in that mundane tour, with 202 runs, average 28.85, and two half-centuries. Tendulkar was fourth in the Indian averages with 331 runs, average 41.37, with one century and two half-centuries. He had three ducks (fourth, second and first balls) and Lara one.

The champions of East and West both had concerns about their physical state and neither of them was in confident mood. Tendulkar, after years of being harassed and chased, wasn't exactly a recluse but he no longer wanted to carry out the role of the Prince of Indian cricket. Lara, too, had tried to cut himself off from the general public, spending most of his time with his close friends who offered protection. Tendulkar's 117 in the second Test was a patient innings, not like his more flamboyant innings of earlier days.

Lara showed unusual signs of anxiety in his second innings in the second Test at Port of Spain when the West Indies were poised to go for a win. He was 40 not out on the final day with his side needing 145 with eight wickets in hand and the crowd was building past the 10,000 mark ready to rise to him. The loud music of the Trinnie Possee was blaring away – a traditional extra at all matches at the largest of the Test grounds in the Caribbean – when Lara stopped play and with a downward wave of a hand told them to keep quiet. To silence the Possee… well, it was unheard of! But they obeyed. Lara spent a further hour adding seven more runs and he was eventually out. India went on to win a close match by 37 runs. Six wickets fell for 39 runs with Chanderpaul stranded on 67.

The fourth Test was played on the customary St John's slab of light-coloured marble but Tendulkar contributed nothing, a nought, and Lara just four in a drawn, one-innings-apiece match which produced 1,412 runs. With Lara failing in the fifth Test at Sabina Park, scoring 9 and 35, Tendulkar moved ahead again with 41 and 86, yet the West Indies won by 153 runs to take the series 2-1.

Lara was back in Sri Lanka in September 2002 for the ill-conceived ICC Champions Trophy when the ICC introduced several experiments using more technology. They wanted to see if the cameras could spot an lbw or a disputed catch more accurately than the naked eye and their conclusion was that the responsibility for lbws should be left to the umpires. Venkat refused to allow the third official to rule on two lbw appeals and Asoka Ellewalakankanamge de Silva, the Sri Lankan umpire who was one of his country's best leg-spinners, upset the Kenyans when he gave Lara not out when most of the commentators thought that the ball touched the bat into the gloves of Collins Obuya. As Lara walks normally, the personable de Silva may well have made the right decision. Like most of the de Silvas who have played for their country, he boasts one of the longer names ever in Test cricket.

This close encounter, won by the West Indies by 29 runs, was played in distressingly demanding conditions and Lara had to call for treatment. He resumed, only to collapse, and when he was finally out for 111 from 120 balls, his fifteenth ODI century, he was transported to a hospital nearby with suspected hepatitis. Skerritt said, 'Brian had discoloured eyes, they were yellowy-orange, there was weakness and he was totally dehydrated.' The next day the patient was diagnosed as having hepatitis A and for the second time, he was evacuated back to Trinidad. But you couldn't call it an *annus horribilis* because his early batting was heavenly in the three Tests.

twenty-two

Shoot-out at the Queen's Park Oval

On 23 April 2003 Brett Lee bowled two bouncers at Brian Lara which some people rate as the most brutal pair of deliveries ever bowled in the history of cricket. Ian Bishop, the former Trinidad and West Indies fast bowler, now commentator and student, said, 'I haven't seen anything as fast as that and the Queen's Park pitch isn't renowned for its pace.'

Lee was twenty-six and in his prime. He was as fit as any fast bowler around and the heat, up to 35°C, and the humidity, up to seventy per cent, wasn't worrying him. He is one of the fairest and most motivated cricketers of his generation. He was bowling around 90-95mph and only Pakistan's Shoaib Ahktar has bowled faster. While Shoaib is always breaking down, Lee has kept going after overcoming his back problems earlier in his career. Lara was thirty-three and wasn't at his fittest and in the second Test at Port of Spain the West Indies were heading for another loss under his captaincy – 407 runs were needed for them to win.

Just before lunch Lara was approaching his century and he and Ramnaresh Sarwan had almost doubled the score to 210 for three when the players went in to down several pints of soft drinks and have a light lunch. In those intervening overs, Australian captain Steve Waugh brought Lee back and the battle between the fast bowler and Lara brought back memories of other cricketing bare-knuckle contests, like Michael Holding *v.* Geoff Boycott, Jeff Thomson *v.* Richie Richardson and Allan Donald *v.* Mike Atherton. But in many people's view, including the author's, the nineteen deliveries Lee hurled down the pitch at Lara exceeded those of the other three contests in terms of pace, sheer intimidation and fear. Lara's score was 94. It would have been a nervous time for many batsmen, but maybe not for Lara. Twice he was struck in the body and needed to rest until he regained his breath.

Sweat was pouring down his face under the helmet and he was staring ahead like a man under acute physical and mental pressure. Waugh's fielders were shouting encouragement… and Lara never flinched. The first brutish ball came straight at his face. He jerked his head back as he flung his body backwards, missing the ball by an inch, no more. Spectators sat up straight with the shock of it and some were heard saying 'whoah'. An inferior player might well have been laid out and put in hospital. A bad player could have been killed. Only a great player could escape the consequences.

Waugh recalled in his book *Never Say Die*:

> Bing [Lee] tried everything – lightning speed, yorkers, slower balls, bumpers – but the great batsman, on his way to his first Test century on his home ground, was up to the considerable task. He took fiery balls on the body, refused to hook with fieldsmen out on the fence, and withstood the barrage.

Lee's second thunderbolt delivery was just as fast and just as dangerous. Again Lara jabbed his head backwards, his back arching parallel to the ground. The ball flashed past, just missing his helmet as Adam Gilchrist caught it high above his head. It was another frighteningly near miss. The crowd were jabbering away. They knew cricket and they acknowledged that this was drama of the highest order. Lara's courage stood out: in that position many batsmen would try to grab a quick single to pass the responsibility to the batsman at the other end, in this case Sarwan. He never did. Twice he pulled short deliveries, not quite as quick, to the square leg boundary and each time a fielder saved the four. He was giving Lee a message – 'I've taken your best shots and I'm still out there punching away!'

On 99 he missed one chance to reach his century, failing to put a full toss away from Lee but in the next over Stuart MacGill bowled a full toss and he made sure of the coveted honour. It was remarkable that he took thirteen years before scoring a Test hundred, his twentieth, on his home ground. Almost everyone in the ground rose to their feet, cheering and stamping, waving flags, blowing horns and dancing to the music of the Trinnie Possee.

At a lunch given by Willie Rodriguez, the president of the Trinidad and Tobago Cricket Board, everyone in the room, including Wes Hall, Viv Richards, Joey Carew, Nigel Comacho, all experts, and the ambassadors from the USA, Canada and the UK, not so knowledgeable, all agreed that they had seen something of an extraordinary nature. 'That was one of the most exciting sessions I've ever seen,' said Carew, the former West Indian opener and Test selector who played a major part in Lara's early development. 'And I've seen a few.'

'You can't doubt that boy's guts,' said the US ambassador. Steve Waugh was quoted as saying, 'When Brett was spelled, wicketless, I had to think that the opposing captain had had the better of a fantastic duel. It was a thriller while it lasted, reflecting the fact that these two superb cricketers showed why Test cricket is called Test cricket.'

Lara survived nine lbw appeals, three in an over from MacGill, in his innings and it is generally acknowledged that being captain gives him the benefit of the doubt in the minds of some umpires. He might dispute that and still does. Later in his career he found himself the victim of a string of bad decisions. Were they down to understandable human error? Or did some officials not like him anymore? We will never know.

After lunch he appeared to be extremely tired and trying to cut a delivery from MacGill, the ball bounced over the head of Matthew Hayden and the first slip fielder turned and made the catch. He was dismissed for 122 out of the second innings' 288, and the West Indies soon collapsed, losing by 118 runs. In his first innings he had been on the way to a first Test century on home territory when Brad Hogg, who often troubled him during that series with his stock ball which moved away from the left-hander, bowled him round his legs for 91. Lara was dismissive of Lee's threat saying:

> He is very fast and keeps the ball at your head and this is Test cricket, you expect that. I am now looking forward to Glenn McGrath. I met him in the dressing room and I am glad to learn that his wife Jane is well again. Glenn keeps you probing outside the off stump and is definitely more demanding. I think McGrath *v.* Lara is definitely more decisive.

To talk about McGrath and be slightly critical of Lee was typical of Lara. He is an honest man and he tells it straight. He recognised McGrath as a great bowler, with far better figures than Lee, who is the more explosive and less consistent performer in Test cricket.

Geoff 'Henry' Lawson, the former Australian Test bowler, said of him:

> Fast bowlers are accused of many things when they aim to maim or dismiss. The vast majority is jealous piffle from those who purvey medium-pace pop, or offspin. Of all the very fastest through the years, Lee could almost qualify as the most polite. He is, by nature, easygoing, friendly and affable, and that is to teammates and opponents alike.

Lara has a good relationship with him. They respect each other.

As for the chuntering, sledgy McGrath, Lara understood the stresses in the McGrath household when Glenn's English-born wife Jane suffered three bouts of breast cancer. McGrath had a nasty reputation for making offensive comments to opponents and has softened in his approach after Jane's misfortunes. He told Ian Stafford of the *Mail on Sunday*:

> Jane is the one with the inner strength, not me. She has such a strong character. It's all been a massive leveller. Losing the Ashes isn't life and death. This thing won't get Jane, no matter how hard it tries, because of the person she is. She made a decision inwardly about surviving or not. She's chosen survival.

The couple have set up the McGrath Foundation to provide more breast cancer care in rural areas of Australia. When he scored runs against England extra money was raised by sponsors. It is a heartening story.

After the World Cup in South Africa that winter Lara was reinstated as West Indies captain for the first time since 1999, replacing Carl Hooper. He was appointed captain for the first two Tests, as though he was on probation. The first Test was at Georgetown where Hooper was born and brought up and he was furious. The Board's decision caused ructions all round the country and the angry Hooper refused to make a decision about whether he would be available to play. After three days, he declined to play under Lara, ending his Test career of 102 appearances at the age of thirty-six. They had been good friends in South Africa earlier in the year, often practising together and neglecting the younger players. Now a firm friendship was ended. Home supporters barracked Lara when he led the side on to the field but he silenced them with a knock of 110 in the second innings. Without McGrath, Waugh's bowlers still bowled out the West Indies twice on a slow, low-bouncing pitch to win by nine wickets. Lara was out hit wicket after an attempted sweep. Not many top-class batsmen get themselves out that way. Lara has a habit of moving his left foot back almost on to the stumps and that time he went too far.

Geoff Boycott wrote in his book *Geoffrey Boycott on Cricket*:

> Simple mistakes confirm to me that his judgement of length has all but deserted him. He now stays on the back foot to balls of fullish length. Against fast bowling his feet are finishing up in the wrong place, so he cannot get his body into the correct position. As the bowler gets into the delivery stride, Lara jumps back and plants his feet firmly. Forced to move again when the ball is delivered, he lets his head dip and he jumps back ever further. All this

movement puts him dangerously close to the stumps, and it came as no surprise recently when Allan Donald went around the wicket to him in South
Africa and Lara, for the first time in his career, actually trod on his stumps.

Bradman played 669 innings in his career and he was dismissed hit wicket
on only one occasion.

The only other time Lara did it was in the first innings of South Africa *v.*
West Indies at Newlands in Cape Town in the fourth Test. Boycott was right.
At the time, Lara was jumping around like a jack-in-the-box and he had a
bad tour. His mental state was in turmoil and Clive Lloyd, the manager, and
Malcolm Marshall, the coach, couldn't do much for him. As a self-made,
instinctive batsman he had to sort things out for himself and he has done
that on most occasions. He has reduced his foot movement and eliminated
his exaggerated jumps. The late and lamented Sir Conrad Hunte, the Moral
Rearmament preacher, coach and ICC referee, said shortly before he died
at the age of sixty-seven, 'I don't think Brian is seeing the ball as early as he
used to.'

Steve Waugh, reared from the same tough New South Wales stable as
McGrath, had six stitches in his left hand after splitting the webbing in the
Georgetown Test. Before the touring squad was picked, his position after
ten years as captain had been under severe pressure. He was left out of the
Australian one-day squad and it was an indication that his days as Test skipper were running out. But his determination and mental strength won him
a reprieve. Six days later, after damaging his hand, he picked himself for
the second Test and he recalled, 'I scored no runs, took no wickets and no
catches but I will still always fondly remember this match. We had retained
the Frank Worrell Trophy.' It became a favourite quiz question: 'Which Test
captain won a Test without scoring a run, taking a wicket or holding a
catch?' Lara was the loser that time and he might have learned something
from the steely Waugh.

Eight days later there was no sign of Lara being ill when the toss took place
on the slowest, grassless pitch Waugh ever encountered at the Bridgetown
Oval, Barbados, the real centre of West Indian cricket. Lara won it and to
the astonishment of everyone present he asked Waugh to bat. 'It was, at best,
an act of negativity which fitted West Indies' publicly stated aim of being
hell bent on a draw,' said *Wisden.* Lara and his selectors chose the least experienced bowling attack in the history of the West Indies. Tino Best, short on
height, high on confidence, and the 6ft 5ins off-spinner Omari Banks were
given debuts and Jermaine Lawson, the twenty-two-year-old fast bowler

from Jamaica who had a kink in his bowling action, and Vasbert Drakes, the experienced medium fast bowler, mustered just nine international appearances among them. Lawson was quick, in the nineties, and some Australian batsmen found difficulty in picking his deliveries. After the match he was sent back to the coaches to sort his action out.

The cricketing public of Barbados, which is almost the whole population of the island, were horrified. 'Worse than the charge of the Light Brigade,' said one observer. Lara was slated on the radio, on television and in the newspapers and not a single Bajan, unless they were deranged, agreed with his decision. It must have discouraged him and it showed in his face. His two centuries in the previous two Tests were overlooked and all the rage was directed at him personally. Late on the second day, when the Australians were heading to 605 for nine declared, he twice came off the field complaining of a virus. It was his thirty-fourth birthday and what a day not to celebrate. There were rumours sweeping around the old-fashioned ground that he had chickenpox, though this was later disproved. Whether he was genuinely ill or not, his behaviour starkly contrasted with the approach of Steve Waugh. Slowed down by a sore left arm and still troubled by his hand, the Australian captain battled his way to 115, his thirtieth Test hundred, passing Sir Don Bradman's record 29. He was dropped three times and physiotherapist Errol Alcott came out to give him treatment out in the middle. Lara's fielders missed a total of eight catches, a sure sign of mental fatigue. When an inspiring leader was needed later, he wasn't there. He was back in his bed at the team hotel.

At lunch on the third day he returned to the dressing-room and indicated that he would bat at eight, the lowest position he had held. The capacity 13,000 crowd gave him a generous reception when he came in and six overs from the end, after eking out 14 in seventy-nine minutes, he was given out lbw by umpire Venkat. Television replays clearly showed that the ball nicked the bat before it hit the pad. Lara showed no anger or resentment, only resigned acceptance. Except for very rare instances, he has always left the crease without complaint. Venkat made another mistake in that Test, with Sarwan the victim, but he said: 'No umpire can go through his career without making mistakes. I get around ninety per cent right and it's very hard to improve that percentage.'

In the second innings, Lara – 'now apparently restored to health,' said *Wisden* – came in at six and showed plenty of fight, helping Sarwan put on 93 before being lbw to Andy Bichel for 42. Waugh described his side's nine-wicket win as:

one of our best because it was difficult to prevail on such an unfriendly pitch. All the stress, emotion and effort that went into such an exhausting victory came to the surface when the team and its support staff gathered spontaneously on the pitch after we won, locked arms, and broke into a rendition of 'Under the Southern Cross.' We love to win!

Badly led since the great West Indies sides of the 1980s were on the wane, Caribbean cricket has yet to match the team spirit and comradeship of the Australians, but then the players come from different parts of the Caribbean and it is hard to create a proper unit. Lara and Waugh agreed on one thing: the slowness of the pitches. 'They don't encourage fast bowlers in this part of the world any more,' said Lara. Chin music, with bouncers flying past the helmet, is dying out and the chief thrill of traditional West Indian cricket, exemplified by bowlers like Andy Roberts, Michael Holding, Joel Garner, Malcolm Marshall, Curtly Ambrose, Courtney Walsh and the fastest of the lot, Sylvester Clarke, now lying in a grave in Barbados tended by Surrey cricket lovers, has almost disappeared. A new breed of young, quick bowlers has appeared but without more grass on the pitches and better prepared cricket surfaces, they will never match the feats of the greats.

The St John's Recreation Ground at Antigua has been one of Lara's favourite arenas, as one would expect, but he puts four others ahead of it: Queen's Park, Newlands, Melbourne and Lord's. From 9–13 May, he was chiefly responsible for yet another amazing comeback. He was in a mean mood. His side faced a 4-0 whitewash and his hold on the captaincy was again under threat. The Australians were chipping away at him with taunts and he decided to take the initiative and strike first. Lawson's questionable action was the subject of debate on the first day when the young bowler took a career-best 7-78 in the first Australian innings of 240 and their comments upset Lara and his younger players. There were a few pointed remarks in the middle and Lara took it personally. On the second day, when he came in at five with the score 73 for three, he had three confrontations with the Australian fielders before he faced his first delivery. The first was with Matthew Hayden, a veteran master of sledging, and Waugh positioned himself at short cover to keep up the fusillade of abuse. Umpire Shepherd intervened briefly to appeal for calm. Waugh said afterwards that Lara came out looking for a blue (a grand sledging contest) and that it was a way of firing himself up. 'He's done that before and it's worked for him,' he said. Waugh compared it to the way some heavyweight boxers or wrestlers, have to gee themselves up. Cassius Clay, now Muhammed Ali, was the real King of Sledge.

Brett Lee was the bowler and, now thoroughly steamed up, Lara hit his first ball for six over point. It brought gasps of astonishment and high glee. What a cheek! After the day's play, following Lara's dismissal for a rapid 68, Procter told the Press that he wouldn't be reporting the incidents:

> Both teams have been very competitive and we saw it with Brian Lara and Steve Waugh. David Shepherd, a very experienced umpire, stepped in at the right time, before anyone got carried away. There was a little gamesmanship which is great, that's what Test cricket is all about. It's being played in a very competitive spirit.

Brett Lee said, 'It's not backyard cricket, it's Test cricket.' Whether it is beneficial to the game is, however, debatable.

Soon the match developed into one of the greatest Tests of all time with the West Indies matching Australia's first innings 240 – the seventh time in the history of Tests that the first innings were exactly equal – and a strategic withdrawal of Lawson, ostensibly because of 'a back sprain', gave some impetus to the home side's bowlers, particularly Mervyn Dillon. A first-wicket stand of 242 by Justin Langer, 111, and Hayden, 177, effectively ended the West Indies' chances of preventing a whitewash, and a second innings of 417 left them a daunting task to win in more than two days. The world record for winning in the last innings was 406 set by India in Port of Spain in 1976 and with Lara bowled by MacGill for 60, going for a fourth six at 165 for four the chances of an upset were slim. Chanderpaul, handicapped by a fractured finger, and Sarwan both edged to their centuries as the Australians began to lose their composure. McGrath, who had returned to the side although he wasn't match fit, was becoming increasingly frustrated and Waugh was about to take him off. He was known as a tough man but he showed some compassion and gave him an extra over.

In Waugh's two-kilo book *Out of My Comfort Zone* he wrote:

> I sensed the telltale signs that the kettle was on the boil. My encouraging words were the ones that had inspired him in the past but when he delivered the last ball of another unsuccessful over, his emotions boiled over, resulting in a sledge a lunatic would have cringed at. He said 'What does Lara's cock taste like?' Why that question came out not even Glenn could fathom. Quick as a flash, young Sarwan barked back 'Why don't you ask your wife?' Well, the dog was off the leash, launching a machine gun offensive that essentially had nothing to do with Sarwan, who was merely the vehicle for Glenn to vent his spleen.

Out in the middle, McGrath asked Shepherd to do something about Sarwan's conduct. Shep, one of the most orderly and unemotional of the Test umpires, appealed to both men to stop insulting each other and get on with the game. Eventually, the game was restarted and neither the umpires, Shep and Venkat, nor the referee, Mike Procter, took any action, which was surprising. Waugh admitted that it had gone too far:

> Glenn had worries about his wife and he was under a lot of pressure at the time. Some angry words were picked up on the on-field camera and microphones and it offered a negative image that I concede cricket doesn't need. But these things happen. It gave a false impression about the relationship between the sides because we really got on well.

Afterwards, the two men made it up and McGrath said, 'If I had a time machine I would change the things I haven't been happy with and that was one.' When Sarwan was caught and bowled by Lee for 105, the contrite Australians congratulated him on his brilliant innings. Sarwan, an extremely personable young man, said, 'It shouldn't have happened but I apologised and we soon made it up.'

It was another case of Caribbean crowds overheating and causing unnecessary trouble. As Ridley Jacobs, the equable wicketkeeper, came in on 288 for five with the match evenly poised he was given out caught off his elbow off the first ball he received, a flier from Lee. Bottles were hurled on to the pitch and the proceedings were suspended for a minute or two. Chanderpaul kept cool only to lose his wicket on 104 at the start of the final day. West Indies needed 46 with three wickets remaining, and none of the batsmen were highly rated. Drakes, the nightwatchman, stuck it out to 27 and the twenty-year-old Omari Ahmed Clemente Banks helped to win an historic victory with a steadfast 47*. Peter Roebuck had brought him over to Devon the previous summer to open the batting for Budleigh Salterton, the other side of the county to Instow, the home of Shep. Lara was back on his pedestal, but only for a short time. Shep's autobiography failed to mention the Sarwan *v.* McGrath fracas: he isn't a man who breaks the unofficial code of 'what happens in the middle stays in the middle'! But, with skilled lip readers around, it is difficult to keep these rows out of the media.

Waugh's men won the first four one-day internationals, with Lara malfunctioning as he scored just 72 runs, to take their unbeaten ODI record to 21 games. Back at his home ground at Port of Spain, the Prince stirred himself, top-scoring with 80 and put himself on to bowl the last over, which cost 15, as his side ended a run of eleven successive ODI defeats. The West Indies won the next two to make it 4-3 against a tired Australian team. Lara specialises in making comebacks, both on the field and off it. In the first Test at Georgetown he was outdone by the local left-hander Chanderpaul who hit up exactly 100, the third fastest century of all time in terms of balls, while Lara made only 26. Viv Richards, with 56 balls against England in 1986, has the fastest, with Australia's Jack Gregory second with 67 against South Africa in 1921. Lara calmed the crowd who were still calling for Hooper, not him, as skipper, scoring a second innings 110 before his side went to victory by nine wickets. Geoff Boycott has continually called for Lara to open in one-day matches but he resists his pleas. Chanderpaul, the man with the black patches under his eyes (he claims he needs them for night matches, although he still wears them during the day!) has been opening recently instead and as Alvin Kallicharran, a former Test star from Guyana now living in England, said, 'He can play both games, quick scoring or doing the anchor role.' Chanderpaul and Lara aren't great friends but they respect each other.

twenty-three

A New World Record

St John's Recreation Ground, Antigua, 12 April 2004
B.C. Lara 400*
778 minutes, 582 balls, 43 fours, 4 sixes

Some people who experience powerful coincidences believe that they have extra-sensory perception and Brian Lara is probably numbered among them. For he set a world Test record 375 at the St John's Recreation Ground, Antigua, in 1994 and ten years later on the same ground, in the same month, against the same opposition and at almost the same time of the day, 11.43 a.m., he swept a single off the bowling of Gareth Batty to lift the record to 400 not out. The statistics were very similar. In 1994, his 375 came off 766 minutes (his 400* came off 778 minutes), took 538 balls (582 ten years later), hit 45 fours (against 43) but in 2004 he scored four sixes and was credited with a five. When he beat Sir Garfield Sobers' record in 1994 he hit the boundary off England's Chris Lewis at 11.46.

On 18 April 2004, he beat Matthew Hayden's record of 380 for Australia against a county-standard bowling attack of Zimbabwe at Perth on 10 October 2003 to give some credibility to international cricket records. Wearing a heavy vest because of a back strain, the left-handed opener Hayden had struck 11 sixes and 38 fours and batted 622 minutes, facing 437 balls. Of the Zimbabweans, only Heath Streak was Test class, Andy Blignaut, Sean Irvine and Ray Price had played part-time county cricket in England and the leg-spinner Trevor Gripper had played club cricket in the UK. Zimbabwean cricket was sadly disintegrating and its Test status was about to be suspended. If that record had stayed, it would have been a travesty. Lara sent a message to the soon-to-be-deposed record breaker: 'A standard has been set which we must strive to achieve to pass. I wish Matthew and his family peace and happiness.'

Bryan Davis gave an interesting insight into Lara's self-motivation:

> When he spoke to Hayden he wanted to continue the conversation but Hayden cut him short saying 'Thanks but I can't say more, sorry.' Brian wasn't too happy about that. It hurt him. He vowed he would win the record back and make sure it would stay a record a long time. He went past the 380 record but went on to 400* before declaring. These things motivate him.

One hundred and eighty-five days later, Lara was back on top of the pile. He gave an interview to Mark Nicholas saying:

> I have a lot to offer and one day it will come to the surface but I am too human to tell you in what capacity, for it will take its course. What happens, happens for a reason. What people say, they will say, but they are too judgemental. I need room, need space to be a catalyst. As things stand I have no control but a greater being will take me through.

Asked if that was a reference to religion, he said, 'Not directly, religion has often confused me but there is something there for sure, someone is watching over me.'

Lara was taken to church regularly by his parents and does not attend frequently now but he has belief, not just about life and a possible afterlife, but in the goodness of what he does, to raise it to the very highest level and persuade others to try to follow. He told Nicholas, 'the word is trust. People such as Sir Viv Richards and I are put in positions without the full backing of the people who put us there. It is all about trust, if they trust us we can do something, if not, well, then…'

A few days later he spoke about his father:

> He was my driving force. He watched every game I played in while growing up and when I was first called up for the Test in Port of Spain in 1989 I was left out on the morning of the match. Having previously suffered minor heart attacks, Dad had a fatal one of the first day of that game. He told one of my brothers to tell me not to worry anymore, that I had made it and would go on to great things. He is the person I miss the most.

Many great men were inspired by their fathers and he was lucky. So many West Indian fathers take little interest in their children, leaving the hard work to the mother, the grandmother or other relatives. Leasel Rovedas brings up their daughter Sydney alone but when Lara is at home he devotes as much time as possible to her and after his 400* she was asked what Sydney had said about it. She replied, 'She cried and cried, she cried her eyes out – tears of joy, of course. We both cried.' A proud Prime Minister of Trinidad, Patrick Manning, said, 'No amount of accolades can truly say how we feel about Brian Lara. This innings is symbolic of what we are capable of achieving when we harness our strength and persevere with grit and determination in pursuit of excellence.'

Not everyone welcomed the news. Andy Roberts, the fast bowler, former coach of the West Indies team who was in charge of the preparation of the supine pitch, said scathingly, 'It was a great achievement but he should have declared at lunch when he was on 390 rather than batting on afterwards because the game is bigger than any individual.' Ricky Ponting, who had a rough time in his early years before maturing into one of the outstanding Australian skippers, said, 'Their whole first innings might have been geared around one individual performance, and they could have let a Test match slip because of it. They ran out of time in the game. That's not the way the Australian team plays.' Mike Atherton said, 'I think Brian is quite statistically minded so it seemed likely he would have a go at getting the record back. This wasn't as pure an innings as the one ten years ago but considering the strain he has been under this is probably more of an achievement.'

Lara defended himself, saying:

> If I could chop my 400 four times, over the four Tests, in order to have won the series and celebrated with winning the Wisden Trophy, I would do so. I don't want to be remembered for records. We were facing a whitewash and preventing that was my priority. It was nothing to rant and rave about. I don't want to be remembered for records, I want to be remembered like Clive Lloyd and Sir Vivian Richards, who must have such joyous memories of series won and happiness through the team and all across the islands of the Caribbean. Cricket has been my life and it has given me so much.

He has given critics a hard time over the years because of his chaotic career and a few days before his 400* Colin Croft wrote in the *Daily Mail* calling for him to be sacked. 'Sport at this level is psychological warfare, not selfishness and cowardice,' he said. 'Lara failed in his first stint as captain and he has failed again now. Miserably. He has shirked responsibility and is presiding over the degeneration of the West Indies tradition.' At that stage, Lara's record as captain was only nine wins out of 32 matches, with 18 lost and five drawn. It was woeful but there were other former West Indian cricketers, including Clive Lloyd, Gordon Greenidge, Desmond Haynes, Lance Gibbs, who blamed the lack of work ethic and enthusiasm of the new generation of players, not the man in charge.

Tony Cozier wrote in the 2005 *Wisden*:

> In letters, columns and phone-in programmes, the home team was accused of lethargic practice routines, poor leadership, a lack of pride and passion, too much pay and too little hard work. There may be some truth in all of these things but the essential problems for Lara's side were brittle batting, fallible coaching and a lack of penetrating bowlers of sufficient experience and fitness.

Except for Lara, most of the players were receiving less than £100,000 a year, a quarter of the sums paid by the ECB. The West Indies Board, so short of money, had to put a levy of £160 on English supporters who wanted to purchase Test tickets and many of them bought their tickets from locals who saw it as a chance to cash in. More than half of the audience were English and the Barmy Army were backing their men but the average English cricket fan respects either side if the game is played properly. They aren't like football supporters, abusing the opposition.

There was some dispute among experts about which was the better innings, his 375 or his 400*. Ian Bishop, his former teammate, said of his 400, 'I think when you look at what has happened before in this series, his innings is certainly the best I've seen.' Michael Holding said, 'Even though this bowling attack is a lot better than the one in 1994, to say he is better now than then is probably pushing it a bit. But it is still a fantastic knock, especially from someone of thirty-four years old.' David Lloyd, the former England coach, said, 'It's a stunning effort, a remarkable achievement. Lara said before this series that he is a better player now than ten years ago and I think he is.'

England's attack at St John's in 1994 was Gus Fraser, Andy Caddick, Chris Lewis and Phil Tufnell, whereas ten years later they had four of the bowlers who went on to win the Ashes in 2005, Matthew Hoggard, Steve Harmison, Andrew Flintoff and Simon Jones, backed up with moderate offspin from Gareth Batty. Christopher Martin-Jenkins said:

> The West Indies prepared unexpectedly lively pitches for the first three Tests, playing into the hands of the best group of England fast bowlers to have

toured together for a long time. Impressively led by Steve Harmison, they were the best pack since the briefly invincible years of the 1950s and certainly since John Snow, Jeff Jones and David Brown led the attack on England's last triumphant tour in the West Indies in 1967/68.

Lara dislocated the little finger of his right hand after dropping a catch in the slip cordon in the first Test on a lightning-fast, white pitch at Sabina Park and that undoubtedly affected him in the opening three Tests. When he batted he found it difficult to hold the bat and he only made 23 out of his side's 311. He had to come off for a short spell and his deputy Sarwan took over and let things slip. On the second day, with England's batsmen trying to survive against the raw pace of twenty-two-year-old Fidel Edwards, the fast bowler from the north of Barbados, and his partner Tino Best, Lara was involved in an unseemly incident after umpire Billy Bowden warned him that too much short stuff might curtail the day's play. One observer said, 'Lara went loopy. He thought the light was just the same when his side batted the day before and England weren't given the same warning.' Bowden, a gentle soul, failed to report Lara's outburst otherwise the West Indies skipper could have faced ICC referee Mike Procter with a view to being docked some of his match fee.

Steve Harmison, so erratic in his younger days, and also latterly in the 2006/07 Ashes series, suddenly found the precise target with his 90mph risers on the fourth day and his 7-12 was the cheapest seven-wicket haul in Test cricket. Rob Smyth described it 'as a bolt from the blue' with the West Indies being shot away in their second innings for their lowest Test total, just 47. Lara lasted just five balls in his second visit to the crease. He was one of five batsmen who were out for a duck and England, who led by 28 on first innings, only needed fifteen balls to win by ten wickets.

Lara's captaincy soon came under examination by former players, TV experts and rum shop pundits all around the Caribbean and one of the more sober judges, the *Times* correspondent Christopher Martin-Jenkins, said:

> Just occasionally his tactics were unfathomable. He was polite and articulate with the media, supportive of his young team in selection meetings, and often very clever in his direction of them in the field but more baffling was his reluctance to use his fastest bowlers Best and Edwards in tandem when England were allowed to settle down while Gayle bowled 11 overs in succession.

Four days later, the wounded Lara was out on the Port of Spain pitch winning the toss in the second Test and his second dismissal for a duck in succession, the first time it had happened to him, was a pivotal moment in the series. Harmison hit him on his injured hand with a delivery which rose sharply off a capricious pitch – they tend to be capricious there these days – and his next ball was a fearsome bouncer which he fended into the hands of Ashley Giles at gully. Out for 208, the game followed a similar pattern with England gaining a lead of 111.

Lara lost his temper when Graham Thorpe was offered the light and his behaviour cost him half his match fee when ICC referee Mike Procter ruled that he was guilty of dissent. In the second innings, the stricken Lara dropped himself down to six and had reached eight when Darrell Hair gave him lbw from Harmison's cutting-back delivery. There was another row about light between the captains before play was resumed on the final day when England won by seven wickets. West Indies had now lost six matches out of seven on Lara's own territory and the highly respected Skerrett resigned, citing his inability 'to instil in the entire team the fullest understanding of their obligations on and off the field to the people of the West Indies'. It was a damning verdict on Lara as much as his players. Tony Howard, a fifty-seven-year-old off-spin bowler from Barbados who played one Test, took over as manager.

Lara moved himself back to three in the batting order in the third Test at Kensington Oval which was packed with British supporters and his misery continued. Surprisingly, Michael Vaughan put the West Indies in and despite dropping three slip chances, England bowled them out for 224. Lara was hoping for a major score but at 36 he was caught at gully by Mark Butcher off Andrew Flintoff, whose 5-58 was his first five-wicket haul. Edwards accounted for Trescothick, Vaughan and Butcher cheaply and only Graham Thorpe's unbeaten 119 kept England, with a first innings lead of just two runs, in the game. Again, Lara played himself in and then got out, caught by Vaughan off Harmison for 33, and his fledging batsmen folded yet again, all out for 94 with Matthew Hoggard taking his first Test hat-trick. An eight-wicket win was sealed within three days and the only consolation for Lara was that there were no demonstrations from the local fans. Their seats had been taken by the Brits.

When he arrived in Antigua, he told a massed press conference, 'The next five days are very important in terms of my future as captain. No captain, no team, wants to go down for the first time in their history as losing all their Test matches at home.' A year before, he had avoided the disaster against the

Australians. Two hundred and twenty years previously, Horatio Nelson, the senior captain of the British naval detachment, sailed into English Harbour in the hurricane season and he wrote in his diary, 'Were it not for Mrs Moutray [the wife of the Naval Commissioner in Antigua] who is very, very good to me, I should almost hang myself at this infernal hole.' There were no hurricanes in 2004 but if Lara had lost this engagement, one might have blown up, hurling him out of his job. Winning the toss, he chose to bat. The fourth ball he received when he came in at 33 for one brought an instantaneous mass appeal from the England side as he tried an impetuous drive. Geraint Jones and his fielders behind him were certain there was a faint touch to Harmison's delivery. Umpire Darrell Hair shook his head and afterwards the television replays confirmed his decision.

It gave Lara a jolt: cut out risk, play sensibly. He had had problems with his technique in the three preceding Tests and he told Nicholas:

> Maybe it was just a weak period. It's happened before and will happen again. In many ways I have an unstable technique, which from time to time needs unravelling. From the start of the series I felt the ball would dominate the bat and England bowled very well, perhaps better than we expected. As a principle, I work on keeping my head steady but have always had a bit of an up and down movement with that little jump across the crease as the bowler delivers. It is a question of degree and for a couple of weeks the degrees were slightly out.

At the end of the first day, the West Indies were 208 for two with Lara on 86 and Sarwan 46 and the master and his pupil put on 232 for the third wicket as the total leapt to 595 for five at the end of the second day. Lara was 313 not out and 227 of them came from him in the day – it was almost Bradmanesque. Ashley Giles had gone down with stomach trouble before the start which was why Batty was in the line-up, weakening an already deteriorating England strike force. Hoggard retired briefly from the field with the same symptoms and four other players followed during the day, overworking the substitute fielders.

Harmison bowled with great heart and dismissed Sarwan for 90 and he was the only bowler to force Lara to defend. Hair angered him by warning him about running down the pitch and Vaughan and Trescothick had to bowl twenty overs to take the pressure off the ailing main bowlers. Geraint Jones said he was amazed at Lara's physical state. 'He didn't look tired,' he said. 'And he wasn't pouring with sweat.' One of the reasons for that was because he was able to remove his helmet frequently. Vaughan had to over-use Batty, who eventually bowled 52 overs with figures of 2–185.

In 1994, Lara couldn't sleep and went off to a golf club before he resumed his world record breaking 375. Having gone through that barrier he was in a much more assured state when he woke early at the team hotel and there was an air of inevitability about the day. England's last card disappeared when Harmison was given his third and final warning for transgressing on the pitch and was banned from bowling again in the innings after sending down thirty-seven overs. He should have been a very relieved man. Lara had just advanced to 359. Ridley Jacobs stood guard with him in the middle, chiselling away to 107* in five hours and they put on 282, a sixth-wicket record.

Just before lunch, Lara danced down the pitch and lofted a straight drive over long on for six off Batty, passing 375 and equalling Hayden's six-month record of 380. Immediately, Batty lost his composure and his next ball, short outside leg, was swept down to fine leg to regain the record for the second time. And with his helmet in his right hand and his bat in his left, Lara jumped with joy. The sun was glinting off his shaven head and his huge smile showed up his near-perfect teeth. Derek Pringle said:

> The series is dead but rumours of the demise of Lara and West Indies cricket have clearly been exaggerated. West Indies supporters are an excitable lot at the best of times but the tumult that followed Lara's reclamation of his record was not just joy, it was the release of years of frustration in which the left-hander has carried the batting more often than anyone can remember.

The individual Test record has changed hands ten times and Lara is the only person to hold it twice. The majority of supporters were English and they rose with their polite applause but on the popular sections flags of all the Caribbean countries were waved, hooters hooted, the music machines were turned up at full pelt and the joyous and noisy shouts and screams swamped the boring, incessant chants of the Barmy Army. First he shook hands with Jacobs and they embraced. Then he shook hands with Vaughan and his players and, as in 1994, he bent down to kiss the pitch, which by that time was rather dusty. There was no wild stampede out to the middle and Andy Roberts was one of the first to come on after intimating to his fellow Antiguans that no mischief would be allowed on the square. Hosts of police gathered as Antigua's new Prime Minister, Baldwin Spencer, strolled out to congratulate the national hero. After a jig of honour around the square, play resumed.

He wanted 400 before he declared and duly got it. After almost thirteen hours at the wicket, Batty bowled just outside the leg stump and, kneeling on his left knee, he nurdled the ball down to fine leg for a single which brought up the immortal 400th run. He played exactly the same shot when he reached his 9,000th Test run in his 115 against South Africa at Newlands. He said at the time: 'and I've reached the target faster than the others.'

West Indies declared on 751 for five, the highest total England had conceded in 820 Tests, beating the 729 for six at Lord's against the Australians. If he had caught Flintoff off Sarwan when he started to throw the ball up and dropped it, the West Indies might have won. Flintoff was on 27 and batted nearly five and a half hours over his unbeaten 102 in England's first innings 285. He was missed three times. In the Clive Lloyd era, their fielders hardly missed a single catch. Without a spinner, they failed to make inroads into England's second innings which dawdled along to 422-5 before time was called.

Lara still had plenty of energy afterwards, conducting long interviews with radio, television and Press. He said:

My goal and the team's goal is to get our cricket back on top. One individual can't do that. We have to see team performances. People will rejoice in the Caribbean because of my innings. But I think it will be more appreciated if we can get a collective effort from everyone. Achieving what I did here is great for me personally but I also hope it brings the team much closer and even brings the islands closer together.

Maybe my leadership has been under scrutiny and maybe it still is. But as a batsman I back myself all the time to go out there and get runs. I learnt from the older heads about what cricket truly meant to our people, about the pride and the passion at every corner, about representing the West Indies in the right way. Though it is only a game, it becomes more than that here and is sensationalised perhaps even beyond its place. The modern player does not see it the same way, which is not that he does not regard it as a great honour to play for the West Indies because he does. It is just that, well, in those days the players had to pay for their own tickets. Nowadays they get paid for every item they wear on their body. It is different, that's all, and not really better for it.

twenty-four

Was He Really Out?

Brian Lara came out with an odd comment when he was given out caught behind by Geraint Jones off the bowling of Ashley Giles in the first npower Test at Lord's on 23 July 2004. Obviously he thought the ball came off the pad, not his bat, and he lingered at the crease before returning to the pavilion with just 11 on the electronic board. He may have risked another ICC penalty so he asked Imran Khan, the press officer of the West Indies team, to put out a short statement to clarify his position. This is what he wrote: 'I still find it impossible not to walk when I know I'm out.' What he was saying constituted dissent and some referees might have taken action but Rajan Madagulle, the compassionate former Sri Lanka batsman, made a sensible decision. He knew that Lara is one of the very few cricketers who walk when he knows he is out and with the ICC trying to further their Spirit of Cricket philosophy around the world, there is a need for more to follow Lara's example. If every batsman was honest about tricky decisions, umpires would have an easier life, the number of runs would be lower and the balance between bat and ball would move back towards the bowlers. Over the years, pitches have been made flatter to occupy the five days of Tests, for economic reasons, and the bowlers have suffered as a result.

Lara was skippering England for the third time in England and he hit a low trough in the Tests, losing by a margin of 4-0 but he rose up at the end of the season to lead his men to victory in the fourth ICC Trophy, beating England by two wickets in the final through the all-round talents of his younger players. But there was plenty of criticism at the start of the tour. It was said that Lara had little confidence in his young players and left them in awe of him and it was also claimed that he often travelled in a silver Mercedes to matches instead of going in the team's garishly decorated coach. But, by the end, his youngsters were backing him and their unexpected success lifted the spirits of cricket lovers throughout the Caribbean.

As an occasional gambler, he took a punt on asking England to bat first at Lord's on an overcast morning and with the sun soon emerging, he lost his betting chips. At the end of the first day, Michael Vaughan's side were 391 for two, almost unheard of, and next day they eventually finished up on 568 with the skipper, Robert Key and Andrew Strauss all scoring centuries. Vaughan set his opponents an improbable target of 478 in around 130 overs and won by 210 runs. It might have ended differently had Lara not charged down the pitch and been bowled by Ashley Giles for 44. His supporters gave Giles the credit for bowling one of his best ever deliveries – fizzing back and squeezing the ball through the gap.

Giles was on target again in the second Test on his home ground at Edgbaston, taking 9-122 following his 9-160 at Lord's as the West Indies went under, losing by 256. Today, too many sceptics call him an ordinary bowler with little spin to offer but in that summer but he had class. Flintoff, too, displayed class of the highest order, especially with the bat as he pummelled 167 in England's unmatchable 566-9. Coming in at four with his side 12 for two, Lara was greeted with warm applause around the ground when he reached fifteen and rival skipper Vaughan went up to congratulate him. As a statistical man he must have been surprised because he needed 115, not 15, to become the fourth Test player to 10,000 Test runs. It was a practical joke and he soon recognised it with a broad smile. Five short of his century, he slashed to slip and was caught. The players' dining room, next to the dressing-rooms, is used for Press interviews after the day's play and Lara had a doleful look when he appeared there after the presentations. Ten years ago, after his 501*, they had difficulty in stopping him talking. Now he was speaking in a soft voice and he stiffened as someone asked him whether he would resign. He dismissed the idea and left.

There was a glimmer of light for him when he won the toss and decided to bat in the third Test at Old Trafford. A declared total of 395 for nine was defendable even though he failed again, being bowled by Flintoff for nought. Lara managed to pass 10,000 runs in his 111th innings – much faster than the previous three batsmen, Gavaskar, Border and Steve Waugh – before Flintoff dismissed him a second time, this time for seven. Flintoff was probably at the peak of his career at the time; Lara was at one of his lowest points. His weird fielding placements were being criticised and Jonathan Agnew described his side as 'the worst West Indian team I've seen'. To add to the gloom, Lara was fined forty per cent of his match fee for presiding over a slow over rate and his team were fined twenty per cent of theirs.

Fazeer Mohammed, one of the travelling West Indian journalists, called his team 'a ragtag bunch masquerading as Test players' as England wound up the 4-0 whitewash in three days with a ten-wicket win. Dropped catches helped England post 470 and Lara scored almost half the runs in the humiliating reply of 152. Writing in *Wisden*, Fazeer reported:

> Crashing 14 fours in his 79 off 93 balls, he gave glimpses of his masterful best but such was the internal turmoil that he seemed unaware there was still one batsman to come when he was eighth out, to a top-edged hook off Harmison. His confusion probably owed something to the absence of Dwayne Smith, recalled to strengthen the batting but visiting a nearby hospital with a side injury. The capitulation Lara had witnessed at the other end was bewildering enough anyway. The entire innings lasted less than 37 overs.

Chris Gayle blazed away to a defiant century off 80 balls but a second-innings total of 318 only left England needing only one run to win. When Lara was out for 15 the crowd rose to applaud. They all thought that this was his final curtain at the Brit Oval as a Test player but he has proved them wrong. His captaincy was under debate again after losing 23 out of the 40 Tests in which he was in charge, one more than Border's tally of 22 out of 93 matches. Without trained, fit troops, even Napoleon lost a few battles, including Waterloo.

With their miserable ODI record, England failed to reach the final of the NatWest series in high summer and the West Indies lost easily in a rain-ruined final against New Zealand. Lara and his selectors chose nine batsmen and only managed 159 in 41.2 overs against New Zealand's 266 off 49.2 overs. Half the audience had gone home when the last rites were performed at 8 p.m.

Two months later, the West Indies were back in England to play in the ICC Champions Trophy and it gave them the chance to win their first global ODI tournament. They were rated as outsiders but to everyone's surprise they won through to the final and beat England by two wickets. Three days earlier, Lara had failed to pick up a short delivery from Pakistan's Shoaib Akhtar in the semi-final and was painfully struck in the side of the neck and had to retire on 31. He wanted to bat on but his head was spinning and he went off. As he came in to start his innings, Shoaib said to him, 'I am going to kill you.' Later, the Pakistan bowler called it a joke between friends. Lara had the last laugh, though, as Pakistan's 131 off 38.2 was abysmal and the West Indies won by seven wickets with 21.5 overs remaining.

The tournament was badly organised and the idea of trying to play highly competitive cricket when darkness was closing in at 6.30 p.m., as it was on the day of the final, 25 September, was plainly dangerous.

The West Indies needed a lift after two damaging hurricanes, Ivan and Jeane, had caused widespread damage to some of the islands and when Ian Bradshaw struck the winning run in near darkness with two balls remaining, every player in the squad raced out on to the Oval pitch hugging and kissing each other in rapturous joy. Lara played a minor role, scoring 14 in his side's 218 for eight and holding a brilliant low, one-handed catch off Flintoff at mid-wicket for his 100th Test catch. The young all-rounders Brayshaw, 34*, from Barbados and Courtney Browne, 35*, born in Lambeth, took the decisive winning roles in an exciting finish.

Morale zoomed up for a while until the following May when Lara's side struggled to beat Bangladesh on their first tour to the Caribbean. Out-scored in the first innings at Gros Islet in St Lucia, the Test newcomers were able to declare in their second innings and Lara was so upset that he promised to resign as captain if his side failed to win at Sabina Park in the other Test. He had criticised the selectors, administrators and ground staff in a newspaper column, displaying a somewhat churlish approach towards the guests from the Subcontinent. But there was no danger of him losing his job – the West Indies won by an innings and 99 runs.

Between November 2003 and February 2004, his erratic side had a big fall, almost losing to Zimbabwe in the first Test and losing 3-1 to South Africa. They were outclassed by the Proteas but Lara topped the averages with 66.37 from 531 runs including 202 at Johannesburg and 115 at Newlands. He was still holding the side up and the strain was showing.

twenty-five

The Prince Beats Allan Border's Record for Test Runs

	Tests	Runs
B.C. Lara	121	11,187
A.R. Border	156	11,174

On a cool day at the Adelaide Oval, a batting paradise, on 26 November 2005, Brian Lara passed Allan Border's record of Test runs at 11.22 a.m. He had completed a full house: the highest Test score, the highest first-class score and the highest aggregate of Test runs. Will anyone match that? One doubts it. Deryck Murray said:

> Brian's sheer mental capacity, and his concentration, is unbelievable and I can't see anyone beating his 501 and 400. Each record was almost predictable. He set himself to do it and he had the advantage of playing in a weak side. If he had been playing in a good one he wouldn't have had the chance to play these long innings. Other good players would make big contributions and the captain would declare.

Border described him as 'a genuine genius. I would rank him as one of the three best batsmen in the world. I have had the pleasure of seeing him play a lot of cricket and there is no doubt about that.' The gritty Border, not a man to overuse praise, set the previous record on 23 February 1993, beating Sunil Gavaskar's 10,122 runs from 125 Tests at an identical average of 50.56. A month earlier, Lara burst on to the stage with his 277 at Sydney. Now the two men were on the field at Sydney and fifteen years and 213 innings later, Lara had taken his record. There was another meaningful link: at the age of fourteen Lara was at the Queen's Park Cricket Club ground at Port of Spain when he saw Border defy the West Indian fast bowlers Joel Garner, Malcolm Marshall and Wayne Daniel in March 1983 when he eked out 98* out of 255 and 100* from 299 for nine in nearly eleven hours to gain a draw. He said, 'As a West Indian, I wanted him out but I admired his fighting spirit and it was a tremendous effort. He was an icon for me and his spirit was in me from the first day I played Test cricket. Thank you, AB!'

Sadly, Border's career ended in bitterness. He wanted to play 100 Tests but the selectors, showing a ruthless streak, decided to end his 93-Test span at the age of thirty-eight. He is the same height and build as Lara but their personalities are totally different. The New South Wales left-hander, born in Cremorne, typified the Australian approach to cricket – remorseless, relentless, forsaking any possible risk and acquiring his runs like a machine that hardly ever broke down. He brought results but not a lot of fun. Like Lara, his ambition was to lead his country. The author remembers edging a Border full toss for two in a benefit match in 1977, when the nineteen-year-old future captain of Australia was guesting for Gloucestershire's Second XI. He clearly didn't like it. Two runs had come off his figures and he wasn't even a proper bowler. When he came in, he patiently built a sound fifty which failed to provoke much applause. He was firstly a winner, not someone eager to please.

Lara has been the opposite, an extravagant entertainer who has spectators jumping to their feet in joy. One minute he will square cut with exquisite timing through the gaps on the off side, perfect a series of rippling extra cover drives, played with awesome power and then, to change the mood like in a piece of classical music, he will gently deflect a leg glance down to fine leg. West Indians have an expressive phrase to describe a Lara shot which beats the field: 'Not a man move.' The shot to fine leg was the one he used to reach 400* and he beat Border's record with a similar shot, a caressed paddle sweep shot to the same area. His virtuosity is unequalled: he is the king of classical cricket which is why the purists love him as well as the rank and file who cherish his genius. Glenn McGrath was the bowler, his prickliest adversary. After the second Test at Hobart, McGrath said that Lara was much shakier at the start of his innings now he was thirty-six. The Australians love to rouse their opponents and their Board encourage it whereas the ECB tutor their Test players to confine themselves to 'safe' comments which won't produce controversy.

Not for the first time, a criticism from an opponent gave Lara the spur to go on and play a memorable innings. He didn't look nervous as he came in at 19 for two and played himself in with the utmost caution. He was given the benefit of an lbw appeal by Pakistan umpire Aleem Dar at 15 and Peter English wrote in his report in *Wisden*: 'Lara was unperturbed and the exhibition, which included 22 fours, was one of unbending concentration as he showed satisfaction in sweating for runs instead of merely waving his magic wand.' In short, it was more Border than Lara. At the end of the opening day he was 202★ having scored fifty-seven per cent of the runs. His eighth double century passed Walter Hammond's seven and only Bradman's 12, probably taken off some less challenging attacks, lay ahead. He pulled Brett Lee for four to pass 200 and looked up to the sky. Television viewers could detect him saying 'thank you' to the Lord, and possibly to Bunty.

When the record was achieved, most of the Australian fielders came up to him to shake his hand. McGrath had a mite of consolation, bowling him for 226 out of 405 – the next highest scorer was Dwayne Bravo with 34 – and if Lara was planning to take a few naps he was soon disappointed. He did a round of interviews lasting for almost an hour and he started by mentioning his father:

> He was my number one. From when I was six or seven he lived vicariously through me. It is special here, with Allan Border being an Australian [Border wasn't there, he was watching his son in an under-11 match in Brisbane]. The reception was excellent and it is touching to be appreciated by a country I have had great battles with. I've had my ups and down but I've stuck it out.

If any proof was needed that he was Australia's greatest opponent it came from more of his stats: his 226 was his ninth century, including three doubles, in 31 Tests against them – the other two were 277, his early favourite, and 213, which set up victory in Kingston in 1999. But the innings some experts thought was his finest was in Barbados where he scored 153★ to pluck an almost impossible victory with 311 for nine on the last day. The other ten players contributed only 130. Researcher Philip Bailey revealed that Lara now has another record, slightly obscure: he is the only batsman to have scored three double centuries while being on the losing side, the 226, 221 in Sri Lanka in 2001/02 and 202 against South Africa in 2003/04. Fourteen batsmen in total have achieved this feat and Lara is second behind Ricky Ponting who recorded 242 against India at Adelaide in 2003/04.

In the Adelaide Test, Australia raced to 428 and with the aid of two grossly bad umpiring decisions, Lara's side were bowled out for 204 and beaten by seven wickets. Second time to the crease, Lara was stupendously caught by Matthew Hayden at slip off the bowling of Shane Warne for 17. An alert statistician noted that it was the first time Test cricket's record wicket-taker had dismissed the highest run-getter since 1886/87 when England's Arthur

Shrewsbury faced Australia's 'Demon' Fred Spofforth. Lara was presented with a framed picture of himself by Richie Benaud and the South Australia Cricket Association awarded him life membership. That meant a lot to him. Bradman was a long-time member and he lived in Adelaide for most of his life.

The Test series was reduced to three matches from the usual five and though the decision upset the West Indian authorities, the players weren't too unhappy as they avoided an authentic whitewash. Lara was the victim of two dreadful decisions, undermining the credibility of the ICC neutral umpires concept. In the first Test at Brisbane he was given lbw by South African Ian Howell for 30 when the replays showed that the delivery pitched outside the line of leg stump. The ensuing collapse led to a comprehensive 379-run defeat. Another mistake by a South African umpire, the more experienced Rudi Koertzen, gave him caught by Adam Gilchrist for 12 as the ball brushed the pad, not his bat. Each time, Lara walked off without a fuss but manager Tony Howard and Australian coach Bennett King complained to the ICC and the umpires' committee and the ICC admitted there had been mistakes.

On the eve of the match, Lara learned from Dwight Yorke that the Trinidad and Tobago soccer team, the Soca Warriors, had qualified for the World Cup finals in Germany and when fellow Trinidadians Dwayne Bravo, 113, and Denesh Ramdin, 71, put on 182 they dedicated their stand to the football team. 'Our goal is to play for fourteen and fifteen years to ensure that when Brian and Shiv Chanderpaul and the senior guys move on, we can turn things round,' they said. Shiv averaged only 14.50 and was relieved of the captaincy. Trinidad are taking over from Barbados as the nation to provide the most Test players for the West Indies. They have a blossoming training scheme which is beginning to develop well-adjusted and talented players.

Lara was captain for the VB ODI series that followed and was victim to a third cruel umpiring decision in a no-result game against Australia at Brisbane. He played and missed and there were appeals for a catch behind off the belligerent bowling of the revived Brett Lee, who was voted Man of the Series. Sir Gary Sobers said, 'I have lost count of the number of bad decisions Brian has had in his career, it must be fifty or more.' The West Indies won only one match and failed to qualify for the final. Australia beat Pakistan 2-0 in close matches. They also complained to the ICC about the umpiring, calling for two neutral umpires instead of one in ODIs.

twenty-six

One Last Strike and Out for the Rebel Leader

Before the 2005 tour of Australia, Lara was reinstated as captain after playing a major role in leading another cricketing war, this time over contracts, which proved to be one of the most damaging episodes in the history of West Indies cricket. Former Test all-rounder Willie Rodriguez, the only international sportsman to represent Trinidad in both cricket and football and a man who devotes much of his time, unpaid, to serving the interests of both sports, said:

> It was a very nasty war but I don't know why it got as bad as it was because these superstars like David Beckham and the American stars have lots of individual contracts themselves while they were still representing their country. Beckham's biggest one was with Vodafone while Real Madrid's shirt sponsor was Siemens before he went to the US. It should have been resolved but it is still dragging on.

The issue of image rights in cricket first erupted in India a few years ago and it is still causing immense problems. Technically, sports governing bodies can capitalise on the image of players so long as they do not breach existing contracts or trademarks. The major snag for the West Indies Cricket Board was that they were budgeting a loss of US$7 million at the end of September 2005 and needed every dollar. Tony Cozier wrote, 'They found themselves between many rocks and many hard places.'

The sad saga started a year earlier, just after the West Indies won the Champions' Trophy in England. The West Indies Board decided not to renew their contract with Cable and Wireless after eighteen years and Digicel, owned by Irishman Denis O'Brien, which had moved into the Jamaican mobile telephone market, bid £10.5 million for the rights to market the Test squad over the next five years. Cable and Wireless, with most of their business being conducted in the West Indies, were distinctly unhappy. There may not have been a problem if the WICB had not also sold Digicel the players' individual image rights. The players refused to sign theirs away without compensation. The West Indies Players' Association, headed by their president Dinanath Ramnarine, the former West Indian spin bowler, issued a damning press release and the row turned into a series of public wrangles which brought no credit to the sport in that part of the world. He wrote, 'We are facing a tyrannical and despotic WICB that has suspended its discretion, jettisoned all reasoning and is hell bent at all costs to do the bidding of its sponsor.'

Lara had been contracted to Cable and Wireless since 2002 and was wearing their advertising motif. In 2004, he signed a contract to extend it for a further four years and C&W signed up seven other players: Ramnaresh Sarwan, Chris Gayle, Dwayne Bravo, Devon Smith, Fidel Edwards and Ravi Rampaul. In his report in *Wisden*, Cozier wrote:

The Players' Association objected to clauses relating to the Digicel sponsorship in the team's contracts for a one-day series in Australia, claiming that they infringed players' rights to sign individual endorsements with other companies, and it advised members not to sign. The dispute was eventually referred to the cricket sub-committee of the Caricom [Caribbean Community] Governments. A provisional ruling enabled the WICB to pick its best team for the tournament in January, though they won only one of their six matches and failed to reach the finals.

But the issue resurfaced once the squad returned home from Australia, leading to the end of Lara's second stint at the helm. When six players were disqualified from selection for the First Test against South Africa because of their individual contracts with C&W, Lara withdrew in protest. Though he had not been banned because his deal pre-dated the sponsorship switch, Shiv Chanderpaul, the vice-captain, took over.

C&W freed its players of their obligations so that they were eligible for the Second Test. But, even after their reinstatement for the rest of the home season, the issue would not go away. When the Board named thirteen players to tour Sri Lanka in July, ten, including Lara, withdrew. Obliged to fulfil the ICC's schedule, the Board hurriedly assembled replacements, mostly from an 'A' team already touring Sri Lanka. As it was, eight members of the 'A' team joined the Test squad the day after signing a collective declaration refusing the summons to do so, which created such internal wrangling that the management felt obliged to move the two teams into separate hotels. Chanderpaul was the only one of the new squad with more than ten Tests to his name.

Back in the Caribbean, there was a public war of words between C&W, who accused the WICB of unfair practices, and Digicel. In what was seen as an unusual sign of openness on the Board's part, a three-man commission, chaired by retired Judge Anthony Lucky, was set up to review the negotiations that led to the change of sponsors. Their 50,000 word report, delivered in August, criticised the WICB and particularly their then president Teddy Griffith, for their handling of the matter and concluded that C&W had been unjustly treated. But it was compromised when Lucky's fellow commissioners disagreed with his contention in a separate report saying that the Digicel contract was legally flawed. The Board adamantly rejected several of the Commission's points, but by then Griffith had resigned for 'personal and family considerations.'

He was succeeded by Ken Gordon, a seventy-five-year-old media executive and former Minister in the Trinidad and Tobago Government who had a high reputation in the corporate world but little cricketing background. Gordon soon faced yet another resignation and another crisis. In September, Rawle Brancker quit as chairman of the World Cup organisers less than two years into the job, citing his frustration over differences with his chief executive Chris Dehring and a lack of support from Griffith and other Board members. Controversially, Gordon appointed himself to the position and added Griffith to the new Board.

Not surprisingly, West Indies continued to falter on the field. In the calendar year 2005, their record was eight defeats against one win (at home to Pakistan) in 11 Tests. It was even direr in ODIs: 15 defeats, with an unprecedented run of 11 including all eight at home to South Africa and Pakistan, against just two victories. It was a nightmare for the new Australian coach Bennett King, the first foreigner to hold the post. He and his all-Australian support staff of assistant coach, physiotherapist and fitness trainer never knew from series to series which players they would be working with, if any: more than thirty players represented West Indies during the year. The discontented players finally returned to the fold for the Test series in Australia in November, 2005, after the warring parties agreed to turn to the ICC and the Federation of International Cricketers' Association to settle the dispute.

Tim May, the FICA chief executive, said, 'I am surprised the situation ever arose, given that there were very similar conflicts around the World Cup and Champions Trophy.' The Board risked a US$1 million fine from the ICC if tours were cancelled and Dr Keith Mitchell, the Prime Minister of Grenada, intervened to stave off that threat. Justice Adrian Saunders, the independent arbitrator appointed by Mitchell, found in favour of the players. He ruled that they had the right to pursue endorsements as private citizens so long as they did not use the WICB or its logos to market products. Lara wasn't blamed in this affair. All he was doing was supporting his senior players to force a conclusion to the impasse. He was neither hero nor villain.

The absence of Lara in the tour to Sri Lanka in July denied the home supporters another rousing contest between the world's best batsman and the world's leading doosra and off-spin bowler. Muralitharan was back after eleven months following his shoulder operation and he captured 17 wickets in the two Test victories over a West Indies Second XI. The earlier tour by South Africa, starting in late March, was still soured by the contracts war and by racial disputes among some certain players but a pseudo-West Indian team, shorn of Lara and five of his compatriots, should have won the first Test at Georgetown after Wavell Hinds, 213, and Chanderpaul, 203, compiled Lara-like totals in a declared innings of 543. Jacques Kallis, who averaged 98 in the four-Test series, denied them with an unbeaten 109. Lara and his disciples returned for the Test in Port of Spain and they were spanked by eight wickets by Graeme Smith's side. After an eight-month furlough caused by the Digicel row, a refreshed Prince came in at 12 for three and retired five hours later with 159* out of a first innings 281 for six. Next morning an expectant Trinnie Possee were about to turn up the volume to honour another double when Andre Nel clipped his off stump on 196, his highest Test score at his home ground.

He trod the same path in the third Test at Bridgetown, coming in at 12 for three, and almost reached the same total, 176, rivalling the brilliance of his 153 against the Australians in 1999 on the same lucky ground. Trelford Vine wrote in *Wisden*, 'Again, Lara delivered an innings that will be remembered forever by those who saw it.' Those watching at the end saw a familiar conclusion: a West Indies collapse, beaten by an innings and 86 runs. Vine beautifully captured the mad-eyed Nel with the description: 'The maturing galumpher hissed, glared and bowled his way to a career-best 10-88.' He went on to say that Nel had got rid of Lara seven times out of the previous eight encounters, though seven of the innings produced 626 runs from Lara's MRF bat.

Lara was seen having a few drinks with the South Africans after the close of play but relations were strained later when Dwayne Bravo accused Graeme Smith of making a racial comment to him. Jeff Crowe, the ICC referee, found there was no evidence to support Bravo's assertion but in the second innings Wavell Hinds tossed in a head-high beamer at Smith at medium pace and spat at the ground to express his disgust. Crowe fined Hinds his match fee.

Several incidental but nevertheless fascinating records were recorded in the final Test at Lara's old glory ground at St John's, none by him. They included the highest number of centuries in a Test, eight, including Chris Gayle's 317, the fourteenth highest individual total in Tests and the fourth instance in Tests where all eleven bowlers were used. Two of the four occasions were at St John's and bowlers all around the world were able to celebrate the digging up of the square at the end of the season, ready for a new, livelier square and a redeveloped ground for the start of the first World Cup to be held in the Caribbean.

Three days after the end of the fifth and final ODI, which concluded in a whitewash for Smith's combative players, Chanderpaul presided over a 0-3 ODI defeat at the hands of Inzamam-ul-Haq's Pakistan side. Lara didn't play in these three matches. He wanted a break, ready to continue his pyrotechnics at his favourite cricketing theatre, Kensington Oval, which was to be renovated in the coming months. He didn't let down his audience, careering past the hundred mark off only eighty-eight deliveries, with the final two balls being hit for sixes. His 130, his twenty-ninth Test century, bettered Pakistan's first innings of 146 and the West Indies won by 276 runs, their first win for nearly a year. Attendances were poor in the series which ended 1-1. The public were becoming fed up with the Digicel shenanigans.

In the other Test, at Kingston, Lara scored 153, a fourth century in five matches that took him past Bradman's total of 29. He might well have gone on to a double until a lethal lifting delivery from Shabbir Ahmed reared up into his face and was caught by wicketkeeper Kamal Akmal. Shabbir was later reported to the ICC and was ordered to undertake a period of retraining on his bowling action. A worrying few months had ended with personal happiness for Lara, but not for the West Indies. The ineffectual Chanderpaul was sacked as captain and Lara was recalled as captain to tour Australia in November. That was yet another record. He was the first Test captain to be called up as skipper for a third time after being sacked twice.

twenty-seven

Lara as Captain

Thirty-one days before the start of the 2007 World Cup, Brian Lara had one of his worst days as captain of the West Indies. The match was the fourth and last ODI held at Baroda and he had a miserable day in the field. He dropped an easy catch, put some of his less capable fielders in key positions, presenting the opposition with extra runs, he failed to inspire his players and was run out backing up as the ball came off the bowler for two. It was the first time he had been out in that way. India piled up 341 for three, their highest total against the West Indies, and won by 160 runs to win the warm-up series 3-1. And worse, Lara's thirty-three-year-old arch rival Sachin Tendulkar returned to form, reaching his 41st ODI century on the final ball, 100★ off 76 deliveries.

Eleven months before, Tendulkar beat Sunil Gavaskar's record of 34 Test centuries in Delhi against Sri Lanka. At thirty-eight, five years older than Tendulkar, Lara has now scored 34 Test hundreds and he will have to improve his century rate to beat Tendulkar. That record may well now be out of his reach.

The tipping point at Baroda came in the thirty-eighth over when Lara decided to bring back Ian Brayshaw, the slightly-built Bajan left-arm medium-pace bowler when Tendulkar and Dravid were about to open up with their big batteries. Having decided to put India in to bat on an excellent batting pitch, the only way to take an early wicket or two was to use his swing bowler at the start. But Brayshaw wasn't given the new ball. Now he was back, with no swing to help him, and Tendulkar took three successive boundaries off him in an over which brought 15 runs. Several times Tendulkar turned his bat as he played the ball wide of mid-on and there was no fielder on that boundary to save the four. Most captains would have moved the straight mid-on to a wider position.

Off went Brayshaw until the last over was approaching and Lara signalled to him to take it. With the capacity 15,000 screaming and shouting their joy, Tendulkar steered the final ball to mid-wicket to reach three figures. But at least Brayshaw went round the wicket to vary his line. Before, he persisted in bowling over the wicket. Lara might have told him to switch it around and use the whole width of the pitch: little things that distinguish between a moderate captain and a good one.

The most baffling decision Lara made in that innings was to put Shiv Chanderpaul, who had an arm bandaged after an earlier injury, on the boundary at backward point, a key position. Tendulkar pushed a single towards him and realising that Chanderpaul couldn't throw, he ran two. Chanderpaul had to lob the ball in with an under-armed throw. He should have been placed in a less demanding position, like short fine leg.

Brayshaw, a useful close-in fielder and an average one on the boundary with a poor arm, found himself in the deep, another mistake. Paul Allott, the perceptive Sky commentator, said, 'They don't seem to mind what's going on out there. Lara looks resigned to it.' He was right. The captain's body language resembled Andrew Flintoff's in Australia in the 2006/07 Test series. Even in the final ten overs, Lara was still using five fielders in the ring instead of four. That extra fielder would have been useful on the ropes. There were throws almost everywhere except over the stumps and there were countless inefficient pick-ups.

Lara made little attempt to come up and encourage the bowlers. He made rapid bowling changes, not always the right ones, and after a splendid one-handed stop at wide mid-off off Mahendra Dhoni, stinging his hands, he dropped a catch shoulder height to his left which, as Allott said, 'he would have taken nine times out of ten.' He is one of the soundest catchers in world cricket, showing great athleticism despite his Tendulkar-size bulk, but he was at fault on that occasion. Devon Smith failed to hold a difficult, high catch on the square leg boundary off Dhoni's extravagant Highland Games-style swing of his bat and almost immediately he missed an extremely easy one in the same position off the same batsmen. No words were offered from the skipper to the shaken fielder.

Just how good is Lara as an international captain? Many critics believe he is only average, if that. For someone who started captaincy when he was at school in his third form he should have matured into being one of the best. Peter Short, the former Bajan administrator, knew most of the West Indian captains and said:

Frank Worrell was by far the best. His man management was excellent, he had good tactical sense and he never panicked. But I have to say there isn't a string of good ones following behind. Clive Lloyd and Viv Richards had very good records but they played in great sides. Jeff Stollmeyer was the outstanding tactician.

Brian is pretty shrewd as a captain but rather defensive which is surprising. Gary Sobers was the same. Except for that declaration which enabled Colin Cowdrey to win the series in 1968, Gary didn't take too many gambles on the field. Brian has made some incredible bowling changes, like not giving the new ball to Curtly Ambrose and Courtney Walsh and taking bowlers off after one over. Some of them have worked. Others not. In the field he chooses some unusual positions for his players.

Gary Sobers defends Lara. 'If the West Indies lose, which they do often, he is blamed but he doesn't let the criticism upset him,' he said. 'That's a good sign. It's easier to captain a winning team than a losing one and he is still learning.' Bob Woolmer said:

> He was going to be a mitigated flop or a big success as captain when he was appointed captain at Warwickshire in 1998 and he was neither. He wasn't a great tactician and had a few good ideas. He would put fielders in strange positions and people questioned his judgement. I felt he was charismatic as a man but not a real leader.

Bryan Davis, the technical director at Queens Park CC, said:

> Joey Carew wanted him to be captain of Trinidad when he was twenty and some others thought it was too soon. Gus Logie was the better candidate and when he didn't get it, he walked out. I was on the selection panel and I was against it. Joey said he's been captain through the ranks and he's got the credentials to do it. I think I was proved right. Brian took the West Indies 'B' to Zimbabwe at that age and found it tough to handle older players like Patrick Patterson, Jimmy Adams and Clayton Lambert. Now he is back as captain for the third time and I still think he is poor. He doesn't have the charisma to motivate the players and encourage them enough. And he had a bad record of timekeeping earlier in his career. As captain you need to be there and make decisions. And for a period he preferred to drive to matches instead of travelling in the coach. That sends a wrong signal to players.

During the short visit to India some observers were surprised to see that Lara left the group to fly to the Maldives for two days. Neither Ponting nor any of the Test captains would have left their players on a tour.

Davis recounted an incident about Lara's youth which presented him in a much better light, saying:

> I was impressed when I was working with him at the age of seventeen when I said to him, 'You ought to read a book written by Mike Brearley about captaincy which would help you' and he said, 'I've read it.' He said he had read Don Bradman's chapter about captaincy in his book *Art of Cricket* as well. It showed he was keen to become a good captain. We lack good leadership in the Caribbean. There are no people around today with the social background of Worrell, Walcott or Lloyd to take charge, people you want to fight for.

Clive Pantin also has praise for his former pupil:

> Brian is a keen student of the game and he believes in trying new things. He doesn't copy what captains do which people think that is the way to do it. He initiates and he asks questions. I am still very close to him and we speak quite often. I think he attracts more criticism than most captains because he is in charge of a weak side that loses more than it wins. But if he had some better, more experienced players under him he would be much more popular!

One of the reasons the West Indies lack outstanding captains is that players like Lloyd, Richards, Rohan Kanhai and Gary Sobers were great, instinctive players who didn't have to study the game and pass examinations. They did what came naturally. Average players without that talent have acquired knowledge over the years like potential professors of cricket and Brearley is the best example. If you examine the records of Test captains around the world, only a small elite have been naturally gifted, such as Bradman and Worrell. In the next group are Richie Benaud, Ian Chappell, Ray Illingworth, Lindsay Hassett, Steve Waugh, Bobby Simpson, Douglas Jardine, Imran Khan, Javed Miandad, Sunil Gavaskar and Brian Close, who should have played many more games but for being disciplined for an offence which a multitude of captains have committed, that of slowing the game down to try to avoid defeat.

Ignoring the top five England captains who had 100 per cent records for wins – they played a handful of matches with Lord Hawke having played eight, the most – Close was England's top man with six victories in his seven matches. Next came Brearley, with 18 wins out of 31, including two over Australian second teams in the Packer era. He summed up his approach to captaincy by saying, 'I like to be bossy. I hate to get bored. I want to be doing something all the time and the tactics of the game fascinated me. I liked the idea of interrelation with people and above all, I like trying to get the best out of people.' That last point escaped B.C. Lara for years but now he is catching up.

Bradman was fourth in the Australian list (again, ignoring the 100 per centers who played ten matches between them) with 15 wins out of 24 matches as captain. Warwick Armstrong, with eight wins out of ten, headed the list and his successor Hassett won 14 out of 24. Ian Chappell was successful in 15 out of 30 matches compared to Benaud's 12 out of 28 while Greg Chappell won 21 out of 48. Allan Border, who holds the record of 62 appearances as captain, had 17 wins and Simpson's tally was similar, 12 out of 39.

Worrell won nine out of 15 to lead the West Indian field. He should have been given the job years before but racial prejudice kept him out. Lara shared the same penchant – to drop off to sleep at any place, any time. Viv Richards is second with 27 wins from 50 appearances and Lloyd 36 from 74 matches, both men benefiting from using four great fast bowlers. Sobers is down to thirteenth with nine wins from 39 appearances. Lara's record is 10 wins out of 47 matches, with 11 draws and 26 losses up to the start of the England series in 2007 but it is not the worst record of any West Indian. That is held by Chanderpaul. Gavaskar's tally is nine wins from 47 matches and most of these were played on good batting pitches which often prevented a result. No other Indian has an outstanding record. The same applies to the captains of South Africa, Sri Lanka, New Zealand, Zimbabwe and Bangladesh. Javed Miandad's score was 11 out of 28 and Imran Khan's was 13 from 45.

Wes Hall is a fervent admirer of Lara's captaincy he said:

> I don't buy that he isn't a good captain. He's an intelligent man, he's adventurous, he knows what he wants and he's not pushed around by coaches. Chanderpaul captained the side and was supposed to be in charge but he wasn't because they had to send out messages to him. Any captain is as good as the players who are under him. Everyone in the current Australian side is a match-winner. We don't have match-winners. Put in Lara in place of Ricky Ponting and you'd see a difference. When we had our great sides under Clive Lloyd and Viv Richards it wasn't too hard to captain them. We had match-winners right through the team.

> Brian scored more than half the number of runs in a Test in Sri Lanka and still finished on the losing side. Give me a break! We now have some talented players emerging but they need to be more competitive, more consistent. Brian has had to play long innings to save matches and he hasn't won many Tests. West Indies haven't won any, full stop.

Lara's captaincy, like his form, goes up and down, ranging from awful days to encouraging ones and his moods can swing either way. In 2006, when India visited the West Indies, he was in good form in every aspect of his game. He showed his class when he scored 120 out of 252 for five against India his bogey side, at the new ground in St Lucia, the most scenic of the Caribbean islands. He showed little emotion when he reached his thirty-second Test century but twenty runs later, when he was given out lbw, wrongly, he burst out laughing. Earlier, Pakistan umpire Asad Rauf turned down an lbw appeal from Anil Kumble and countless replays showed that only a millimetre saved him from dismissal. This time the delivery, from Kumble bowling round the wicket, pitched an inch or two outside the leg stump. It was clear to the naked eye that the batsman wasn't out yet Rauf had bowed to pressure. Three close-in fielders, all wearing helmets, turned to him with arms aloft, screaming and shouting. As Rauf raised the finger, Lara walked off with a broad smile.

Up to that time, Lara had only scored two centuries against India and his average against them was the lowest of the major countries. But the cricket lovers of India adore him which is why he visits there regularly. Tony Cozier said of him in that series, 'I've never seen him bat like this before. He's fought through a bad spell and showed the stamp of a champion, battling through adversity and coming out on top again.' Ian Bishop said, 'He thrives on the responsibility of being captain again.' As captain of the West Indies, Lara averaged 57 at the time. As a player, not as a skipper, he averaged 52.

Though he was out near the close, the West Indies drew a second Test in a row when they were outplayed and faced defeat. He was the motivating force, inspiring his younger colleagues and making them curb their normal instinct to play risky shots. Shiv Chanderpaul was caught off a miscued pull from a high full toss from Kumble – it must have been one of the very few he bowled in his career – and he looked distraught as he trudged off. Some captains would have been annoyed. Chanderpaul's carelessness could have cost the series. Instead, Lara went up to him and put his arm round him. That was management of the highest order. If only he could captain the side in this upbeat manner all the time!

twenty-eight

Summing Up the Enigma

Many who know Brian Lara call him a genius while others brand him an enigma, a puzzling man, a riddle. Well, he is puzzling to some but his goal was to become one of the greatest cricketers that ever played the game and he succeeded despite the pitfalls he suffered on the way. When sudden fame enveloped his life after his 375 he could have gone down the road that many geniuses have trodden and ended in dishonour. He could have been an alcoholic like George Best, whose football career was effectively over by the time he was twenty-seven. He could have been like Paul Gascoigne, who is still striving to attain a stable life after a ghastly series of self-inflicted disasters. Matthew Le Tissier, one of the sane ones, said of Gascoigne: 'In his pomp he had the legs to play the holding role in midfield and still contribute to the attack. Was he daft as a brush? Of course. Yet I have never met anybody with a bigger heart. He just surrounded himself with the wrong people.'

An ever better parallel could be drawn to Diego Maradona, whose playing career was blighted by drug use. Maradona is still loved by the vast majority in Argentina and he has a corporate box on the halfway line at his old club Boca Juniors in the poorest part of Buenos Aires. He has the same appeal as Eva Peron and lives on his name. Lara has admitted that drugs and crime could have caught up with him in Trinidad where they are rampant. But he never thought of it and the whole of his life was consumed with cricket and the pursuit of excellence. As Dennis Amiss said, 'You've got to tolerate geniuses sometimes' – there is a delicate balance between being too lax with them and being too strict. The various members of the West Indies Board have tried all kinds of accommodation with Lara, sending him warning letters, fining him and banning him but in the end, he is still doing it his way, more or less. A more authoritarian approach might have cut short his career and with added maturity, he is still unchallenged as the top man in Caribbean sport.

Asked by *The Wisden Cricketer* to describe himself, Lara said:

A very simple person thrust into an overwhelming situation in terms of his cricket life. It shaped my life. You are going to read or hear things about me, and some would be good, some great and some bad. At the end of the day you still have a human being. I've enjoyed bringing a smile to people's faces. Just to hear someone say that there was a joy in watching Brian Lara is enough for me. If it is thousands of people, even bettter.

Still reasonably fit, except for a recurrent knee problem, and mentally strong, he could follow the example of the first great Caribbean batsman, George Alphonso Headley who played his last Test against England in Kingston in 1954 at the age of forty-four years and 236 days to become the oldest West Indian cricketer. Born in Panama in 1909, Headley was going to study dentistry in the USA until he decided to make a career out of cricket in Jamaica. A small man, about the same size as Lara, he was an essentially back-foot player who scored ten centuries in 22 Tests and averaged 60.83. He is still third in the all-time Test averages behind Bradman and Graeme Pollock. Like Lara, one of his nicknames was 'Atlas' because he carried the West Indies batting when they started playing international cricket.

Lara was cast in the role of 'Atlas' when the ICC World Cup started in 2007 and he couldn't sustain it. On the opening day on 13 March, he led his young side to a comfortable victory over Pakistan and there were excitable scenes all over the Caribbean. Pakistan then lost embarrassingly to Ireland, while two easy wins over Zimbabwe and Ireland propelled Lara's men into the Super Eight stage of the competition, provoking more joyous celebrations. Dwight Yorke was spending a few days with Lara and they shared the excitement. Yorke was enjoying a revival in his career, playing a pivotal role in Sunderland's midfield and helping Roy Keane's side to take over the leadership of the Coca-Cola Championship. He has had to cope with the death of his sister Verline from cancer and the health problems of his five-year-old son Harvey. In an interview with Matt Dickinson of *The Times* he said defiantly, 'If I was such a playboy, how come I am still going at my age?' He was thirty-five at the time.

The celebrations were abruptly curtailed on 18 May when Bob Woolmer's body was found lying unconscious on the floor of his bedroom at the Pegasus Hotel in Kingston and two hours later he was pronounced dead at the University of West Indies Hospital. It cast a dreadful pall over the whole tournament, and all around the cricketing world. Lara was staying on the twelfth floor, just across the corridor from where Bob, his former coach at Warwickshire, had been staying. Various alarmist theories were put forward to explain the mysterious death of the much-lamented and loved Pakistan coach, who appeared to have been strangled.

Malcolm Speed, the ICC chief, insisted that the tournament should go ahead and that was a sensible decision, backed by the Woolmer family. Just how this tragedy affected Lara and his players was not easy to judge. There was no comment from the West Indies camp but it must have been a terrible dampener. They must have been relieved to move on to Antigua to take on the Australians in the Super Eights at the new, out-of-town Sir Vivian Richards Stadium.

The idea of awarding the competition to the West Indies was to revive their cricket and provide greater wealth through tourism. Sadly, it didn't work out. The Antiguans would have preferred to remain at their old Recreation Ground where Lara made his name. The shuttle vans taking supporters to the ground were inefficiently run, security was oppressive and when the match went into the second day, the small number of spectators had to come up with another £13 or more to watch the conclusion. The West Indies lost three wickets for 20 chasing the Australian total of 322 for six and Lara took up the challenge single-handedly before he was lbw for 77 out of a meagre total of 219. Mark Nicholas wrote in the *Daily Telegraph*:

> As ever, his batting caught both eye and imagination. His wrists are like rubber, his feet like quicksilver and his brain almost always a step ahead of his opponent. There were rasping cuts and delicate deflections to savour. There were thunderous, winner-takes-all drives at which to marvel and whips off legs and body that found the vast legside spaces. But sadly, there was no one supporting. He was a lighthouse in the desert – bright but ultimately without value, for nobody had the nous to stay with him.

West Indies lost by 103 runs, not quite a humiliation but close to it. That defeat was swiftly followed by another hiding, by seven wickets, by the New Zealanders and on the eve of the match Lara was involved in controversy after dropping fast bowler Jerome Taylor and replacing him with the young, inexperienced Trinidadian batsman Lendl Simmons. Andy Roberts, a frequent critic of Lara's captaincy, said: 'I can't find the words to describe it. If you play an extra batsman at number eight, he has to be able to bowl. All I can say is that Simmonds must have changed roles since I last saw him.' Lara's hunch turned out to be a major mistake. If he wanted to bring in a new, talented player from his home country a better candidate would have been nineteen-year-old Kieron Pollard, the 6ft 5ins all-rounder who is an outstanding fielder, bowls at the same pace as England's Paul Collingwood and scored several centuries in his first first-class season, in which he struck more than 30 sixes. The first shot he played in his first-class career, at the Queen's Park ground, was a six high into the newly built pavilion.

Lara made a composed 37 against the New Zealanders and with so much criticism flying around the morale of his team was low going into the third, decisive game against Sri Lanka at the new Providence Stadium in Guyana, the biggest ground in the Caribbean. Many of the matches were affected by rain and this was no exception. Lara won the toss and put the Sri Lankans in on a pitch yet to dry out, under low cloud which should have helped his pace-based attack. Upul Tharanga, a twenty-two-year-old left-hander whose family home in the fishing village of Ambalangoda was swept away by the tsunami of Boxing Day 2004, and Kumar Sangakkara, the wicketkeeper-batsman signed up to play for Lara's old club Warwickshire, were soon removed but Lara lost a grip on things as shoddy fielding allowed Sanath Jayasuriya, 115, and skipper Mahela Jayawardena, 82, to put on 183 from 30 overs. Lara fell and missed the chance to stop two runs and his poor example was soon followed by his younger colleagues. When Jayasuriya was bowled by Darren Powell, hardly any of the players went up to congratulate the bowler. There was no animation, no spark. Tony Cozier said, 'If they can't do it on their own grounds, and this ground is almost full, when can they do it? Where has it gone?' Colin Croft said, 'Lara is the worst West Indian captain there has ever been.'

Lara gambled by promoting Dwayne Bravo, born in Santa Cruz, Lara's birthplace, to open, demoting Shiv Chanderpaul to first wicket down, and it proved to be a wrong decision. The languid Chris Gayle sacrificed his wicket with a big heave straight down the pitch and was caught off a skier which might have struck the closed roof of a modern football stadium like Wembley or the Millennium Stadium. Lara had himself down at five but swopped with Sarwan. After scoring two, he missed the fourth delivery he faced and was stumped by Sangakarra who was bravely standing up against the bowling of Chaminda Vaas. Normally, Sangakarra would have been standing back but it was a sign that more method is being incalculated into Sri Lanka cricket by their Australian coach Tom Moody. Trevor Penney, who played with Lara at Warwickshire, was in charge of the fielding practice and he has made a tremendous improvement in the Sri Lanka fielding. Next to the late Colin Bland, Penney was the greatest fielder of recent times. The Sri Lankans showed up the lamentable standards of Lara's players, who proved to be the worst fielders in the tournament with the exception of the Kenyans.

Lara has rarely been stumped, taking his lead from his idol Sir Garfield Sobers, who was stumped just once in his career. 'I don't believe in giving the fielding side a chance,' said Sobers. Lara looked totally disillusioned when he was summoned up to the presentation dias afterwards and his mood wasn't improved to see his old enemy Lance Gibbs, the former manager of a West Indian side who had criticised him on a previous tour to England. Gibbs was there as the chief guest presenting the Man of the Match award. Asked what went wrong, a muted Lara said, 'Well, it's been pretty tough out there. This is our fourth match in ten days and we're not fresh and the fielding wasn't too good. We're now going to have a couple of days off in Grenada before the next game against South Africa on the tenth.' Actually, it was four days' cricket in the past six days and at Guyana the temperature out in the middle was well above 90°F with the humidity eighty-eight per cent, similar conditions to those experienced in Colombo. The Sri Lankans were fitter, faster and more enthusiastic, although the West Indians also grew up in a hot, humid part of the world.

Sangakarra was asked about his team's next move. 'We'll be getting down to more work,' he said. 'We were complacent before our defeat by the South Africans and we've got to be sure our preparation is right for the next game.' That was the difference between the mental state of the two sets of players. Willie Rodriguez believes that lack of fitness is the reason why the West Indians are lagging behind countries like Sri Lanka, New Zealand, South Africa and Australia. 'When they were top of the tree their players trained extremely hard under Dennis Waight, their Australian trainer,' he said. 'I don't see that happening now. They can't last the pace. The other countries have improved and the West Indies have gone backwards, and their fielding isn't up to it.' Lara is the only player in the side who bats the same way in one-day cricket, technically correct. The previous generation of West Indian batsman also batted that way but today's players aren't close enough to the ball when making their shots. 'They try to belt the ball and they're not over it,' said Rodriguez.

The danger now is that the West Indies probably have the best medium-size grounds in the world and, except for the visit of England, accompanied by prosperous English supporters, they are unlikely ever to be filled. After the Ashes disaster of 2006/07, fewer English cricket lovers went to the World Cup, adding to the cash problems. And the early exits of India and

Pakistan also contributed to a largely chaotic and unsuccessful tournament. The pressure will be on Lara to make big scores to rekindle interest among boys who are quickly losing the urge to take up the game. Chris Gayle was looked on as a possible successor as captain but his manner in the World Cup convinced most experts that he is not ready for it. Chanderpaul hasn't the necessary qualities and that leaves Sarwan, who had a poor start in the competition. However, he has been heir apparent for some time and is still the favourite to succeed Lara.

One of the reasons why Lara is not held in such high regards as West Indies greats of the past is the absence of someone like the eminent West Indian writer C.L.R. James to write about him. James would certainly have improved Lara's reputation had he lived long enough to savour his great innings. 'CLR', as he was always known, was the equivalent of Sir Neville Cardus in England and wrote eloquently about Learie Constantine, George Headley and other West Indian heroes. At a meeting with him at his small flat in Brixton, his eyes lit up as he spoke about of one his proteges, Frank Worrell. A brilliant lecturer and writer, CLR successfully campaigned for the appointment of Worrell as the first black man to lead the West Indies on tour. This happened in Australia in 1960/61 and it turned out to be the greatest Test series of any in the Southern Hemisphere.

Worrell became a senator in the Jamaican Parliament and in his monumental book *World Cricketers* Christopher Martin-Jenkins wrote: 'He was a great cricketer, a great captain, an exemplary ambassador for West Indies cricket and a man of strong convictions. Had he lived he would surely have been a statesmen in world affairs.' He died of leukemia at the age of forty-three. But for that, much of the turmoil in West Indies cricket might well have been avoided. Headley and Worrell were the two most inspirational figures in West Indies cricket. Will people look back on Lara's career and say he was the third? We will have to see. He still has something to give to the game he loves so deeply.

If you are interested in purchasing other books published by Stadia, or in case you have difficulty finding any Stadia books in your local bookshop, you can also place orders directly through the Tempus Publishing website
www.tempus-publishing.com